"*Gender and Leadership: Shattering the Status Quo* reviews, critiques, and advances the state of the science on gender and leadership. It debunks popular myths and misconceptions to offer practical insights, backed up by an impressive body of research. This book is an essential reading for anyone interested in leadership—be they students, scholars, supervisors, or senior leaders."

Lilia M. Cortina, *University Diversity and Social Transformation Professor, Department of Psychology and Department of Women's and Gender Studies, University of Michigan, USA*

Gender and Leadership

Gender and Leadership brings together a diverse team of leading scholars who provide critical insights into the key topics of debate and research on gender in leadership.

These expert voices break down key issues and even correct popular misconceptions. Each chapter contains a state-of-the-art review of a critical topic within the field, such as the work–life interface, glass cliff, communication, negotiation, and networking. Importantly, they provide thought leaders' perspectives and experiences throughout. Written in an approachable style, this text provides an engaging take on foundational issues of gender in leadership. Intersectional, cross-cultural, and non-corporate approaches are highlighted throughout the book. To support student learning, this textbook includes pedagogical features such as chapter summaries, discussion questions, and case studies with accompanying reflection questions linked to key topics in the book. Online instructor resources include quizzes for each chapter.

This book is suitable for learners of management, organizational studies, leadership, psychology of gender, women in leadership, human resource management, business ethics, and anyone looking to advance their understanding of gender in a business context.

Lisa A. Marchiondo is Associate Professor at the University of New Mexico's Anderson School of Management. Her research centers on leadership, diversity, and workplace mistreatment.

Gender and Leadership

Gender and Leadership

Shattering the Status Quo

Edited by
Lisa A. Marchiondo

Routledge
Taylor & Francis Group
LONDON AND NEW YORK

Designed cover image: michaklootwijk / Getty Images

First published 2026
by Routledge
4 Park Square, Milton Park, Abingdon, Oxon OX14 4RN

and by Routledge
605 Third Avenue, New York, NY 10158

Routledge is an imprint of the Taylor & Francis Group, an informa business

British Library Cataloguing-in-Publication Data
A catalogue record for this book is available from the British Library

ISBN: 978-1-032-78581-3 (hbk)
ISBN: 978-1-032-78575-2 (pbk)
ISBN: 978-1-003-48859-0 (ebk)

DOI: 10.4324/9781003488590

Typeset in Helvetica Neue and Avant Garde
by Apex CoVantage, LLC

Access the Support Material: www.routledge.com/9781032785752

To my two little leaders—may you spread your lively spirits and creative dreams. And to the many people who have served as inspirers, guides, and supporters to me and the authors of this book.

Contents

Contributors

Jennifer L. Berdahl
Department of Sociology, University of British Columbia
Canada

Jennifer L. Berdahl is Professor of Sociology at the University of British Columbia. She earned her PhD in social psychology at the University of Illinois and was a faculty member in business schools in the USA and Canada. She studies gender, race, and power in the workplace.

Hannah Riley Bowles
Harvard Kennedy School, Harvard University
USA

Hannah Riley Bowles is Roy E. Larsen Senior Lecturer in public policy and management at the Harvard Kennedy School (HKS). She is a leading expert on gender in negotiation and a scholar of women's leadership advancement. She co-directs the Women and Public Policy Program (WAPPP) at HKS.

Suzette Caleo
E. J. Ourso College of Business, Louisiana State University
USA

Suzette Caleo is Associate Professor of Public Administration at Louisiana State University. In her research, she examines the conditions under which men and women are evaluated differently at work, using these conditions to understand the psychological processes underlying gender bias. She holds a PhD in social psychology from NYU.

Nicole Capehart
Anderson School of Management, University of New Mexico
USA

Nicole Capehart, SHRM-CP, is Lecturer at UNM's Anderson School of Management. She combines over a decade of teaching experience with industry expertise to guide students in leadership, ethical decision-making, and professional growth. Her pedagogy emphasizes DEI, transformational leadership, mentorship, and student-centered, experiential learning.

Siri Chilazi
Harvard Kennedy School, Harvard University
USA
Siri Chilazi is a senior researcher at the Women and Public Policy Program at Harvard Kennedy School and an internationally recognized expert in advancing women and promoting gender equity in organizations. She is the coauthor, with Iris Bohnet, of *Make Work Fair: Data-Driven Design for Real Results* (HarperCollins, 2025).

Alison Cook
Huntsman School of Business, Utah State University
USA
Alison Cook is Professor of Management at Utah State University. Her research examines diversity in the workplace, specifically focusing on the factors that either facilitate or hinder promotion opportunities for women and racial/ethnic minorities and factors that facilitate or hinder their post-promotion success.

Ash Francisco
Dilin Duwa Centre for Indigenous Business Leadership, University of Melbourne
Australia
Dr. Ash Francisco is the engagement lead at the Dilin Duwa Centre for Indigenous Business Leadership at the University of Melbourne and Melbourne Business School in Australia. Ash is a proud Wiradjuri woman whose passion lies in advancing regional economies.

Katherine Giscombe
Giscombe & Associates
USA
Katherine Giscombe has a PhD in organizational psychology from the University of Michigan and trained at the Institute for Social Research. With over 20 years in research and consulting, Dr. Giscombe directed a series on race and gender in the workplace sponsored by the Ford Foundation and the Catalyst organization.

Christy Glass
Department of Sociology, Utah State University
USA
Christy Glass is Professor of Sociology at Utah State University. Her research and teaching focus on the ways gender and race shape access to and mobility in professional work organizations. Her collaborative work with Alison Cook and Alicia Ingersoll explores the glass cliff, the risk tax, and the impacts of representation on elite careers.

Alicia Ingersoll
Goddard School of Business and Economics, Weber State University
USA
Alicia Ingersoll is Assistant Professor at Weber State's Goddard School of Business and Economics. Alicia's research examines the connections between corporations and society with specific focus on the link between organizational performance

and corporate practices, such as diversity, leader attributes, and sustainability initiatives

Priyanka Joshi
Lam Family College of Business, San Francisco State University
USA
Priyanka Joshi is Lam Larsen Distinguished Research Professor at San Francisco State University. Her research examines the effects of psychological distance from the audience on communication patterns and has been published in reputed journals including *Academy of Management Journal*, *Psychological Science*, and *Personality and Social Psychology Bulletin*.

Fred Macoukji
Corporate Sherpa, LLC
USA
Dr. Macoukji is on the product development team at GeniusMesh, where he designs HR technology solutions that advance leadership development, succession planning, and 360 feedback. He is also the founder of Corporate Sherpa LLC., a consulting practice focused on enterprise-wide talent interventions, performance management, and data-driven approaches to developing leaders.

Lisa A. Marchiondo
Anderson School of Management, University of New Mexico
USA
Lisa A. Marchiondo is Associate Professor at the University of New Mexico's Anderson School of Management. Her research centers on leadership, diversity, and workplace mistreatment. She has served on numerous federal grants aimed at institutional transformations totaling over $20 million. She earned a PhD at the University of Michigan.

Zhihe Allan Ren
McGill University
Canada
Zhihe Allan Ren is an undergraduate student at McGill University, majoring in Statistics and expects to graduate in 2026. He contributed to this project through the Integrated Management Student Fellowship (IMSF), an initiative of the Marcel Desautels Institute for Integrated Management (MDIIM) within the Desautels Faculty of Management.

Brian Rubineau
Desautels Faculty of Management, McGill University
Canada
Brian Rubineau is Associate Professor of Organizational Behavior at the Desautels Faculty of Management of McGill University. His research examines the social dynamics of inequality in organizations, occupations, and labor markets. He employs social network analysis and mathematical and computational modeling, in addition to traditional quantitative and qualitative methods.

Marionne Sevilla
Leeds School of Business, University of Colorado Boulder
USA
Marionne Sevilla is pursuing her PhD in Organizational Behavior at the Leeds School of Business at the University of Colorado, Boulder. She received her undergraduate degree from San Diego State University's Psychology program with an industrial–organizational emphasis.

Parisa Sharif Esfahani
Schulich School of Business, York University
Canada
Parisa Sharif Esfahani is a PhD student in organization studies at the Schulich School of Business, York University. Her research focuses on women in leadership, specifically women's leadership development and women's wellbeing at work.

Winny Shen
Schulich School of Business, York University
Canada
Winny Shen is Associate Professor of Organization Studies at the Schulich School of Business, York University. She conducts high-impact management and psychological research on leadership, diversity and inclusion, and worker health and well-being and is devoted to teaching in an effort to promote inclusive, productive, and healthy work organizations.

Shan Sherwan Hussein
Harvard Kennedy School, Harvard University
USA
Shan Sherwan Hussein is Research Fellow at Harvard Kennedy School, supporting Hannah Riley Bowles with work on negotiation and women's participation in labor and conflict resolution. She has nearly a decade of humanitarian experience in Iraq, Ukraine, and Jordan and teaches negotiation workshops in the USA, India, Afghanistan, and the Kurdistan Region of Iraq.

Richard Tan
McGill University
Canada
Richard Tan is an undergraduate student at McGill University, completing a BCom in Business Analytics and Computer Science with an expected 2026 graduation. He worked on this project through the Integrated Management Student Fellowship, an initiative of the Marcel Desautels Institute for Integrated Management within the Desautels Faculty of Management.

Sabrina D. Volpone
Jindal School of Management, University of Texas at Dallas
USA
Dr. Volpone's research at the University of Texas at Dallas develops and tests theory about sociolinguistic practices in organizations. Her work on discursive practices

examines how organizations use language to reproduce/dismantle power. Then, her research on narrative practices investigates how individuals use language to manage their identities in workspaces.

Daniel S. Whitman
E. J. Ourso College of Business, Louisiana State University
USA

Daniel S. Whitman is Associate Professor in the Rucks Department of Management at Louisiana State University's E. J. Ourso College of Business. His research centers on multilevel theory and examines topics such as organizational justice, counterproductive work behaviors, and dark triad traits. He holds a PhD in industrial–organizational psychology.

CHAPTER 1

Introduction to Gender and Leadership

Lisa A. Marchiondo

Let's begin with a riddle:

> A father and his son are in a car accident. The father dies. The son is rushed to the ER. The attending surgeon looks at the boy and says, 'I can't operate on this boy. He's my son!' How can this be?

Have an answer? Brainstorm a bit longer.

More than four out of five Americans cannot provide the correct answer to this 50-year-old riddle, often finding themselves stumped or suggesting it is the boy's stepfather (Morehouse et al., 2022). The answer is that the surgeon is the boy's mother. This puzzle is an engaging and often surprising reflection of the persistence of gender stereotypes in jobs and organizations to this day, even when considering that women[1] constitute 40–43% of physicians in the USA and Canada, respectively, and approximately a quarter of general surgeons in these nations (Pickel & Sivachandran, 2024; Robert Wood Johnson Medicine, 2025). These percentages are notably higher in the European Union, where over 50% of physicians and 30–40% of surgeons are women (Eurostat, 2024). And in many Eastern European countries, women constitute the majority of physicians, exceeding 70% (Eurostat, 2024).[2] Nonetheless, this "think surgeon-think man" effect remains prevalent and generalizes to non-Western countries (Morehouse et al., 2022).

Looking outside the medical field, women began earning more bachelor's degrees than men approximately 40 years ago in Western countries (Buchmann et al., 2025). University attendance and graduation rates are now notably higher for women than men (e.g., 58% of graduates were women in the European Union in 2023; Eurostat,

DOI: 10.4324/9781003488590-1

2025), and this trend exists across most racial/ethnic groups (Hurst, 2024). Clearly, women are succeeding academically—and have consistently demonstrated their scholastic achievements and knowledge for many decades.

An important caveat is that women collegiate students are still underrepresented in certain disciplines, notably STEM fields like engineering and math, where larger racial/ethnic divides are also present (American Academy of Arts & Sciences, 2025; Fry et al., 2021; Society of Women Engineers, 2025). These gaps are narrowing, albeit gradually. A number of chapters in this book will discuss possible reasons for areas in which gender gaps persist.

In business programs, however, gender gaps are closing more quickly: 42% of MBA graduates were women in 2023–2024 (Fore & Suarez, 2024; Forté Foundation, 2023). A growing number of the most elite business schools worldwide, including the University of Oxford Said Business School, ESSEC Business School in France, and University of Pennsylvania Wharton School, have achieved gender parity (Fore & Suarez, 2024; Kefford, 2024). In China, women make up substantially more than 50% of many MBA cohorts (e.g., 56% at the Shanghai University of Finance and Economics: College of Business; Kefford, 2024).

Like business school trajectories, gender gaps have substantially narrowed in law schools, particularly in the past decade (American Bar Association, 2024). In 2016, more than half of US law students were women, who now constitute over 56% of US law students (American Bar Association, 2024). The International Bar Association has investigated women's representation in legal fields across 12 countries, finding that 47% of all lawyers are women (International Bar Association, 2024). Countries like Chile, the Netherlands, and Ukraine have the highest percentages of women lawyers (International Bar Association, 2024).

Despite women's notable academic achievements across fields for decades, consequential disparities—notably, leadership barriers and pay gaps—exist once women are practicing within their fields. In business, women occupy 41–42% of management positions in Australia, the UK, and USA[3] (which varies depending on specific fields; Fry, 2025; International Labour Organization, 2025), yet these numbers quickly decline with organizational ascent. In particular, women comprise only 10% of CEOs of the most profitable and powerful companies (i.e., Fortune 500 companies; Catalyst, 2025). Although this double-digit number has been celebrated, it means that 90% of the most dominant corporate leaders are men. Representation in these prevailing positions is even lower for women of color (Catalyst, 2025). Although women's representation on boards of directors in top companies is higher, men occupy two-thirds of these positions and report substantially greater influence in these roles (Catalyst, 2025).

Similarly, in the legal profession, although women have made noteworthy gains as practicing lawyers and law firm associates, they remain underrepresented in senior positions (American Bar Association, 2024; International Bar Association, 2024). Internationally, men hold almost two-thirds of senior law positions. In the USA, 72% of law firm partners, 88% of managing partners, and 66% of federal judges are men (American Bar Association, 2024). Many leadership positions, such as firm partnerships, have been proportionally slow to change, inching upward at rates far slower than those for women's law school graduations and associate hires (American Bar Association, 2024).

The underrepresentation of women in top legal positions likely helps explain the staggering gender gap in the political empowerment facet of the World Economic Forum's Global Gender Gap Index (2025). The Global Gender Gap Index annually measures four dimensions of gender parity across 148 economies. Although minimal gender disparities remain in health and education, politics contains a notable gender gap (only 23.4% of the gap is closed). Globally, then, women wield limited political influence, particularly within the most powerful spheres (World Economic Forum, 2025).

Along with women's underrepresentation in the highest leadership positions, a gender pay gap persists globally: for every dollar men make, women receive 77 cents (Holder, 2025). Like leadership gaps, pay gaps are even wider for women of color (e.g., especially Black and Latinas/Hispanic women in the USA; DeCourcy & Gould, 2025). Across education levels and socioeconomic statuses of jobs, pay gaps endure (DeCourcy & Gould, 2025). The good news is the gap is narrowing, particularly in certain countries and among groups of younger workers (Holder, 2025). The disappointing news is that at the current rate of gap reduction, women and men will not earn equal pay, on average, until the year 2159 (Holder, 2025).

The goal of this book, then, is to explore the many reasons for gaps like the ones outlined here. As the opening riddle exemplifies, our gender stereotypes tied to jobs, organizations, and leadership are stronger than we might think. It is as important as ever to learn about the dynamics operating within our minds. Education and understanding allow us to gain control of how we think, behave, and lead—ultimately, making us more productive contributors to our organizations and societies. The goal of learning about gender (and other identity) disparities is not to prompt guilt or shame, contrary to some popular media messaging. Instead, learning about organizational barriers—and ways to rectify them—promotes collective benefit: individuals are happier, teams are more effective, and organizations are more profitable. As this book's experts will explain, though, narrowing gender-based organizational gaps can, at times, be more nuanced and challenging than it may seem. Before giving the book's experts the floor, we will quickly visit the concepts of the glass ceiling and the labyrinth of leadership.

THE GLASS CEILING AND THE LABYRINTH OF LEADERSHIP

Multiple people have been credited with coining the famous "glass ceiling" term. Marilyn Loden first used the term in a speech in 1978 (100 Women: 'Why I invented the glass ceiling phrase', 2017); Gay Bryant referred to it in an *Adweek* interview as well as her book in 1984 (Bryant, 1984; Frenkiel, 1984); Carol Hymowitz and Timothy Schellhardt discussed the concept in their 1986 *Wall Street Journal* article and included a sketch of a woman standing on a desk, pushing upward on a translucent ceiling (Hymowitz & Schellhardt, 1986). The term drew critical attention to the absence of women—and people of color—in leadership positions. However, it also insinuated that once a woman broke through this so-called ceiling, other women could—perhaps readily—ascend the same ladder to leadership in a field. Not so.

Decades later, Eagly and Carli (2007) published a notable book, *Through the Labyrinth*. In it, they contend that women's ascension to leadership is not about linearly escalating through a barrier but rather, winding through a maze of hurdles often present only to women, rather than men, during their leadership journeys. The book—formative for me during my doctoral education—elucidates the twists and turns that many women navigate throughout their careers—all rooted in high-quality research.

Dr. Alice Eagly has been a particularly formative leader in exposing the nuanced role of gender in workplaces, especially as women strive to ascend leadership. In her and Carli's book, they detail research showing that few to no gender differences exist in general intelligence and the personality traits that matter for leadership success (see Chapter 3 of Eagly & Carli, 2007). When gender differences in sub-facets of leadership-related qualities do emerge, a handful favor women and a handful favor men. Overall, though, the argument that "men are more likely than women to have what it takes for leadership" is unfounded. Yet, nearly 20 years since *Through the Labyrinth* was published and almost 50 years after the "glass ceiling" was coined, hurdles to women's leadership ascension persist.

An important distinction, often not discussed enough in educational and popular press contexts, is that of leadership emergence versus leadership effectiveness. We often see people with exclusive social connections, swagger, or "gift of gab" ascend to leadership positions before or instead of their competent peers. The factors that lift individuals to leadership do not always equate to *good* leadership practices that promote the success of both the organization and its employees. Instead, certain qualities linked to effective leadership, like ethical decision-making (Den Hartog, 2015) and individualized consideration (Bass, 1990), can be overlooked during leadership promotions. Skills considered "soft" but that are foundational to successful leadership can be scorned (e.g., advocating for others; Bosak et al., 2018), particularly in male-dominated fields, and dismissed as "too feminine."

Indeed, Eagly's work has demonstrated that women leaders face a "double bind": they are socially penalized if they act either too communally or too agentically (Eagly & Karau, 2002). Men, too, face challenges in terms of "precarious manhood" (Bosson & Vandello, 2011). This notion encompasses the idea that reputational "manhood" can be lost if men do not routinely adhere to prescribed gender norms. Therefore, the qualities and experiences that springboard individuals to leadership can be gendered, and they are not necessarily the qualities and experiences that prompt *effective* leadership. Readers are encouraged to consider this distinction, particularly when drawing on real-world examples.

INTRODUCING THE BOOK CHAPTERS

This book deviates from the status quo of gender-related leadership books by bringing together organizational experts who provide cutting-edge and engaging evaluations of foundational gender and leadership topics. These experts' voices uniquely unveil pressing issues within this vast literature, even correcting misconceptions in the popular press. The chapters contain state-of-the-art reviews while providing many of the thought leaders' perspectives and experiences.

In Chapter 2, Shen and Sharif Esfahani begin by outlining how leadership styles are conceptualized in organizational research and the extent to which gender differences—both desirable and undesirable—exist in these manifestations of leadership. They also review gender-related predictors and outcomes of leadership styles. In Chapter 3, Glass, Ingersoll, and Cook review the history and current state of the glass cliff phenomenon as it pertains to women and men of color, as well as White women. They explore theoretical mechanisms for the glass cliff, issues leaders face following glass cliff appointments, and recommendations for scholarly advancement.

In Chapter 4, Giscombe details the unique experiences of women of color, particularly African American, Asian, and Latina/Hispanic women, and their important contributions to businesses and economies. She explains the "outsider within" experiences of many Black women executives and concludes with implications of politically charged efforts to dismantle DEI efforts for women of color. In Chapter 5, Francisco turns our attention to the histories of Aboriginal and Torres Strait Islander women in contemporary Australia, including how they intersect with current political and social events to shape women's organizational opportunities and treatment.

Chapter 6 by Caleo and Whitman addresses multiple types of workplace mistreatment. They outline why observers perceive mistreatment differently based on whether women or men enact it, highlighting the importance of prescriptive gender stereotypes. In Chapter 7, Joshi explains how stereotypical social role expectations shape gender differences in communication. She underscores the importance of context for the emergence of these gendered patterns and provides recommendations for gender parity in organizations. In Chapter 8, Sherwan Hussein and Bowles detail when and how gender most often shapes career-related negotiations. They walk readers through a proven framework for preparing for and mitigating biases in negotiations. Chapter 9 by Rubineau, Tan, and Ren then centers on the role of gender in networking processes. They outline three stages through which gender-related differences in networking shape women's workplace success.

In Chapter 10, Volpone, Macoukji, and Sevilla provide an overview of the work–life balance literature. They boldly emphasize that little research has been paid to the experiences of women outside white-collar positions, including women with criminal histories, and proceed by uncovering barriers to these women across the human resource management lifecycle. Chapter 11 by Berdahl introduces masculinity contest culture (MCC) and its underlying components. She provides an engaging application of the concept to academia, explaining how institutions assumed to be progressive and logical often breed MCC, which affects faculty, students, and worldviews.

Chapter 12 by Chilazi concludes by analyzing strategies for supporting women's organizational success, differentiating evidence-based methods from popular but unsupported tactics. Her analysis contains a research-centered guide for overcoming many of the barriers outlined throughout this book. Chapter 13 by Capehart provides five case studies through which readers can demonstrate their knowledge of gender issues in organizations and practice applying strategies for overcoming biases and barriers.

BOOK-WIDE APPLICATIONS AND DISCUSSION QUESTIONS

Below are discussion questions for readers to consider across chapters, as well as ideas for applying book concepts to meaningful and personal scenarios. Questions and ideas vary in applicability based on readers' learning goals and educational stages.

1. Make a chart of recurring concepts, theories, or research findings, the chapters in which they appear, and how they are applied in each chapter.
   a. Which concepts, theories, or research findings are consistent across chapters?
   b. Which recur most frequently, highlighting their importance?
2. Are there any differences in research findings or conclusions between chapters, and if so, how could you reconcile them? Read the reference articles from which they draw.
3. For each chapter, select additional readings from its references section. Download them from your library. Provide an overview of each article's primary findings and share them with peers to help them learn more about particular concepts or theories.
4. After reading each chapter, apply one of its concepts or theories to a scenario that resonates with you. This could be a work experience you've had, work experiences you've overheard (e.g., from your parents or friends), organizational issues in the media, or job scenarios in TV shows,

movies, books, and video games. Describe how a concept unfolded in one of these applied scenarios.

5. Identify experiential opportunities to actively observe the book's concepts, whether being observant at your own workplace, shadowing friends/family at work, or witnessing dynamics in public venues (e.g., restaurants, stores, museums, libraries, schools).
6. If you are in a research-based program, develop a research proposal through which you could investigate a certain topic in the book more deeply or expand on it.

NOTES

1 In this chapter, "woman" and "man" are used to refer to anyone who identifies as a woman or man, respectively. Most empirical research in peer-reviewed journals has centered on cisgender women and men. However, non-binary and transgender employees frequently face exclusion and discrimination (Out Leadership, 2023). Readers are encouraged to read references like the following to learn more about the experiences of non-binary and transgender employees: Office of the High Commissioner for Human Rights (n.d.), Out Leadership (2023), Randstad (2024), Rastogi and colleagues (2025), and Sears et al. (2024).

2 Readers are encouraged to research statistics in additional countries and global regions through resources like the International Labour Organization or the Organisation for Economic Co-operation and Development.

3 Canada's proportion of women in managerial positions is notably lower at 35.6%, although this was last measured 2021, as opposed to the 2024 statistics for the other three countries (International Labour Organization, 2025).

REFERENCES

100 women: "Why I invented the glass ceiling phrase". (2017, December 12). *BBC News*. https://www.bbc.com/news/world-42026266

American Academy of Arts & Sciences. (2025). *Gender distribution of bachelor's degrees in the humanities*. https://www.amacad.org/humanities-indicators/higher-education/gender-distribution-bachelors-degrees-humanities

American Bar Association. (2024). *Women in the legal profession*. https://www.americanbar.org/news/profile-legal-profession/women/

Bass, B. M. (1990). From transactional to transformational leadership: Learning to share the vision. *Organizational Dynamics*, *18*(3), 19–31.

Bosak, J., Kulich, C., Rudman, L., & Kinahan, M. (2018). Be an advocate for others, unless you are a man: Backlash against gender-atypical male job candidates. *Psychology of Men & Masculinity*, *19*(1), 156–165. https://doi.org/10.1037/men0000085

Bosson, J. K., & Vandello, J. A. (2011). Precarious manhood and its links to action and aggression. *Current Directions in Psychological Science*, *20*(2), 82–86. https://doi.org/10.1177/0963721411402669

Bryant, G. (1984). *The working woman report: Succeeding in business in the 80s*. Simon and Schuster.

Buchmann, C., Dwyer, R. E., & Yao, M. (2025). The deepening gender divide in credentials, 2000–2020: Continuity, change, and implications. *The Russell Sage Foundation Journal of the Social Sciences*, *11*(1), 154–177. https://doi.org/10.7758/RSF.2025.11.1.08

Catalyst. (2025). *Spotlight on women CEOs*. https://www.catalyst.org/insights/featured/women-ceos

DeCourcy, K., & Gould, E. (2025, March 25). *Equal Pay Day: Gender pay gap hits historic low in 2024-but remains too large*. Economic Policy Institute. https://www.epi.org/blog/gender-pay-gap-2024

Den Hartog, D. N. (2015). Ethical leadership. *Annual Review of Organizational Psychology and Organizational Behavior*, *2*, 409–434.

Eagly, A. H., & Carli, L. L. (2007). *Through the labyrinth: The truth about how women become leaders*. Harvard Business School Press.

Eagly, A. H., & Karau, S. J. (2002). Role congruity theory of prejudice toward female leaders. *Psychological Review*, *109*(3), 573–598. https://doi.org/10.1037/0033-295x.109.3.573

Eurostat. (2024, December). *Healthcare personnel statistics—physicians*. European Union. https://ec.europa.eu/eurostat/statistics-explained/index.php?title=Healthcare_personnel_statistics_-_physicians

Eurostat. (2025, June). *Tertiary education statistics*. European Union. https://ec.europa.eu/eurostat/statistics-explained/index.php?title=Tertiary_education_statistics

Fore, P., & Suarez, J. (2024, October 31). *Women are breaking enrollment records at top MBA programs—but more progress is needed, report says*. Fortune. https://fortune.com/education/articles/women-mba-enrollment-forte-foundation-2024/

Forté Foundation. (2023). *Forté's 2023 report reveals record-breaking success: Women in full-time MBA programs on the rise*. https://www.fortefoundation.org/fortes-2023-report-reveals-record-breaking-success-women-in-full-time-mba-programs-on-the-rise/

Frenkiel, N. (1984, March 15). The up-and-comers; Bryant takes aim at the settlers-in. *Adweek: Magazine World 1984 Supplement*. New York, NY: A/S/M Communications: 30, oolumn 2.

Fry, R. (2025, July 17). *Women are a rising share of U.S. managers and professionals*. Pew Research Center. https://www.pewresearch.org/short-reads/2025/07/17/women-are-a-rising-share-of-us-managers-and-professionals/

Fry, R., Kennedy, B., & Funk, C. (2021, April 1). *STEM jobs see uneven progress in increasing gender, racial and ethnic diversity*. Pew Research Center. https://www.pewresearch.org/social-trends/2021/04/01/stem-jobs-see-uneven-progress-in-increasing-gender-racial-and-ethnic-diversity/

Holder, M. (2025, March 18). *Gender pay gap statistics 2025: A comprehensive analysis*. Equal Pay Today. https://www.equalpaytoday.org/gender-pay-gap-statistics/

Hurst, K. (2024, November 18). *U.S. women are outpacing men in college completion, including in every major racial and ethnic group*. Pew Research Center. https://www.pewresearch.org/short-reads/2024/11/18/us-women-are-outpacing-men-in-college-completion-including-in-every-major-racial-and-ethnic-group/

Hymowitz, C., & Schellhardt, T. C. (1986, March 24). The glass ceiling: Why women can't seem to break the invisible barrier that blocks them from top jobs. *Wall Street Journal, special supplement 1*, 4.

International Bar Association. (2024). *50:50 by 2030: A longitudinal study into gender disparity in law*. https://www.ibanet.org/document?id=IBA-Gender-Progress-Report-2024

International Labour Organization. (2025). *ILOSTAT data explorer* [Data file]. https://rshiny.ilo.org/dataexplorer39/?lang=en&id=SDG_T552_NOC_RT_A

Kefford, M. (2024, March 6). *The 25 best MBA programs for women*. GMAC Business Because. https://www.businessbecause.com/news/mba-rankings/6775/25-best-women-mba-programs

Morehouse, K. N., Kurdi, B., Hakim, E., & Banaji, M. R. (2022). When a stereotype dumbfounds: Probing the nature of the surgeon=male belief. *Current Research in Ecological and Social Psychology*, *3*, 100044.

Office of the High Commissioner for Human Rights. (n.d.). *The struggle of trans and gender-diverse persons*. United Nations. https://www.ohchr.org/en/special-procedures/ie-sexual-orientation-and-gender-identity/struggle-trans-and-gender-diverse-persons

Out Leadership. (2023, September). *Out to Succeed 2.0: Realizing the full potential of LGBTQ+ talent*. https://outleadership.com/wp-content/uploads/2023/09/Out-to-Succeed-2.0-FINAL_9_27.pdf

Pickel, L., & Sivachandran, N. (2024). Gender trends in Canadian medicine and surgery: The past 30 years. *BMC Medical Education*, *24*, 100. https://doi.org/10.1186/s12909-024-05071-4

Randstad. (2024, May 22). *41% of LGBTQI+ workers face discrimination—How do we turn the tide?* https://www.randstad.com/workforce-insights/future-work/41-percent-of-lgbtqi-workers-face-discrimination-how-do-we-turn-tide/

Rastogi, A., Menard, L., Miller, G. H., Cole, W., Laurison, D., Caballero, J. R., Murano-Kinney, S., & Heng-Lehtinen, R. (2025, June). *Health and wellbeing: A report of the 2022 U.S. Transgender Survey*. Advocates for Transgender Equality. https://ustranssurvey.org/download-reports/

Robert Wood Johnson Medicine. (2025, Winter). *Women in surgery: Increasing in numbers—and influence*. https://rwjms.rutgers.edu/magazine/winter-2025/women-surgery-increasing-numbers-influence

Sears, B., Mallory, C., Lin, A., & Castleberry, N. M. (2024, November). *Workplace experiences of transgender employees*. UCLA School of Law Williams Institute. https://williamsinstitute.law.ucla.edu/publications/transgender-workplace-discrim/

Society of Women Engineers. (2025). *U.S. degree attainment*. https://swe.org/research/2025/us-degree-attainment/

World Economic Forum. (2025, June 11). *Global Gender Gap Report 2025*. https://reports.weforum.org/docs/WEF_GGGR_2025.pdf

CHAPTER 2

Gender and Leadership Styles

Winny Shen and Parisa Sharif Esfahani

People often claim, "Men are from Mars, Women are from Venus." This implies that men and women are fundamentally different. However, research paints a more complex picture. Although men and women can differ (Hyde, 2005), many times, these differences are magnified or distorted through our perceptions. In other words, our beliefs that men and women are (or should be) different can influence what behaviors we notice alongside how we interpret them.

In turn, this makes investigating and understanding gender differences in leadership styles a tricky endeavor. This is because leadership is a process of social influence whereby leaders motivate others to fulfill collective goals (Kaiser et al., 2008). Therefore, leadership is inherently about people and relationships. Not surprisingly then, researchers have relied on the people around leaders (e.g., subordinates, peers, superiors, customers) to provide us with insight as to how a leader acts and how effective they are. Yet, as described, these informants may not be entirely accurate or objective. Although we can deal with idiosyncrasies that may be unique to a given person by asking a larger number of people to provide us with information about a leader's behaviors to get closer to the truth, more systematic biases that most—if not all—people are subject to (e.g., societal tendencies to overlook women's contributions) are difficult to identify and would be embedded in these responses.

However, all is not lost. Although relying on others' impressions may be flawed in that they may not always accurately capture true gender differences in leadership behaviors, they still provide us with valuable insight as to leaders' social or lived realities; that is, to the extent that leaders are impactful via their influence on those around them, understanding how others view leaders—even if they

DOI: 10.4324/9781003488590-2

overlook or misinterpret their actions—helps us understand the landscapes that men and women leaders need to navigate as they seek to make a difference in their organizations.

To this end, in this chapter, we first review what is known regarding gender differences in leadership styles. Then, we discuss the downstream implications of men's and women's differential enactment of leadership behaviors. Finally, we examine the evidence to support different explanations of why men and women lead differently.

GENDER DIFFERENCES IN LEADERSHIP STYLES

Leaders can engage in a variety of actions that influence the degree of effort that others put forth toward meeting collective goals. Leaders are typically expected to engage in task-oriented behaviors, such as crafting team priorities, setting deadlines, and rewarding the behaviors they want to encourage amongst their followers. Leaders also need to attend to relationship-oriented behaviors, including providing ethical or moral guidance, demonstrating care, and understanding subordinates' values, goals, and motivations (Shen & Joseph, 2021).

Task-oriented leadership behaviors are more agentic in that they reflect a desire to master or control the environment. In contrast, relationship-oriented behaviors are more communal in that they appear to reflect desires to nurture others or promote their growth and well-being (Paustian-Underdahl et al., 2024). Although both are recognized as important components for effective leadership, people still tend to view agency as a "need to have" characteristic for leaders, whereas communality is often perceived as a "nice to have" trait (Vial & Napier, 2018). Additionally, traditional gender roles dictate that men should be agentic (e.g., assertive, dominant) and women should be communal (e.g., warm, caring). This then contributes to a perceived misfit between women and leadership roles (Eagly & Karau, 2002).

Yet, perhaps somewhat surprisingly, gender differences in task- and relationship-oriented leadership behaviors do not match gender stereotypes that men are more agentic and women are more communal. Rather, the evidence suggests that women are perceived as exhibiting both more effective task-oriented and relationship-oriented leadership behaviors than men (Shen & Joseph, 2021). This could be because perceptions of misfit between women and leadership roles create double standards of competence (Biernat & Kobrynowicz, 1997), such that women need to be especially competent or qualified to get the chance to lead in a formal capacity.

Beyond task- and relationship-oriented leadership, leaders can also engage in other actions. Scholars have argued that change-oriented leadership behaviors are another important way that leaders can motivate followers to achieve group goals (DeRue et al., 2011). These leadership behaviors encourage followers to think beyond the status quo and try new approaches. However, these actions are less clearly aligned with agency or communality and may be considered relatively gender neutral (Paustian-Underdahl et al., 2024). These gender differences tend to be a bit less pronounced than for task- or relationship-oriented leadership behaviors, but again, women leaders are rated as slightly more likely to communicate a vision or challenge people to consider assumptions more deeply than their men counterparts.

Finally, although most research focuses on what leaders can do to empower followers to achieve collective goals, the literature also recognizes that leaders can engage in problematic behaviors (e.g., taking undue credit, berating followers) or fail to take action, demotivating followers from pursuing group goals. Generally, people are more likely to report observing these passive and destructive leadership behaviors from men than women (Paustian-Underdahl et al., 2024; Shen & Joseph, 2021). Overall, the pattern of gender differences in leadership styles generally supports a female leadership advantage (Eagly & Carli, 2003); on average, women are perceived as engaging in more positive or effective leadership behaviors as well as fewer negative or ineffective leadership behaviors than men.

This pattern of gender differences is generally consistent across various levels of leadership (e.g., first-line supervisors vs. executive-level leaders; Paustian-Underdahl et al., 2024). There is also limited evidence that this gender gap has narrowed over time (Paustian-Underdahl et al., 2024). However, some research suggests that gender differences in communal leadership behaviors may depend on culture. Specifically, women leaders appear to engage in more consideration (i.e., approachable, supportive behaviors) than men leaders primarily in Western contexts (e.g., USA, Europe; van Emmerik et al., 2008).

Although there is evidence of consistent gender differences in leadership behaviors, it is important to acknowledge that these differences are generally modest or small. This means that even though, on average, men and women do not engage in these behaviors with the same frequency, these two distributions exhibit more overlap than divergence. Functionally, this means that many men and women lead similarly. It is also worth keeping in mind that there is a wide diversity of leadership behaviors amongst both groups.

DOWNSTREAM CONSEQUENCES ON LEADERSHIP OUTCOMES

Given the pattern of female advantage when it comes to leadership behaviors, you might assume that this would translate directly to women being more effective leaders than men, leading their teams or organizations to better performance or profits. Yet, this is not the case. Instead, research has found that there are no meaningful gender differences in overall leadership effectiveness (Eagly et al., 1995; Paustian-Underdahl et al., 2014).

Digging deeper into these results provides possible explanations. Although there are no gender differences when examining leadership effectiveness overall, differences do emerge based upon whose perspective is taken. Specifically, when asking others (e.g., peers, subordinates, supervisors), women are reported as slightly more effective leaders then men. However, when asking leaders *themselves*, men report that they are more effective leaders than women (Paustian-Underdahl et al., 2014).

This pattern suggests that men may be overconfident in their leadership capabilities. Yet, high levels of confidence, even if unwarranted, can yield some benefits. In particular, it often propels individuals to continue to seek promotions and other high-status opportunities (Mayoral et al., 2024). This may also help explain why men continue to be overrepresented at the upper echelons of organizations (e.g., executive-level positions). That is, individuals are often only considered for these elite roles if they choose to apply or throw their hat into the ring, and men may be more likely to do so than women. In fact, research has shown that changing the default to considering everyone for a promotion (unless one asks to be removed from consideration) increases the number of women considered for more senior roles (He et al., 2021).

There are also different ways to conceptualize leadership effectiveness. When distinguishing between satisfaction with one's leader versus performance-based indicators of effectiveness, we again see differences. Namely, women appear to garner greater satisfaction through their leadership than men. However, men exhibit a slight advantage over women when it comes to more performance-based metrics of leadership effectiveness (Eagly et al., 1995).

One reason that women's leadership may gain recognition or appreciation from followers but not result in better objective outcomes could be because women often find themselves leading in more trying circumstances than men. Past research has found that women are more likely than men to be appointed to lead during times of crises or poor organizational performance, a phenomenon known as the glass cliff (Ryan & Haslam, 2005). This term signals the risky and treacherous path these women tread. The impetus behind promoting women in these cases is the belief that women are better equipped to help workers endure difficult circumstances or take responsibility for problems, rather than confidence that these women have the capability to turn bad situations around (Ryan et al., 2011). When people compare outcomes without realizing or taking into account that women may be leading under more difficult conditions than men, they may wrongly conclude that women are less suited for leadership roles; that is, the poor performance that either predates them or is outside their control may still be blamed on these women leaders.

Another explanation for why gender differences in leadership behaviors may not equate to gender differences in leadership effectiveness could be that women do not receive due or appropriate credit for their actions. Supporting this point, there is some evidence that women do not always engender positive outcomes from their more communal leadership behaviors, such as being considerate and caring. Gender stereotypes render these behaviors as expected or required from women. Instead, men leaders are sometimes rewarded more than women leaders for these actions (e.g., Loughlin et al., 2011; Reuvers et al., 2008; Wang et al., 2013), likely because they are viewed as "pleasant surprises" and "going above and beyond." Thus, women may not benefit from their more communal leadership behaviors compared to men, who can get away with doing relatively less and receive the same evaluations.

Conversely, there is evidence that the leader themselves (or their subordinates) can benefit from women leaders displaying certain agentic actions (e.g., self-reliance, Schaumberg & Flynn, 2017; initiating structure, Kim et al., 2025). However, women leaders navigate a difficult tightrope in that they are prohibited from showing the agentic behavior of dominance and are strongly socially sanctioned for doing so (Ma et al., 2022). Specifically, research has shown that followers are more likely to accept or even approve of dominant behaviors, such as being controlling, unfair, and abusive, from men leaders but view these same behaviors from women leaders as demotivating or intolerable (e.g., Fiset & Byrne, 2024; Mu et al., 2024; Wang et al., 2013). Therefore, although women may engage in more agentic leadership behaviors than men, they need to be careful that these behaviors do not signal dominance and contravene gender norms. Otherwise, these leadership efforts will backfire, and these women will be punished rather than rewarded. Recent research also suggests that follower support plays an important role in alleviating women leaders' concerns that their gender atypical behaviors are going to be scrutinized or harshly judged, ensuring that women leaders do not experience negative consequences from engaging in agentic leadership behaviors (Lin et al., 2025).

UPSTREAM FACTORS THAT CONTRIBUTE TO GENDER DIFFERENCES IN LEADERSHIP STYLES

When we ask people to speculate why gender gaps or differences exist or persist, they typically invoke one of three explanations (Flynn, 2025). First, individuals might point to external constraints or barriers, such as problematic societal gender norms or unfair organizational policies or practices that differentially disadvantage women versus men. Second, individuals might refer to underlying dispositional gender differences; for example, due to evolutionary pressures, men are more risk-taking than women. Third, individuals may reason that men and women have different choices or preferences from one another. For example, perhaps women are less represented at upper echelons of organizations than men because they are more likely to prioritize family over work.

These explanations lay the responsibility for gender differences in leadership in different places, resulting in different perceptions regarding the need for change (Flynn, 2025). For those who subscribe to external constraints, the problem is the system or environment in which men and women find themselves, which can be biased, and is outside their control. In contrast, those who endorse different competencies may view gender differences in leadership as a reflection of the "natural order" that may not need intervention. Through this lens, nothing "unfair" is occurring, as these gaps result from different strengths and weaknesses between groups. Finally, for those who agree with a personal choice perspective, differences are a matter of personal responsibility, so men or women only have themselves to blame.

Although individuals may believe gender differences in leadership are best explained by a particular reason, reality is complicated, and these different explanations are difficult to truly disentangle. For example, although we observe gender differences in personality traits between men and women (Feingold, 1994), it is unclear whether these are "inherent" differences versus the result of differential socialization; gender stereotypes can create environments in which girls and women are pushed or encouraged to be agreeable. Even when people claim something is their personal choice, that may not necessarily be true. For example, we know that people do not like to believe the world is unjust or unfair (Iatridis & Fousiani, 2009). Therefore, they may justify or rationalize their circumstances as their choice (e.g., Diehl et al., 2020), which may give them a sense of agency or control. With these limitations in mind, below, we briefly review what we know regarding each of these explanations.

External Constraints

Work by Diehl et al. (2020) indicates that gender bias against women leaders manifests in six overarching ways. First, there continues to be male privilege in that organizational cultures and leadership conceptions lean toward masculinity and elevate male interests. Second, there are more constraints placed upon women, including women being discouraged from pursuing certain career choices and being told they need to act and communicate in particular ways. Third, women receive less support than men. Women continue to have more difficulty accessing informal networks, mentoring, and sponsorship. Fourth, women experience more devaluation; their (communal) contributions are often unseen or taken for granted and not rewarded monetarily. Fifth, women experience more hostility, including in the form of sexual harassment and lack of assistance from senior women. Sixth, these negative gender-related experiences and messages are then often internalized and contribute to acquiesce by women. Namely, women end up self-censoring and self-limiting their career options and goals.

Providing some evidence of how these gender biases can negatively affect women, Scott and Brown (2006) found that individuals may have difficulty recognizing and remembering agentic leadership behaviors enacted by women. This suggests that some of women's agentic contributions may be overlooked and fail to be captured in existing assessments of agentic leadership. In turn, if others do not acknowledge these actions, they will not be appropriately counted or rewarded.

Additionally, research indicates that despite minimal gender differences in evaluations (e.g., leadership effectiveness), there are much larger gender differences in leader rewards, favoring men (e.g., bonuses, promotions; Joshi et al., 2014). Moreover, this gap between evaluations and rewards varies by context, suggesting that gender bias is greater in some environments than others. This gap was reduced in industries with stronger representations of female executives, suggesting the importance of female representation at upper echelons for reducing external barriers for women.

Different Characteristics

Prior research has emphasized the central roles that knowledge (i.e., knowing what to do) and skills (i.e., knowing how to do it) play in determining performance or behaviors. However, the particular knowledge and skills that are most critical to leadership have not been clearly delineated. Additionally, it is generally unclear whether men and women leaders differ in knowledge and skill antecedents to leadership performance, such that they explain gender differences in leadership behaviors (Shen & Joseph, 2021).

Instead of focusing on specific leadership-related knowledge and skills, research has generally examined somewhat more distal antecedents of leadership behaviors. Specifically, people often argue that the gender gap in leadership styles is the result of underlying gender differences in personality. In this vein, Hsu et al. (2022) examined to what extent gender differences in transformational leadership behaviors (i.e., behaviors that transform followers and motivate them to transcend current circumstances) can be explained by gender differences in agentic traits, communal traits, or emotional intelligence. They found that although women are more communal and emotionally intelligent, which enhances transformational leadership, men are more agentic, which is also positively associated with transformational leadership and erodes some of women's upper hand. Overall, this research provides some evidence that women's leadership advantage may be due to their more social and emotional tendencies.

Divergent Choices

Differences in choice are often framed as issues of motivation. This is because motivation is typically described as a series of choices: the choice to act, the choice of effort level to expend, and the choice to persist (Campbell & Wiernik, 2015); that is, men and women may differentially attain leadership or lead differently due to different goals and motivations.

Researchers have uncovered three primary reasons why individuals are motivated to lead (Chan & Drasgow, 2001). Individuals may desire to lead because they intrinsically like leading (i.e., affective motivation to lead). Alternatively, individuals may want to lead because they feel an obligation or duty to lead (i.e., socio-normative motivation to lead). Finally, individuals may seek to lead because they think it is desirable or worthwhile to do so, despite potential costs or lack of rewards (i.e., non-calculative motivation to lead). There are small, but consistent, gender differences in motivation to lead (Badura et al., 2020). On average, men express slightly higher affective and socio-normative motivation, and women exhibit slightly higher non-calculative motivation to lead. In other words, men express a greater desire to lead for personal (i.e., enjoyment) and social (i.e., responsibility) reasons than women, but women are more likely than men to cite willingness to lead even in the absence of benefits.

All three types of motivation to lead are positively associated with desirable leadership behaviors (e.g., transformational leadership) and negatively associated with less desirable leadership behaviors (e.g., laissez-faire leadership), suggesting that each acts as a call to action, with the strongest relationships generally observed with affective motivation to lead. However, this pattern of results does not appear to converge with the findings reviewed earlier, where women exhibit an advantage when it comes to leadership behaviors and men exhibit stronger affective motivation to lead (which appears to be most beneficial for desirable leadership behaviors and outcomes). We speculate that one reason could be that in actuality, leadership is often fraught with costs and requires sacrifice. Therefore, since women's motivation to lead appears to be more selfless in nature (i.e., non-calculative), they may continue to invest in leading well even when it is likely they may receive nothing in return or even if it costs them something. In contrast, men may be more likely to withdraw their leadership efforts if they perceive the exchange or consequences to be unfavorable.

One issue with focusing solely on motivation to lead is that it does not capture the other goals individuals may hold. Most individuals have a variety of life goals. However, due to limits on resources, such as time and energy, individuals are not always able to pursue all their goals at once, but rather, need to prioritize and allocate resources among them. Interestingly, research finds that women tend to have more life goals than men. Additionally, relative to men, fewer of women's life goals involve power, including attaining high-status roles like leadership. Women and men are equally likely to report that achieving high-level positions is possible. However, women see doing so as less desirable. This seems to occur because women anticipate more negative outcomes (e.g., conflict with other life goals) of attaining these goals than men (Gino et al., 2015). Thus, differences in goals and motivations could contribute to the underrepresentation of women at upper echelons of organizations to the extent that men may be more likely to pursue these powerful leadership roles compared to women, who may instead choose to pursue other life goals, particularly goals that are more compatible with each other.

Conventional wisdom often highlights family goals as a reason that women choose to opt out of leadership opportunities. Although there is not strong evidence that women generally value family more than men (Shockley et al., 2017), Fritz and van Knippenberg (2018) found that the presence of work–life initiatives within one's organization was more strongly linked to the leadership aspirations of women relative to men. This seems to imply that family goals or concerns may pose an obstacle to women seeking leadership roles. However, other research suggests that perceptions of misfit between women and leadership roles might be exacerbated when women do not have immediate family members. Namely, Merluzzi and Phillips (2022) found that young single women were the least likely to advance, compared to young single men, married men, or married women, because observers assumed they lacked the social and relational characteristics needed for leadership, which marriage helped signal.

Although family goals might pose a barrier to women's choices to pursue leadership roles, that does not necessarily mean that family goals negatively impact women's leadership behaviors if or when they do choose to take on these roles. In fact, Dumas and Stanko (2017) found that having family responsibilities (i.e., being married, having children) promoted transformational leadership behaviors among leaders due to greater identification with family, which then led to greater transference of resources from the family to the work domain. Additionally, women were better able to leverage having family ties to ultimately benefit their transformational leadership compared to men. This suggests that family connections may especially aid and enrich women's leadership styles.

CHAPTER SUMMARY

Our review of the research reveals that there are small, but meaningful, gender differences in leadership styles and behaviors. Specifically, women are perceived as engaging in more effective leadership behaviors alongside less ineffective leadership behaviors compared to men. There is currently ambiguity as to whether these differences are driven by differential external constraints, different competencies, and/or divergent choices of men and women. However, what is clearer is that women often do not reap the benefits of purported female leadership advantages in that women leaders typically are not evaluated more positively nor receive more rewards than men.

DISCUSSION QUESTIONS

1. Think about and describe times you've exhibited (or witnessed) task- and relationship-oriented leadership behaviors.
2. How might perceptions of leadership effectiveness differ based on other identities that intersect with gender, including nonbinary gender identities, race/ethnicity, sexual orientation, disability, or age?

  a. Similarly, how might these perceptions differ based on organizational, regional, or national contexts?
3. Are there ways organizations can better leverage the female leadership advantage?

REFERENCES

Badura, K. L., Grijalva, E., Galvin, B. M., Owens, B. P., & Joseph, D. L. (2020). Motivation to lead: A meta-analysis and distal-proximal model of motivation and leadership. *Journal of Applied Psychology*, *105*(4), 331–354. https://doi.org/10.1037/apl0000439

Biernat, M., & Kobrynowicz, D. (1997). Gender-and race-based standards of competence: Lower minimum standards but higher ability standards for devalued groups. *Journal of Personality and Social Psychology*, *72*(3), 544–557. https://doi.org/10.1037/0022-3514.72.3.544

Campbell, J. P., & Wiernik, B. M. (2015). The modeling and assessment of work performance. *Annual Review of Organizational Psychology and Organizational Behavior*, *2*, 47–74. https://doi.org/10.1146/annurev-orgpsych-032414-111427

Chan, K.-Y., & Drasgow, F. (2001). Toward a theory of individual differences and leadership: Understanding the motivation to lead. *Journal of Applied Psychology*, *86*(3), 481–498. https://doi.org/10.1037/0021-9010.86.3.481

DeRue, D. S., Nahrgang, J. D., Wellman, N., & Humphrey, S. E. (2011). Trait and behavioral theories of leadership: An integration and meta-analytic test of their relative validity. *Personnel Psychology*, *64*(1), 7–52. https://doi.org/10.1111/j.1744-6570.2010.01201.x

Diehl, A. B., Stephenson, A. L., Dzubinski, L. M., & Wang, D. C. (2020). Measuring the invisible: Development and multi-industry validation of the Gender Bias Scale for Women Leaders. *Human Resource Development Quarterly*, *31*(3), 249–280. https://doi.org/10.1002/hrdq.21389

Dumas, T. L., & Stanko, T. L. (2017). Married with children: How family role identification shapes leadership behaviors at work. *Personnel Psychology*, *70*, 597–633. https://doi.org/10.1111/peps.12182

Eagly, A. H., & Carli, L. L. (2003). The female leadership advantage: An evaluation of the evidence. *The Leadership Quarterly*, *14*(6), 807–834. https://doi.org/10.1016/j.leaqua.2003.09.004

Eagly, A. H., & Karau, S. J. (2002). Role congruity theory of prejudice toward female leaders. *Psychological Review*, *109*(3), 573–598.

Eagly, A. H., Karau, S. J., & Makhijani, M. G. (1995). Gender and the effectiveness of leaders: A meta-analysis. *Psychological Bulletin*, *117*(1), 125–145. https://doi.org/10.1037/0033-2909.117.1.125

Feingold, A. (1994). Gender difference in personality: A meta-analysis. *Psychological Bulletin*, *116*(3), 429–456.

Fiset, J., & Byrne, A. (2024). Getting away "Scott" (but not Susan) free: The effects of safety-specific abusive supervision and supervisor gender on follower attributions and safety outcomes. *Journal of Organizational Behavior*, *46*(1), 90–107. https://doi.org/10.1002/job.2837

Flynn, E. (2025). Constraints, competencies, or choices? How lay theories of the gender gap impact diversity support. *Academy of Management Journal*, *68*(6), 1380–1406. https://doi.org/10.5465/amj.2023.0625

Fritz, C., & van Knippenberg, D. (2018). Gender and leadership aspiration: The impact of work-life initiatives. *Human Resources Management*, *57*(4), 855–868. https://doi.org/10.1002/hrm.21875

Gino, F., Wilmuth, C. A., & Brooks, A. W. (2015). Compared to men, women view professional advancement as equally attainable, but less desirable. *Proceedings of the National Academy of Sciences*, *112*, 12354–12359. https://doi.org/10.1073/pnas.1502567112

He, J. C., Kang, S. K., & Lacetera, N. (2021). Opt-out choice framing attenuates gender differences in the decision to compete in the laboratory and in the field. *Proceedings of the National Academy of Sciences*, *118*(42), e2108337118. https://doi.org/10.1073/pnas.2108337118

Hsu, N., Newman, D. A., & Badura, K. L. (2022). Emotional intelligence and transformational leadership: Meta-analysis and explanatory model of female leadership advantage. *Journal of Intelligence*, *10*, 104. https://doi.org/10.3390/jintelligence10040104

Hyde, J. S. (2005). The gender similarities hypothesis. *American Psychologist*, *60*(6), 581–592.

Iatridis, T., & Fousiani, K. (2009). Effects of status and outcome on attributions and just-world beliefs: How the social distribution of success and failure may be rationalized. *Journal of Experimental Social Psychology*, *45*(2), 415–420. https://doi.org/10.1016/j.jesp.2008.12.002

Joshi, A., Son, J., & Roh, H. (2014). When can women close the gap? A meta-analytic test of sex differences in performance and rewards. *Academy of Management Journal*, *58*(5), 1516–1545. https://doi.org/10.5465/amj.2013.0721

Kaiser, R. B., Hogan, R., & Craig, S. B. (2008). Leadership and the fate of organizations. *American Psychologist*, *63*(2), 96–110. https://doi.org/10.1037/0003-066X.63.2.96

Kim, J. (Jenny), Mitchell, M. S., Waldman, D. A., & Siegel, D. S. (2025). Do gender-role violations in initiating structure and consideration help or harm employee stress and well-being? *Journal of Management*. https://doi.org/10.1177/01492063251346400

Lin, S.-H. (J.), Woodall, J. P., Mitchell, M. S., Chi, N.-W., & Johnson, R. E. (2025). The gendered nature of leader behaviors: Navigating stereotype threat from conservation of resources and gender role perspectives. *Journal of Applied Psychology*, *110*(8), 1083–1104. https://doi.org/10.1037/apl0001263

Loughlin, C., Arnold, K., & Crawford, J. B. (2011). Lost opportunity: Is transformational leadership rewarded in all managers? *Equality, Diversity, and Inclusion: An International Journal*, *31*(1), 43–64. https://doi.org/10.1108/02610151211199218

Ma, A., Rosette, A. S., & Zhou Koval, C. (2022). Reconciling female agentic advantage and disadvantage with the CADDIS measure of agency. *Journal of Applied Psychology*, *107*(12), 2115–2148. https://doi.org/10.1037/apl0000550

Mayoral, S., Ronay, R., & Oostrom, J. K. (2024). Overconfidence and the pursuit of high-status positions: A test of two behavioral strategies. *Journal of Business & Psychology*, *39*, 1163–1186. https://doi.org/10.1007/s10869-024-09936-9

Merluzzi, J., & Phillips, D. J. (2022). Early career leadership advancement: Evidence of incongruity penalties toward young, single women professionals. *Organization Studies*, *43*(11), 1719–1743. https://doi.org/10.1177/01708406221081619

Mu, F., Shen, W., Bobocel, D. R., & Barron, A. H. (2024). Investigating gendered reactions to manager mistreatment: Testing the presumed role of prescriptive stereotypes. *Journal of Organizational Behavior*, *45*(5), 720–740. https://doi.org/10.1002/job.2763

Paustian-Underdahl, S. C., Smith Sockbeson, C. E., Hall, A. V., & Halliday, C. S. (2024). Gender and evaluations of leadership behaviors: A meta-analytic review of 50 years of research. *The Leadership Quarterly*, *35*, 101822. https://doi.org/10.1016/j.leaqua.2024.101822

Paustian-Underdahl, S. C., Walker, L. S., & Woehr, D. J. (2014). Gender and perceptions of leadership effectiveness: A meta-analysis of contextual moderators. *Journal of Applied Psychology*, *99*(6), 1129–1145. https://doi.org/10.1037/a0036751

Reuvers, M., van Engen, M. L., Vinkenburg, C. J., & Wilson-Evered, E. (2008). Transformational leadership and innovative work behaviour: Exploring the relevance of gender differences. *Creativity and Innovation Management*, *17*(3), 227–244. https://doi.org/10.1111/j.1467-8691.2008.00487.x

Ryan, M. K., & Haslam, S. A. (2005). The glass cliff: Evidence that women are over-represented in precarious leadership positions. *British Journal of Management*, *16*(2), 81–90. https://doi.org/10.1111/j.1467-8551.2005.00433.x

Ryan, M. K., Haslam, S. A., Hersby, M. D., & Bongiorno, R. (2011). Think crisis–think female: The glass cliff and contextual variation in the think manager–think male stereotype. *Journal of Applied Psychology*, *96*(3), 470–484. https://doi.org/10.1037/a0022133

Schaumberg, R. L., & Flynn, F. J. (2017). Self-reliance: A gender perspective on its relationship to communality and leadership evaluations. *Academy of Management Journal*, *60*(5), 1859–1881. https://doi.org/10.5465/amj.2015.0018

Scott, K. A., & Brown, D. J. (2006). Female first, leader second? Gender bias in the encoding of leadership behavior. *Organizational Behavior and Human Decision Processes*, *101*(2), 230–242. https://doi.org/10.1016/j.obhdp.2006.06.002

Shen, W., & Joseph, D. L. (2021). Gender and leadership: A criterion-focused review and research agenda. *Human Resource Management Review*, *31*(2), 100765. https://doi.org/10.1016/j.hrmr.2020.100765

Shockley, K. M., Shen, W., DeNunzio, M. M., Arvan, M. L., & Knudsen, E. A. (2017). Disentangling the relationship between gender and work-family conflict: An integration of theoretical perspectives using meta-analytic methods. *Journal of Applied Psychology*, *102*(12), 1601–1635. http://dx.doi.org/10.1037/apl0000246

van Emmerik, I. H., Euwema, M. C., & Wendt, H. (2008). Leadership behaviors around the world: The relative importance of gender versus cultural background. *International Journal of Cross Cultural Management*, *8*(3), 297–315. https://doi.org/10.1177/1470595808096671

Vial, A. C., & Napier, J. L. (2018). Unnecessary frills: Communality as a nice (but expendable) trait in leaders. *Frontiers in Psychology*, *9*, 1866. https://doi.org/10.3389/fpsyg.2018.01866

Wang, A.-C., Chiang, J. T.-J., Tsai, C.-Y., Lin, T.-T., & Cheng, B.-S. (2013). Gender makes the difference: The moderating role of leader gender on the relationship between leadership styles and subordinate performance. *Organizational Behavior and Human Decision Processes*, *122*(2), 101–113. https://doi.org/10.1016/j.obhdp.2013.06.001

CHAPTER 3

Shattered Ascent

Navigating the Glass Cliff

Christy Glass, Alicia Ingersoll, and Alison Cook

THROUGH THE GLASS CEILING, OFF THE GLASS CLIFF

The glass cliff refers to the greater tendency for White women, as well as men and women of color, to be appointed to precarious or risky leadership positions, compared to White men. In 1989, when Kimberlé Crenshaw coined the term intersectionality in an academic publication (Crenshaw, 1989), she was careful to note that the concept was a "lived experience before it was a term" (Crenshaw, 2015). This reality gave the term conceptual power because it named a trend that had hitherto been invisible among researchers but very real for those impacted by its consequences. At their best, social scientific concepts serve as nightlights, naming lived experiences so that scholars can illuminate their reality and move toward addressing injustices.

So is the case for the concept of the glass cliff. When Michelle Ryan and Alexander Haslam coined the term in 2005, they were responding to backlash against women's increasing representation in corporate positions which claimed that many of these women leaders harmed their organizations. For example, they quote a journalist from *The Times* who claimed that women's growing presence on corporate boards "wreaked havoc" on performance and share value (Ryan & Haslam, 2005, p. 82). Ryan and Haslam (2005) sought to interrogate such claims by evaluating the direction of the causal arrow: do women leaders harm performance, or alternatively, are women more likely to be appointed to leadership positions in organizations already in crisis?

Their initial study focused on archival analyses of company performance in the Financial Times Stock Exchange (FTSE) 100 before and after women were appointed to

DOI: 10.4324/9781003488590-3

the boards. They found that poor performance preceded women's appointments and that women directors were more likely to be appointed to struggling organizations. In other words, the so-called havoc that women directors were wreaking on their companies predated their arrival.

Like Crenshaw's foundational 1989 article, Ryan and Haslam's (2005) work reflected the best of critical academic work: recognizing problematic assumptions about a marginalized group and using the analytic tools of social science to investigate the validity of that assumption. In doing so, they generated a new interdisciplinary field of study that addresses a vexing problem for gender scholars: what are the barriers women face in seeking leadership roles and how might these barriers be overcome?

Since 2005, scholars have continued to expand our understanding of the glass cliff phenomenon and its consequences. Women face greater precarity in leadership appointments in corporate (Haslam et al., 2010), legal (Ashby et al., 2007), public (Yang et al., 2022) and political contexts (Kulich et al., 2014); Black and other men of color face the glass cliff in appointments to senior roles in corporate (Gündemir et al., 2019) and athletic contexts (Cook & Glass, 2013); and White women and women of color face greater leadership risks across a range of leadership contexts (Cook & Glass, 2014b). Scholars have also provided greater clarity and elaboration of the processes, contexts, and mechanisms that contribute to the glass cliff (e.g., Glass & Cook, 2020a; Ryan et al., 2016). Despite these important advances, scholarship on the glass cliff continues to expand in new and important areas, enhancing our understanding of factors that moderate glass cliff tendencies, expanding our understanding of leadership appointments at the intersection of gender, race, and other axes of difference, and analyzing the post-appointment consequences of precarious leadership appointments.

This chapter is organized in three parts. First, we seek to provide a state-of-the art review of research on the glass cliff, identifying the spheres and contexts in which the glass cliff has been documented. We are careful to note the ways that the glass cliff has been applied to White women as well as men and women of color, so as to expand our understanding of the phenomenon beyond a single axis conceptualization. Second, we review the social psychological and institutional mechanisms that have been identified as contributors to the glass cliff phenomenon. The interdisciplinary nature of research in this field has provided a range of mechanisms that contribute to precarious leadership appointments; illuminating these reveals the various micro- and meso-level processes at work in generating these tendencies and the ways these mechanisms may be gendered *and* racialized in particular contexts. Finally, we review nascent evidence of the impact of glass cliff roles post-appointment. While most research has focused on the point of appointment, precarious appointments are likely to have longer-term consequences. Thus, we review what is known about the effects of the glass cliff on women's short-, medium-, and long-term leadership trajectories. We conclude with a brief outline of ways scholars of the glass cliff can further enhance our knowledge of this phenomenon and pathways for removing barriers to women's ascension to top leadership positions.

THE GLASS CLIFF: A REVIEW OF EVIDENCE

In their preliminary examination, Ryan and Haslam (2005) found that "in a time of a general financial downturn in the stock market, companies that appointed a woman had experienced consistently poor performance in the months preceding the appointment" (p. 86). They concluded by calling on researchers to document the existence of the glass cliff more thoroughly in corporate and non-corporate contexts and to investigate the processes that underlie this phenomenon.

A recent meta-analysis of research on the glass cliff by Morgenroth et al. (2020) concluded that archival and experimental studies consistently demonstrate evidence of the glass cliff. They further concluded that the glass cliff phenomenon is more pronounced in countries with higher gender inequality and extends to White women, as well as men and women of color. Next, we briefly detail the evidence of glass cliff appointments across a range of contexts.

Corporate Contexts

Most research on glass cliff appointments has focused on corporate contexts and, in particular, on the appointments of senior executives and board directors. In their analyses of appointments of women to corporate boards in the FTSE 100 between 2001 and 2005, Haslam et al. (2010) found women directors were more likely than men to be appointed to firms whose stock performance was suffering. Cook and Glass (2014a) analyzed appointments of White women and men and women of color CEOs in the Fortune 500 over a 15-year period. They found that, compared to White men, non-traditional leaders were more likely to be appointed to firms experiencing performance declines. They further found that when non-typical leaders were unable to solve performance declines quickly, they were at risk of being replaced by White men CEOs, a phenomenon they termed the savior effect (Cook & Glass, 2014a).

Further studies have confirmed the presence of glass cliff appointments in the USA. For instance, Gündemir et al. (2019) found Asian American CEOs were more likely to be appointed during performance declines. They predicted that a preference for Asian American leaders during times of crisis is due to stereotypes that these leaders are more suitable for short-term leadership stints. Related research finds that Asian leaders may be more likely to be viewed through feminized stereotypes (Galinsky et al., 2013) and thus more likely to be selected for crisis leadership roles that require communal traits.

Sanchez and Frey's (2020) cross-sectional analysis of multiple industries in California found that while women CEOs remain underrepresented, women CEOs tend to be underrepresented in large firms with stronger performance trajectories. Reinwald et al. (2023) focused on executive appointments across the USA and found women executives were more than 50% more likely to be appointed to firms in crisis compared to men.

Some studies have reached conclusions contrary to the glass cliff in corporate contexts. For example, Bechtoldt et al. (2019) relied on performance measures for 233 large firms in Germany and the UK between 2005 and 2015. They found that performance was not significantly associated with the appointment of women directors. Significantly, however, the authors were careful to note that their findings may reflect the paucity of women directors as well as firms' hesitance to appoint women directors to large corporate boards.

Law and Politics

Research has confirmed the presence of glass cliff assignments in law and politics. An early study by Ashby et al. (2007) concluded that women lawyers are more likely to be assigned risky or hard-to-win cases. Similarly, Ryan et al. (2010) analyzed the selection of women candidates in the UK and found that within the Conservative Party, women candidates were more likely than men to run for more difficult-to-win seats or seats likely to be contested. As a result, they predicted that women candidates are less likely to win elections compared to men candidates. In 2014, the authors replicated their study among non-White candidates and found that racial and ethnic minorities were more likely than White candidates to run for hard-to-win seats (Kulich et al., 2014).

Aelenei et al. (2020) found that the tendency to put forward non-traditional candidates for hard-to-win seats extends to Black candidates and other candidates of color in leftist parties in France and Switzerland as well. They found that White women as well as men and women of color were more likely to run for seats that were more difficult to win, compared to White men candidates, thereby creating a more precarious path to political leadership.

These findings reinforce concerns about women party leaders' tenure and risk of turnover in the political sphere and may explain part of the gender gap in political representation. A study by O'Neill et al. (2021) found that women leaders in Canada hold shorter tenures than men and are at greater risk of involuntary departures and resignations.

Sports

Beyond corporate and political-legal contexts, scholars have analyzed whether glass cliff appointments extend to appointments of head coaches in collegiate sports. Cook and Glass (2013) analyzed all head coaching appointments in NCAA Division 1 basketball over a 30-year period and found that compared to White coaches, Black coaches were more likely to be appointed to losing teams. Wicker et al. (2019) conducted a similar study of women college soccer coaches, finding that women coaches were more likely than men to be hired on teams with weaker winning percentages during prior seasons. Thus, while the gender of the coach is not associated with team performance (Gomez et al., 2019), team performance is predictive of the gender of a newly selected head coach.

Public and Non-Profit Contexts

Finally, scholars have analyzed glass cliff appointments in non-profit and public contexts. While indicators of crisis or performance declines are more difficult to assess in these contexts, scholars have adopted a range of measures to understand the appointment contexts of non-typical leaders, including White women and men and women of color.

An important study by Yang et al. (2022) examined the context of women's leadership in municipal government roles in Florida. They found that women, compared to men, not only tend to be concentrated in roles in smaller municipalities with smaller staffs but that they are also more likely to be hired during periods of budget cuts. Consistent with the savior effect phenomenon (Cook and Glass, 2014a), they found that when women (but not men) were unable to address budget issues, they were at heightened risk of being terminated, resulting in higher turnover rates for women compared to men managers (Yang et al., 2022).

At the federal level, Sabharwal (2015) analyzed the appointments of women senior executives across US federal agencies. They assessed a glass cliff position by evaluating turnover likelihood and found that women in senior leadership roles were more likely to anticipate leaving or losing their positions when they had less decision-making authority and when their organizations were predominantly composed of men. A similar study by Smith and Monaghan (2013) found that compared to men, women were more likely to lead regulatory agencies with limited visibility and with a high risk of failure. These studies suggest that institutional context and job characteristics combine to shape leadership experiences for women in public service.

Outside the USA, research on civil service appointments has found evidence contrary to the glass cliff. In a study of Dutch civil service, Groeneveld et al. (2020) found that women's appointments to leadership positions were not associated with resource declines, looking specifically at workforce reductions.

FACTORS CONTRIBUTING TO GLASS CLIFF APPOINTMENTS

In subsequent work, Ryan et al. (2016) carefully noted that the glass cliff does not reflect a theory of social life but rather, a phenomenon in need of explanation. They note that the role of scholars is to explain this phenomenon by applying theory to uncover the tendency to appoint minoritized leaders to precarious leadership positions. To explain glass cliff appointments, Ryan et al. (2016) called on scholars to provide a "nuanced, context-dependent understanding of the conditions under which the glass cliff occurs" (p. 10). Scholars continue to answer this call by drawing on a range of data sources and methodologies, including archival, experimental, survey, and interview designs.

Psychological Factors: Gender Bias, Negative Stereotypes, and Benevolent Sexism

Ryan, Haslam, and their colleagues have conducted several experimental studies (e.g., Ashby et al., 2007; Haslam & Ryan, 2008; Ryan et al., 2016) to examine underlying psychological factors that may increase the likelihood that decision makers will tap women for precarious leadership roles. In a series of studies, participants were provided with scenarios that indicated a company's performance and were asked to evaluate potential candidates for a leadership position within that company. Under these experimental conditions, evaluators were more likely to positively evaluate the woman candidate's resume versus the man's when the company's performance was declining. These findings led the authors to conclude that while the think manager-think man stereotype may remain salient (Schein, 1973), poor firm performance leads to the tendency to think crisis-think woman (Gartzia et al., 2012; Ryan et al., 2011).

A preference for women leaders during times of crisis likely reflects assumptions and stereotypes about men and women. For instance, (White) women are assumed to be more communal, cooperative and warm, while (White) men are assumed to be agentic, assertive and competitive (Eagly & Wood, 2012). Stereotypically masculine traits may be preferred when selecting leaders in general (Schein, 1973); however, in times of crisis, evaluators demonstrate a greater preference for qualities that women are assumed to possess (Bruckmüller & Branscombe, 2010).

In fact, Ryan et al. (2011) found that women were particularly favored as crisis leaders when the expectations of their role centered on serving as a scapegoat for a crisis or when the leader was expected to manage people through the crisis. By contrast, no preference for women emerged when crisis leaders were expected to serve as a spokesperson or improve firm performance (Ryan et al., 2011). This study suggests that rather than viewing women as capable of turning crises around, women may be preferred primarily for their communal or supportive characteristics or as stand-ins for blame and censure.

To explain the tendency to promote women as leaders during crises, Ryan et al. (2011) found that participants were more likely to ascribe feminine stereotypes to the requisite qualities of managers of poorly performing companies. In a similar experimental study, Bruckmüller and Branscombe's (2010) participants rated men and women candidates for a leadership position based on stereotypically masculine and feminine traits. Participants demonstrated a greater tendency to assign women candidates to poorly performing firms in part based on feminine stereotypes.

Institutional Factors: Organizational Context, Representation, and Agency

In addition to psychological factors that drive glass cliff appointments, scholars have also identified institutional factors that may enhance the likelihood that White women, as well as men and women of color, are appointed to precarious leadership roles.

While women and other minoritized groups may view risky appointments as less attractive (Rink et al., 2012), they may nevertheless be inclined to accept such positions in recognition that they may not have abundant alternative opportunities (Darouei & Pluut, 2018; Mashele & Alagidede, 2023). Thus, the relative scarcity of White women and men and women of color in highly visible leadership roles may serve as a nudge for them to accept roles that would otherwise be undesirable.

Yet another way representation affects glass cliff appointments is through the composition of boards of directors. In a study of CEO appointments, Cook and Glass (2014c) found that gender diversity among boards of directors significantly increased the likelihood that a firm would appoint a woman CEO, regardless of firm performance. The study further revealed that board diversity increased women CEOs' tenure and reduced the risk of their being replaced due to poor firm performance. This study suggests that representation (or its absence) among decision makers can be a significant predictor of glass cliff appointments.

Qualitative research with senior leaders identified an additional mechanism, what Glass and Cook term the risk tax (Glass & Cook, 2020a). Drawing on 33 in-depth interviews with senior leaders across a range of sectors, Glass and Cook (2020b) revealed the ways in which gender and racial bias early in careers motivated future leaders to seek opportunities to overcome doubts regarding their abilities to lead effectively. Part of their strategy involved seeking high risk management opportunities starting early in the careers. Over time, successive demonstrations of crisis management contributed to their reputations as effective crisis leaders, leading to the tendency to "think crisis-think non-typical leader."

This study uncovered the career risks White women and men and women of color must endure to be viewed as effective leaders. While risk management enabled these leaders to distinguish themselves to attain highly visible leadership roles, paying a risk tax also results in penalties, including a perfection standard of performance, anxieties regarding career derailment, and performance fatigue (Glass & Cook, 2020a).

FACTORS MODERATING GLASS CLIFF APPOINTMENTS

While most research to date has focused on processes preceding glass cliff appointments, a handful of studies provide some insight into ways that this phenomenon may be reduced or moderated. Glass cliff appointments are not universal; thus, researchers must examine the context-dependent nature of the phenomenon to identify potential interventions. Researchers have sought to identify not just its reality across organizational contexts but also factors that moderate the tendency to place women in risky leadership positions.

A significant body of research has explored the ways in which signaling change motivates glass cliff appointments, suggesting that preferences for women leaders during times of crisis may be contingent on the company's history of leadership. Previous research found that appointing a woman leader during a time of crisis can be intended to signal that the company is headed in a bold new direction (Lee & James, 2007). Indeed, Bruckmüller and Branscombe (2010) found that the think crisis-think woman phenomenon was particularly pronounced in organizations with a history of men leaders. The tendency to prefer women leaders during times of crisis or threat has been confirmed in other studies as well (e.g., Brown et al., 2011).

Signaling change was also a relevant factor in Reinwald et al.'s (2023) study of executive appointments. They found that women executives were not only more likely than men to be appointed during crises but that firms tended to frame these leaders as harbingers of change in press releases announcing the appointment. However, experimental research by Kulich et al. (2015) found that beliefs that women signal change do not necessarily translate into beliefs that women are *effective* change agents. In fact, this study found that women's selection for crisis leadership did not necessarily reflect evaluator confidence in women's leadership ability. In fact, evidence suggests that women may be selected for crisis appointments precisely because these roles are unappealing, and women appointed during times of crisis are unlikely to be successful (Ryan et al., 2011; Ryan et al., 2016).

Firm visibility may also moderate the tendency to appoint non-traditional leaders off the glass cliff. Glass cliff appointments are more likely in firms with low media visibility (Ihmels et al., 2022), suggesting that concerns regarding media scrutiny may dissuade decision-makers from appointing women to precarious leadership roles. Other research has found that the fear of negative media publicity may dissuade firms from ousting women CEOs (Elsaid & Ursel, 2018), again suggesting that media scrutiny may serve as a form of accountability to firms enacting gender bias in leader appointments and dismissals.

Scholars have also identified moderators related to the nature of the organizational field in which appointments are made. In their study of glass cliff appointments among NCAA Division 1 men's head basketball coaches, Cook and Glass (2013) compared coaching appointments at Historically Black Colleges and Universities (HBCUs) to appointments at other Division 1 schools. They found that Black head coaches were less likely to face a glass cliff at HBCUs, suggesting that sector as well as composition of the firm or organization may moderate the tendency to appoint non-traditional leaders to precarious roles.

The nature of crisis may also influence the tendency to seek non-traditional leaders when organizations are struggling. Experimental research by Kulich et al. (2021) examined how the nature of a crisis affected preferences for women leaders. They found that participants were more likely to select a woman candidate to lead a behaviorally based crisis (i.e., a crisis that involved internal conflict) but were less likely to select a woman leader when crises were primarily financial, reflecting gender bias regarding women leaders' financial acuity.

Finally, there is evidence that decision-maker composition can influence the likelihood of selecting a non-traditional leader for a crisis appointment. In their study of CEO appointments in the Fortune 500, Cook and Glass (2014c) found that women's representation on boards of directors reduced the likelihood that women would be appointed CEOs to firms in crisis. Women's representation on boards also granted women CEOs more time to demonstrate their leadership abilities post-appointment. This study suggests that the composition of decision-makers may moderate the tendency to appoint women to risky or precarious leadership roles.

This finding underscores the relevance of an experimental study by Rink et al. (2013), which found the preference for women leaders during a crisis was more pronounced when the leader lacked a strong network of support. When participants were assured that the focal leader would have the necessary and needed support to navigate the crisis, preference for women leaders declined. The presence of women on boards of directors and women CEOs in an industry also alleviate concerns of women CEO candidates (Klein et al., 2021), including concerns about glass cliff appointments.

FALLING OFF THE GLASS CLIFF: POST-APPOINTMENT CHALLENGES

In their original formulation of the glass cliff, Ryan and Haslam (2005) speculated that women appointed to glass cliff leadership roles would suffer negative repercussions as a result, including blame for the poor performance that preceded their appointments. They speculated that real or perceived failure following a glass cliff appointment may result in a loss of reputation for women leaders due to the lack of recognition that their appointments were, in part, a reflection of the performance declines that predated them. They concluded, "if, upon finding themselves in a leadership position, [women] fail . . . they may be singled out for blame and humiliation, at the same time that the propitious conditions of their appointment are overlooked" (p. 88).

These tendencies are likely to be heightened by the performance pressures, negative stereotypes, and hyperscrutiny faced by non-traditional incumbents of leadership positions (Kanter, 1977). Indeed, research finds that non-typical leaders are much more likely to be held accountable for real or perceived errors compared to traditional leaders (Brescoll et al., 2010), thereby enhancing the potential negative consequences of glass cliff appointments. Though very little research has explored the post-appointment trajectories of glass cliff leaders, there is work that confirms the original predictions of Ryan and Haslam (2005).

Tenure and Turnover Effects

Previous research found that women leaders may be particularly vulnerable to performance declines and that performance challenges may inhibit women's abilities to sustain and succeed in leadership roles (Pearson & Clair, 1998). However, findings regarding women CEOs' tenure and turnover relative to men are mixed. In their study of CEO succession in the USA, Elsaid and Ursel (2018) found that while women are more likely than men to be appointed to struggling firms, this precarity does not translate into shorter tenures. In fact, women CEOs are less likely to face turnover following their appointments, compared to men. They further found that firms may be hesitant to dismiss women CEOs for fear of negative publicity (Elsaid & Ursel, 2018). However, in their analysis of boards of directors in the UK, Main and Gregory-Smith (2018) found that women directors experience shorter tenures compared to men and face a higher risk of dismissal (Main & Gregory-Smith, 2018). Gupta et al. (2020) found that women CEOs are more vulnerable than men to short-term performance declines. While Gupta et al. (2020) did not account for firm performance at the time of appointment, their study suggests that performance may indeed shape women's tenure and risk of turnover relative to men's.

The Savior Effect

Performance declines increase the scrutiny of and performance pressure on incumbent leaders, and this is likely more salient for leaders who do not fit the typical leader profile, including White women and men and women of color. Real or perceived failure is likely to be public and highly publicized. In their review of evidence of the glass cliff, Ryan et al. (2016) speculated that negative publicity and scrutiny may be particularly harsh in the context of the glass cliff due to the "co-occurrence of two relatively rare events—a crisis and the appointment of a female leader" (p. 447). In their analysis of the post-appointment experiences of glass cliff appointees, Cook and Glass (2014a) found that when White women and minority CEOs are unable to fix crises in short periods of time, they tend to be blamed and replaced by White men (i.e., the savior effect). In these instances, women CEOs tend to be blamed for crises that predated their appointments and then replaced by leaders intended to signal that companies are once again in stable hands.

Post-Leadership Trajectory

Though very little research to date has traced the post-appointment trajectories of glass cliff leaders, there is research that finds that ousted leaders face limited prospects for future leadership appointments (Ferris et al., 2003). Diminished opportunities may be particularly salient for non-traditional leaders, who are subject to greater scrutiny and negative evaluation bias. In their analysis of all women who have ever served as CEOs in the Fortune 500, Glass and Cook (2016) found that women CEOs experience shorter tenures compared to male peers.

In their qualitative research with glass cliff appointees, Glass and Cook (2020b) revealed these leaders' frustrations regarding the unique challenges they faced. Interviewees occupied highly visible and influential roles, yet most expressed performance fatigue as well as continued hypervisibility and performance pressures. One White women leader referred to the "one mistake rule": her inability to make an error (or perceived error) lest her credibility be undermined. A Black man CEO, who had been appointed during his company's bankruptcy scandal, noted that to survive as a Black CEO "you have to have a flawless run" or risk perceptions that you lack fitness for leadership (Glass & Cook, 2020b, p. 10).

By centering the strategic agency as well as the subjective experiences of glass cliff leaders, this study revealed that leaders experience heightened visibility due to their atypicality and performance challenges. These barriers continue far beyond the stage of appointment, suggesting the need for greater research on the post-appointment trajectories of glass cliff leaders and the factors that moderate their negative experiences.

NEXT STEPS FOR GLASS CLIFF RESEARCH: WHERE DO WE GO FROM HERE?

Evidence of the glass cliff is robust across multiple organizational contexts and over time. Yet in many ways, the field of research is still in its early stages. There is substantial opportunity to expand and develop our understanding of the glass cliff across multiple disciplines and using a range of methodologies. Below, we consider two directions that could strengthen the field by increasing our understanding of the nuances and mechanisms that drive the glass cliff as well as the medium- and long-term consequences of glass cliff appointments for leaders and organizations.

Intersectional Analyses of Leader Appointments

In their seminal article, Rosette et al. (2018) called on scholars of organizational inequality to attend to the ways race and gender intersect to shape workplace opportunities, mobility, and status. Drawing on the rich multidisciplinary history of intersectional thought, Rosette et al. (2018) argued that women's workplace experiences vary widely at the intersections of race, ethnicity, and other axes of difference. For instance, they highlight research that contrasts perceptions of women leaders generally to perceptions of Black women specifically. While White women tend to be viewed as passive and communal—qualities that make them ineffective leaders—Black women face a burden of doubt regarding their competence as leaders. Thus, while Black women are often stereotyped as dominant, perceptions of their incompetence create steep barriers to leadership (Rosette et al., 2018). The authors argue that the absence of intersectional research serves as a significant limitation of research on the glass cliff, noting that stereotypes of Black women position them as least likely to be appointed to lead companies for which managing financial precarity is required. Instead, they note, "although Black women may experience benefits once they access leadership roles because of dominance stereotypes, their presumed incompetence likely impedes their attainment of top roles and at least partially explains their immense underrepresentation in leadership roles" (p. 7).

Analyses that attend to the complexity of difference are better equipped to explain the contexts within which glass cliff appointments occur as well as the mechanisms that drive these appointments. Despite these insights, glass cliff research tends to focus overwhelmingly on White women. However, a few examples illustrate the importance of a broader and more intersectional approach to understanding the context under which non-traditional leaders are appointed. In their quantitative (e.g., Cook & Glass, 2013, 2014a, 2014b) and qualitative studies (Glass & Cook, 2020a, 2020b) examining the glass cliff, Cook and Glass find that race as well as gender contribute to precarious leadership appointments. Similarly, in their recent study of the glass cliff in the context of political candidates, Robinson et al. (2024) find that White women as well as ethnic minority candidates disproportionately run for less winnable seats, suggesting that the glass cliff may impede gender and racial representation among political office holders.

While these studies approach intersectionality in a more additive manner, Gündemir et al. (2019) studied the glass cliff using a nuanced approach. In their archival and experimental analyses of Asian American leaders, they found that stereotypes of Asian Americans as self-sacrificing and submissive contributed to a preference for these leaders during times of crisis. Thus, while racial stereotypes may facilitate opportunities for Asian leaders, these opportunities are rare and short-term. These studies serve as an important baseline from which scholars can build to integrate more analyses that recognize that gendered processes are shaped at the intersections of race, class, sexuality, and other axes of difference.

Understanding the Consequences of Glass Cliff Appointments

In addition to incorporating intersectional frameworks to understand glass cliff appointments, future research must also expand the timeframe within which we analyze precarious leadership appointments. Glass cliff appointments reflect processes at the micro, meso, and macro levels, including the strategic agency of non-traditional leaders across their careers (e.g., Glass & Cook, 2020a), the organizational characteristics that increase the odds of glass cliff appointments (e.g., Ihmels et al., 2022), and the psychological and institutional contexts in which leadership and difference are given meaning (e.g., Rosette et al., 2018).

To refine analyses of the context of glass cliff appointments, scholars must also expand their analytical windows, analyzing the processes that shape potential leaders' careers over time as well as the post-appointment consequences of glass cliff appointments for leaders and organizations. Doing so will build upon and extend our theoretical understanding of the glass cliff as a social process as well as the mechanisms that reduce or increase the salience of racial and gendered differences among leaders.

As previous research finds, White women, as well as men and women of color, are strategic agents in shaping their career trajectories (Glass & Cook, 2020a). The strategies atypical leaders rely upon to negotiate their belonging in White and male-dominated organizations may contribute to reputations and skill sets that enable them to manage crises effectively (Glass & Cook, 2020a). However, high-risk career building strategies, such as seeking out crisis opportunities, may also reduce the pipeline of potential White women and minority leaders for highly visible, senior leadership roles.

Organizational contexts are also important sites to analyze pre- and post-glass cliff appointments to better understand the meso-level factors that contribute to the risk of precarious leadership opportunities for atypical leaders. For example, a comparative qualitative analysis by Dwivedi et al. (2018) found that organizations in which men precede women's CEO appointments vary in terms of the context of support for women leaders. Women CEOs who achieved high performance following their appointments were more likely than other women to benefit from support by their male predecessors. When men CEOs engage in what the authors term "gender-inclusive gatekeeping," they set up women CEOs for success, particularly when the male predecessor is long serving and when the woman successor is internally appointed. This study, as well as Glass and Cook (2020a), underscore the importance of understanding both the organizational context and prior career trajectories of glass cliff appointees.

It is also likely that post-appointment effects of the sglass cliff contribute to a reduced supply of atypical leaders by increasing the risk of dismissal and negative reputational costs for White women and men and women of color. Ongoing research on the antecedents and repercussions of the glass cliff finds that women CEOs are more vulnerable than men CEOs to involuntary dismissals during periods of performance declines and that investors reward firms for replacing dismissed women CEOs with White men successors (Cook et al., 2024). This suggests that atypical CEOs may be more vulnerable than White men to glass cliff appointments and glass cliff dismissals. The vulnerability to dismissal may also enhance perceptions that women are unfit leaders and reduce the supply of highly skilled women leaders by derailing the careers of women above the glass ceiling.

CHAPTER SUMMARY

The glass cliff is a relatively recent academic concept that has become a burgeoning phenomenon. This chapter outlines the contexts in which the glass cliff has been documented and explains theoretical contributors to the occurrence of the glass cliff. It also highlights the effects of glass cliff appointments on the career trajectories of White women and people of color. Moving forward, scholars and practitioners should contemplate these precursors and outcomes of glass cliff appointments to design and implement practices that disrupt the occurrence of glass cliff appointments, thereby shattering the nature of precarious leadership positions for women and employees of color.

DISCUSSION QUESTIONS

1. How might the intersections of race, gender, and other identities (e.g., sexual orientation, disability, social class) create unique experiences of the glass cliff? Can you give examples of experiences that might be missed if we only look at gender or race?
2. The concept of the glass cliff implies that some leaders are set up for failure. From a systemic perspective, what are the organizational benefits of this phenomenon? Who stands to gain when a marginalized leader fails in a high-risk position?
3. Beyond the "glass cliff," what other metaphors or concepts could be used to describe the nuanced challenges faced by non-binary or gender

non-conforming individuals in leadership roles? What systemic barriers might they face that are distinct from those experienced by cisgender men and women?

4. The chapter cites a backlash against women's increasing representation. How do public narratives and media portrayals of corporate leaders contribute to the formation and perpetuation of the glass cliff? What is the media's responsibility in challenging or reinforcing these stereotypes?
5. The chapter suggests that the glass cliff is a "lived experience" that was given a name. Can you think of any unnamed or invisible challenges in your own professional experiences or observations that could benefit from a similar conceptualization?
6. The chapter focuses on formal leadership appointments. In what ways might the glass cliff phenomenon apply to informal leadership, for instance, leading a high-stakes project or stepping in to guide a team without a formal promotion?

REFERENCES

Aelenei, C., Assilaméhou-Kunz, Y., Iacoviello, V., & Kulich, C. (2020). The political glass cliff: When left-wing orientation leads to minority candidate choices for hard-to-win seats. *European Review of Applied Psychology*, *70*(3), 100514.

Ashby, J., Ryan, M. K., & Haslam, S. A. (2007). Legal work and the glass cliff: Evidence that women are preferentially selected to lead problematic cases. *William & Mary Journal of Women and the Law*, *13*, 775–793.

Bechtoldt, M. N., Bannier, C. E., & Rock, B. (2019). The glass cliff myth? Evidence from Germany and the U. K. *The Leadership Quarterly*, *30*, 273–297.

Brescoll, V., Dawson, E., & Uhlmann, E. (2010). Hard won and easily lost: The fragile status of leaders in gender-stereotype incongruent occupations. *Psychological Science*, *21*(11), 1640–1642.

Brown, E., Diekman, A., & Schneider, M. (2011). A change will do us good: Threats diminish typical preferences for male leaders. *Personality and Social Psychology Bulletin*, *37*, 930–941.

Bruckmüller, S., & Branscombe, N. R. (2010). The glass cliff: When and why women are selected as leaders in crisis contexts. *British Journal of Social Psychology*, *49*, 433–451.

Cook, A., & Glass, C. (2013). Glass cliffs and organizational saviors: Barriers to minority leadership in work organizations. *Social Problems*, *60*, 168–187.

Cook, A., & Glass, C. (2014a). Above the glass ceiling: When are women and racial/ethnic minorities promoted to CEO? *Strategic Management Journal*, *35*, 1080–1089.

Cook, A., & Glass, C. (2014b). Analyzing promotions of racial/ethnic minority CEOs. *Journal of Managerial Psychology*, *29*, 440–454.

Cook, A., & Glass, C. (2014c). Women and top leadership positions: Towards an institutional analysis. *Gender, Work and Organization*, *21*, 91–103.

Cook, A., Glass, C., & Ingersoll, A. (2024). Antecedents and repercussions of CEO dismissals in the U.S.: A glass cliff for women CEOs? Unpublished manuscript.

Crenshaw, K. (1989). Demarginalizing the intersection of race and sex: A Black feminist critique of antidiscrimination doctrine, feminist theory and antiracist politics. *University of Chicago Legal Forum*, *1*(8), 139–167.

Crenshaw, K. (2015, September). Why intersectionality can't wait. *The Washington Post*, 24.

Darouei, M., & Pluut, H. (2018). The paradox of being on the glass cliff: Why do women accept risky leadership positions? *Career Development International*, *23*(4), 397–426.

Dwivedi, P., Joshi, A., & Misangyi, V. (2018). Gender-inclusive gatekeeping: How (mostly male) predecessors influence the success of female CEOs. *Academy of Management Journal*, *61*(2), 379–404.

Eagly, A. H., & Wood, W. (2012). Social role theory. In P. A. M. Van Lange, A. W. Kruglanski, & E. T. Higgins (Eds.), *Handbook of theories of social psychology* (pp. 458–476). Sage Ltd.

Elsaid, E., & Ursel, N. D. (2018). Re-examining the glass cliff hypothesis using survival analysis: The case of female CEO tenure. *British Journal of Management*, *29*, 156–170.

Ferris, S., Jagannathan, M., & Pritchard, A. (2003). Too busy to mind the business? Monitoring directors with multiple board appointments. *The Journal of Finance*, *58*(3), 1087–1111.

Galinsky, A. D., Hall, E. V., & Cuddy, A. J. (2013). Gendered races: Implications for interracial marriage, leadership selection, and athletic participation. *Psychological Science*, *24*, 498–506.

Gartzia, L., Ryan, M., Balluerka, N., & Aritzeta, A. (2012). Think crisis-think female: Further evidence. *European Journal of Work and Organizational Psychology*, *21*(4), 603–628.

Glass, C., & Cook, A. (2016). Leading at the top: Understanding women's challenges above the glass ceiling. *Leadership Quarterly*, *27*(1), 51–63.

Glass, C., & Cook, A. (2020a). Pathways to the glass cliff: A risk tax for women and minority leaders? *Social Problems*, *67*(4), 637–653.

Glass, C., & Cook, A. (2020b). Performative contortions: How white women and people of color navigate elite leadership roles. *Gender, Work & Organization*, *27*(6), 1232–1252.

Gomez-Gonzalez, C., Dietl, H., & Nesseler, C. (2019). Does performance justify the underrepresentation of women coaches? Evidence from professional women's soccer. *Sport Management Review*, *22*(5), 640–651.

Groeneveld, S., Bakker, V., & Schmidt, E. (2020). Breaking the glass ceiling, but facing a glass cliff? The role of organizational decline in women's representation in leadership positions in Dutch civil service organizations. *Public Administration*, *98*(2), 441–464.

Gündemir, S., Carton, A. M., & Homan, A. C. (2019). The impact of organizational performance on the emergence of Asian American leaders. *Journal of Applied Psychology*, *104*, 107–122.

Gupta, V. K., Mortal, S., Silveri, S., Sun, M., & Turban, D. (2020). You're fired! Gender disparities in CEO dismissal. *Journal of Management*, *46*(4), 560–582.

Haslam, S. A., & Ryan, M. K. (2008). The road to the glass cliff: Differences in the perceived suitability of men and women for leadership positions in succeeding and failing organizations. *The Leadership Quarterly*, *19*, 530–546.

Haslam, S. A., Ryan, M. K., Kulich, C., Trojanowski, G., & Atkins, C. (2010). Investing with prejudice: The relationship between women's presence on company boards and objective and subjective measures of company performance. *British Journal of Management*, *21*, 484–497.

Ihmels, A., Haslam, A., Shemla, M., & Wegge, J. (2022). *Through a glass cliff darkly*. Zeitschrift für Arbeits-und Organisationspsychologie A&O.

Kanter, R. M. (1977). *Men and women of the corporation*. Basic Books.

Klein, F., Chaigneau, P., & Devers, C. (2021). CEO gender-based termination concerns: Evidence from initial severance agreements. *Journal of Management*, *47*(3), 567–596.

Kulich, C., Gartzia, L., Komarraju, M., & Aelenei, C. (2021). Contextualizing the think crisis-think female stereotype in explaining the glass cliff: Gendered traits, gender, and type of crisis. *PLOS One*, *16*(3), e0246576.

Kulich, C., Lorenzi-Cioldi, F., Iacoviello, V., Faniko, K., & Ryan, M. K. (2015). Signaling change during a crisis: Refining conditions for the glass cliff. *Journal of Experimental Social Psychology*, *61*, 96–103.

Kulich, C., Ryan, M. K., & Haslam, S. A. (2014). The political glass cliff: Understanding how seat selection contributes to the underperformance of ethnic minority candidates. *Political Research Quarterly*, *67*, 84–95.

Lee, P., & James, E. (2007). She'-e-os: Gender effects and investor reactions to the announcements of top executive appointments. *Strategic Management Journal*, *28*(3), 227–241.

Main, B., & Gregory-Smith, I. (2018). Symbolic management and the glass cliff: Evidence from the boardroom careers of female and male directors. *British Journal of Management*, *29*(1), 136–155.

Mashele, W., & Alagidede, I. P. (2023). When spotting the glass cliff matters: A qualitative study focusing on gender inequalities in corporate South Africa. In J. Crawford & T. Choudhry (Eds.), *Leadership: Advancing great leaders and leadership*. https://doi.org/10.5772/intechopen.108102

Morgenroth, T., Kirby, T. A., Ryan, M. K., & Sudkämper, A. (2020). The who, when, and why of the glass cliff phenomenon: A meta-analysis of appointments to precarious leadership positions. *Psychological Bulletin*, *146*(9), 797–829.

O'Neill, B., Pruysers, S., & Stewart, D. (2021). Glass cliffs or partisan pressure? Examining gender and party leader tenures and exits. *Political Studies*, *69*(2), 257–277.

Pearson, C., & Clair, J. (1998). Reframing crisis management. *Academy of Management Review*, *23*(1), 59–76.

Reinwald, M., Zaia, J., & Kunze, F. (2023). Shine bright like a diamond: When signaling creates glass cliffs for female executives. *Journal of Management*, *49*(3), 1005–1036.

Rink, F., Ryan, M. K., & Stoker, J. I. (2012). Influence in times of crisis: How social and financial resources affect men's and women's evaluations of glass-cliff positions. *Psychological Science*, *23*, 1306–1313.

Rink, F., Ryan, M. K., & Stoker, J. I. (2013). Social resources at a time of crisis: How gender stereotypes inform gendered leader evaluations. *European Journal of Social Psychology*, *43*, 381–392.

Robinson, S. L., Kulich, C., Assilaméhou-Kunz, Y., Aelenei, C., & Iacoviello, V. (2024). Women and ethnic minority candidates face dynamic party divergent glass cliff conditions in French elections. *International Review of Social Psychology*, *37*(1), 1–24.

Rosette, A. S., Ponce de Leon, R., Koval, C. Z., & Harrison, D. (2018). Intersectionality: Connecting experiences of gender with race at work. *Research in Organizational Behavior*, *38*, 1–22.

Ryan, M. K., & Haslam, S. A. (2005). The glass cliff: Evidence that women are over-represented in precarious leadership positions. *British Journal of Management*, *16*, 81–90.

Ryan, M. K., Haslam, S. A., Hersby, M. D., & Bongiorno, R. (2011). Think crisis-think female: The glass cliff and contextual variation in the think manager-think male stereotype. *Journal of Applied Psychology*, *96*, 470–484.

Ryan, M. K., Haslam, S. A., & Kulich, C. (2010). Politics and the glass cliff: Evidence that women are preferentially selected to contest hard-to-win seats. *Psychology of Women Quarterly*, *34*, 56–64.

Ryan, M. K., Haslam, S. A., Morgenroth, T., Rink, F., Stoker, J., & Peters, K. (2016). Getting on top of the glass cliff: Reviewing a decade of evidence, explanations, and impact. *The Leadership Quarterly*, *27*, 446–455.

Sabharwal, M. (2015). From glass ceiling to glass cliff: Women in senior executive service. *Journal of Public Administration: Research and Theory*, *25*, 399–426.

Sanchez, D., & Frey, E. (2020). Where do females rise to leadership positions? A cross-sector analysis. *Applied Economics Letters*, *27*(15), 1252–1255.

Schein, V. E. (1973). The relationship between sex role stereotypes and requisite management characteristics. *Journal of Applied Psychology*, *57*, 95–100.

Smith, A. E., & Monaghan, K. R. (2013). Some ceilings have more cracks: Representative bureaucracy in federal regulatory agencies. *The American Review of Public Administration*, *43*, 50–71.

Wicker, P., Cunningham, G. B., & Fields, D. (2019). Head coach changes in women's college soccer: An investigation of women coaches through the lenses of gender stereotypes and the glass cliff. *Sex Roles*, *81*, 797–807.

Yang, L., Connolly, L., & Connolly, J. (2022). Is there a glass cliff in local government management? Examining the hiring and departure of women. *Public Administration Review*, *82*(3), 570–584.

CHAPTER 4

Women of Color in Business Organizations

Katherine Giscombe

Women of color represent a demographic group that has contributed vast amounts of labor to the USA. This chapter highlights both the personal and institutional challenges that women of color face in business organizations, providing insights to the talents, experiences, and contributions to business and civil life that women of color have made.

A BRIEF HISTORY OF WOMEN—AND WOMEN OF COLOR—IN THE USA

Women in the United States of America (USA) experienced major societal inequities in the nineteenth and early twentieth centuries, with no rights to own property, vote, hold public office, control their own reproduction, or pursue a variety of jobs. In the early 1900s, women's legal standing depended on their marital status. A married woman had no separate legal identity from her husband, and no separate standing in courts of law. These statutes defined White women's places in society as mainly domestic (Evans, 2006).

The situation in the USA for women of color in the nineteenth and early twentieth centuries was much more difficult than for White women. African American women, along with African American men, resided mainly in Southern states where they had been enslaved, under typically brutal conditions, until after the end of the Civil War in the late nineteenth century (Kelley, 2023). Given limited educational opportunities and "Jim Crow" laws, which mandated segregation and prompted post-civil war violence in the South, African American women joined African American men in the "Great Migration" (National Archives, African American History, n.d.). Approximately

DOI: 10.4324/9781003488590-4

six million Black people left the South to settle in Northern, Midwestern, and Western states from roughly the 1910s until the 1970s. During the early years of the Great Migration, the labor supply was strained with a decline in immigration from Europe and immigration bans on people of color from other parts of the world. This afforded the Black population an opportunity to be the labor supply in non-agricultural industries (National Archives, African American History, n.d.).

In the late nineteenth century and early- to mid-1900s, Asian groups migrated to the USA from many countries, including China, Japan, Korea, the Philippines, and South Asia. The major impetus for their moves to the USA was to escape imperial wars, colonialism, and homeland disorder. In fact, a notable group of Asian women came to the USA between the 1840s to the 1930s as part of a global movement of people escaping imperialist countries (Fong, 1997). Points of entry included Hawai'i (prior to the region becoming a state) and the Western USA. Asian women were often initially employed on plantations, in agricultural fields and canneries, as domestic workers and seamstresses, and to help operate family businesses (Hune, 2020).

Hispanic/Latino migration to the USA has been significant, with the population growing rapidly in recent decades. Most Hispanic/Latino immigrants came from Mexico, Central America, and South America. In 1970, the Hispanic/Latino population was 9.6 million, making up 4.7% of the US population. Later growth of the Hispanic/Latino population has been fueled by immigration. By 2010, Mexicans made up 63% of the Latino/Hispanic population, while Central and South Americans made up 13%. Many Hispanic and Latino immigrants come to the USA for better opportunities and economic prosperity. Some immigrants, like those from Cuba, fled political repression, dictatorship, and economic hardships.

The Women's Bureau, a US governmental agency, was founded in 1920 to support working women. Early work of the Bureau included determining which women were permitted to take examinations for positions in the federal government (US Department of Labor, 2021). The latter led the Civil Service Commission to issue a ruling opening all examinations to both men and women. The Bureau included studies on the working conditions of African American women workers (US Department of Labor, 2021). The Fair Labor Standards Act, enacted in 1938, set the first minimum wages and maximum working hours. The Bureau had long studied women's work hours, starting with an examination of the eight-hour day in 1921.

In 1969, Elizabeth Duncan Koontz became the first African American woman to head the Women's Bureau and was the highest-ranking African American woman in the Nixon Administration. In this capacity, she helped the Bureau share research and expertise with women abroad, especially in developing countries. The Bureau's primary focus in the 1970s was addressing and eliminating discrimination against women and minorities in the workforce (US Department of Labor, 2021).

FOUNDATIONAL CONCEPTUAL WORK REGARDING WOMEN OF COLOR: INTERSECTIONALITY

Legal scholar Kimberlé Crenshaw (1989) created the term "intersectionality." Motivated by what she saw as the "erasure" of Black women, her work that year, "Demarginalizing the Intersection of Race and Sex: A Black Feminist Critique of Antidiscrimination Doctrine, Feminist Theory and Antiracist Politics," reviewed what she labeled as the single-axis framework in anti-discrimination law, feminist theory, and antiracist politics in the USA.

Crenshaw argued that the single axis framework focused either on race by itself (with Black men identified as representatives of the Black race) or gender by itself (with White women as the standard bearers of women), implicitly excluding the complex identities of Black women. Her work thus brought attention to the multi-dimensional experiences of Black women—and, by extension, other non-White women—in an effort to end these women's "theoretical erasure and marginalization" (Carbado et al., 2013). She called for a rethinking of feminist and antiracist frameworks to include intersectionality, emphasizing the need to center the experiences of the most disadvantaged to achieve broader social justice (Coaston, 2019). Her positions on race and gender influenced academics and practitioners–including the non-profit Catalyst organization whose mission was to better the lives of working women–to more closely examine the work lives of women of color (Carbado et al., 2013). It was the impetus that led Catalyst in the late-1990s to expand their research and consulting to include women of color. The organization received a grant from the Ford Foundation to proceed with this work.

FOCUS ON WOMEN OF COLOR IN THE CORPORATE WORK ENVIRONMENT: FOUNDATIONAL EARLY RESEARCH

In the late 1990s and early 2000s, Catalyst's organizational research helped bring to life the work experiences of women of color, with an emphasis on the interpersonal and intrapersonal aspects of their experiences. Data collection was limited to women of color employees to provide an in-depth understanding of their perceptions and experiences. The goal was to help business organizations gain a more nuanced view of women of color in their employment and to develop recommendations for improving opportunities for women of color employees.

Catalyst fielded a series of major studies on women of color based on data collected in 30 corporate companies and 1,735 women in the positions of managers and professionals who identified as African American, Asian American, and Hispanic/Latina. The work involved re-contacting respondents three years after initial data collections. The work also included a qualitative study of women of color at 16 Fortune 500 companies, containing 59 focus groups and 82 individual interviews (Catalyst, 1999).

The Catalyst team illuminated the unique experiences of women of color as distinct from White women. For example, Catalyst popularized the metaphor "concrete ceiling" for women of color, in contrast to the "glass ceiling" for White women. The exclusivity of work environments for women of color (e.g., difficulty finding mentors and sponsors, senior leaders' risk aversion to support women of color) created a dense, harder-to-shatter barrier to their advancement.

Catalyst presented its business case as a prelude to the study, citing demographic data as one reason organizations need to pay close attention to women of color employees—which is still relevant today. Factors underlying the need for businesses to pay greater attention to women of color include the following:

- Increasing demographic diversity of the labor pool.
- Recognition of women of color as important sources of talent for corporations.
- Competitive advantage derived from diverse perspectives.
- Buying power of women of color as consumers.
- High costs of employee turnover.
- Increasing importance of global competencies.

Analyses of survey findings, in-depth interviews, and focus groups allowed identification of key workplace dynamics for women of color. Results highlighted women of color's (a) organizational representation, (b) barriers to career success, and (c) success factors. Although women of color made up 22.6% of women in the US workforce at the time of data collection, their representation among women who held managerial and administrative positions was 14.3%. Women of color spent more "time in grade" than White women. They were promoted more slowly, with an average of 3.6 years since last promotion, compared to 2.6 years since last promotion for White women.

The most frequently cited barriers to career success reflected a lack of connection with and acceptance by others in the workplace:

- Not having an influential mentor or sponsor (cited by 47%).
- Lack of networking with colleagues (cited by 40%).
- Lack of company role models who are members of the same racial/ethnic group (cited by 29%).
- Lack of high visibility assignments (cited by 28%).

Regarding what led to their successes, approximately half of all women of color surveyed identified the following factors:

- Access to high visibility assignments.
- Performing above expectations.
- Communicating well.
- Having an influential mentor or sponsor.

Among senior professionals, in-depth interviews revealed a personal trait that most women of color had in common: *emotional resilience*. This characteristic enabled these women to defy stereotypes and not take to heart biased impressions that others had of them. This resilience lent women of color the strength to leverage adverse circumstances and form positive relationships (Catalyst, 2002).

Research findings from Catalyst are provided for three subgroups of women of color–African American women, Latinas, and Asian/Asian American women—as well as brief backgrounds to provide interpretive context.

AFRICAN AMERICAN WOMEN

History of Enslavement

African American women's history in the USA is unique from that of Latinas and Asian women, given American enslavement. African slaves endured dehumanizing treatment, having been brought by force from their native countries in Africa in the late 1700s and 1800s and sold to plantation owners in the American South (Kelley, 2023). There, they endured forced labor under brutal conditions including sexual abuse by their White owners. One legacy of the sexual abuse that occurred during slavery is that African Americans vary widely in appearance, from light to dark skin shade and with features varying in terms of how "European" versus "African" one is in appearance.

Drawing on research demonstrating that skin shade and physical features impact socioeconomic outcomes and education among African Americans, Keyes et al. (2020) examined the link between African Americans' physical attributes and their satisfaction with work outcomes. Participants rated their skin shade from 1 (very light) to 7 (very dark) and their facial features from 1 (very European) to 7 (very ethnic). The information was combined to indicate two categories of respondents: lighter skin and fewer ethnic features versus darker skin and more ethnic features. Results indicated that light-skinned/less ethnic-looking African American women tended to be more satisfied with their pay (56%) than dark-skinned/more ethnic-looking women (46%).

African American Women's Barriers to Advancement

Stereotypes

In the Catalyst research, over half of African American women cited negative and persistent race-based stereotypes, such as deficits in intelligence and hypersexuality. These stereotypes were perceived as creating difficulty connecting with others in the workplace, including securing mentors and gaining respect from managers. Many African American women also reported that their personal communication styles were straightforward and direct. However, they also perceived that these direct communication styles were different from those of White women, leading others to stereotype Black women as confrontational. As one respondent stated, *"We express ourselves in an animated way, and that is perceived as emotional and out of control—somebody that frightens whites."*

Other stereotypes that African American women reported stemmed from not having traditional family arrangements. In particular, single mothers reported facing negative stereotypes regarding their marital status.

Visibility, Scrutiny, and Guardedness

African American women felt they were more visible than other employees, given the perception of belonging to an "out" group. They believed that their visibility resulted in their actions coming under greater scrutiny than those of majority employees. African American women reported the need to walk a fine line: attempting to connect with other employees and sometimes responding to scrutiny from coworkers by being guarded in how much they revealed about themselves: *"If my colleague is not at his desk, it's just assumed that he's busy. But if I'm not there, people will think, 'Did she leave early today?' We're not given the benefit of the doubt."*

Perceptions of being scrutinized led some African American women to be guarded in what they shared about themselves, fearing negative reactions from coworkers. Some African American women reported that colleagues seemed threatened when they revealed details about being on par with White employees economically or socially:

> *When they find out you take real vacations, they look at you like, 'We've got one of those kinds; a person who could be equal'. I had to watch what I shared with them because they started to look at me differently, like, 'You can't be on my level, you can't have any money, you can't do anything and you can't know anything'. So I don't share my views.*

Many African American women also perceived that their relationships with White women were conflicted, a finding not as frequently reported by Latinas and Asian American women.

African American Women's Success Factors

African American women in the Catalyst study were able to leverage their strengths to succeed in the workplace by exceeding performance expectations, communicating effectively, connecting with mentors, building positive relationships with managers and others, and using their cultural backgrounds to enhance their job performance. In some cases, being an "outsider" with unique perspectives seemed to help their performance. African American women were also more likely to report a greater connection with community groups than Asian women or Latinas.

The most frequently cited success factors by African American women were high-visibility projects, exceeding performance expectations, good communication style, and an influential sponsor/mentor.

Exceeding Performance Expectations

Eighty-six percent of the African American women surveyed cited exceeding performance expectations as key to success. This result is not particularly surprising, given challenges to their credibility, as reported earlier.

> *You have to really have that confidence in yourself and in your credibility. And you have to get that experience and that exposure. If you're shaky in an area, figure it out on your own-you have to come to the table with the right skills. And if you don't have them, you've got to go get them.*

Communication Style

More than 90% of the African American women surveyed cited good communication as a success factor. Many maintained and leveraged their direct communication styles. Some believed they challenged organizational norms by doing so.

> *I tend to be very direct. I'm bumping up against the unwritten rules about being indirect. My upbringing has led me to respect people, no matter what their place in life is. That is also in conflict here. You're to hold managers in high esteem; I don't see it that way. My preference is to say it as I think it.*

Connecting With Mentors

Three-quarters of African American women reported having a mentor as key to success. Among the women of color surveyed, African American women were the most likely to have a mentor: 38% of African American women surveyed had a mentor, compared to 33% of Latinas and 27% of Asian women.

More than half (54%) of African American women's mentors were also African American: 32% of their mentors were African American men, 22% were African American women, and 29% were White men. The least likely race/gender category for mentors of African American women was White women (16%).

Mentors of African American women were more likely to provide advice on racial issues than are mentors of Asian women and Latinas, which is one indicator of the greater salience of race to African American women's work experiences. Mentors of African American women also were more likely to provide advice on gender issues in the workplace (e.g., strategies for communicating with male managers, appropriate dress), compared to mentors of other women of color.

LATINAS

Diversity of Latinas' National Origins

Given the wide range of nationalities and regions represented by Latinas in the Catalyst research—Central/South America, Cuba, Mexico, and Puerto Rico—some individuals in the study were not identifiable as Latinas based on their physical appearance. While people from these countries and regions are often assumed to belong to a "people of color" cohort, not everyone in this group identifies as such. In fact, some 10% of the Latina subsample in the study identified as White/European. A challenge that was fairly unique among these respondents was whether to reveal their national origin:

> *When people don't know me, (and) I tell them I'm Mexican, they look at me like, why would you say that? Why would you let people know? Because you don't have to admit it. You look Italian or European. You don't need to tell people that.*

Some 33% of Hispanic women in the Catalyst study identified as Chicanas: women of Mexican descent. This number was lower than the US national representation of individuals reporting Mexican origin (66%). It is also notable that politically active Chicanas have historically seen themselves as bridging gaps with other politically active White feminists (Hurtado, 1998). While these actions did not necessarily play out in corporate workplaces based on the Catalyst data, it is worth noting that they are part of the political tradition of many Chicanas.

Latinas' Barriers to Advancement

Stereotypes

More than one-third (38%) of Latinas surveyed reported that stereotypes, such as being poorly educated or lazy, existed for women of their ethnic group. In particular, Latinas who reported a strong connection with their ethnic group (46%) were more likely to perceive that these stereotypes existed than were women with a lower connection (33%). As one participant stated:

> *The managers that I've spoken to think of Mexicans as very lazy because of their notion that in their work habits, they have a siesta time . . . and that they take a break. I try to educate them and say, 'Well, I also understand they're the most productive people because they do have a break. If you look at the quality of what we produce in Mexico, they are the top of our line. So where are you getting your information?'*

One woman noted the stereotyping she experienced due to her accent: *"Some people tend to relate my level of intelligence with my accent, which is wrong."*

The following descriptions of encounters with coworkers illustrate the persistence of negative stereotypes, as well as the difficulty in educating others at work:

> *There's a perception that if you're female and you want to advance, you have to take on some male characteristics. In my family growing up, my being a little girl or woman was just as important as anything else and important to me to preserve. I wasn't going to get into male roles in my manner or in my dress. Sometimes there is this perception that we need to put that aside or we'll be seen as flirtatious.*
>
> *When I first started in this job, whenever there was a Spanish name in the newspaper, a coworker of Polish descent would ask me, 'Did you see—do you know so and so?' It was never good; it was rapes or killings. I would say, 'No . . . why would I know every Puerto Rican in town?' I had to [show] that not everybody from Puerto Rico is poor, is uneducated and works in the fields; there are professionals.*

Lack of Access to Influential Others

Latinas reported being denied opportunities due to smaller networks and fewer connections to influential businesspeople:

> *I had a very good opportunity to work in Latin America, in a very key position. A requirement was that you be bilingual. A White female was hired. I was told*

that the only reason I didn't get the job was because I didn't have a big network in the company. . . . The other person didn't speak Spanish at all, and she's taking classes at Berlitz.

Lack of Support From Managers

At many organizations, diversity initiatives can be perceived as ineffective because individual managers do not implement them well. Individual managers greatly affect the extent to which a work environment is inclusive: one in which employees do not have to conform to narrow styles.

While three out of four Latina respondents in the Catalyst study agreed that their managers were comfortable interacting with them, Latinas were least likely of the women of color groups studied to rate their managers highly on helping them understand organizational politics (49%) and mapping clear developmental goals (34%).

Gender Roles and Commitment to Families

Many Latinas reported that their participation in family life was quite important and that it extended beyond the nuclear family. Some Latinas reported a lack of understanding from coworkers regarding their commitments to extended family:

Whenever someone says, 'Let's go to lunch' or asks me to stay late, I say I can't, I have my family I need to attend to. Yesterday someone told me, 'That excuse is getting to be pretty old'. And I said, 'It's not an excuse'. The person said, 'Well, you don't have a family'. I said, 'Yes I do. It's my brothers, my sisters, my parents, my cousins, my aunts, my uncles'. I think a lot of people don't see that. Your extended family is as high a priority as your children and your husband.

Latinas' Success Factors

Mentoring and Strong Relationships With Managers

While Latinas reported difficulty acquiring mentors, the women who were able to secure mentors reported that they enjoyed positive outcomes. Some Latinas credited a combination of luck and skill in obtaining mentors:

I got on the promotable list strictly by the luck of the draw. I happened to have been invited to a vice president' s quarterly meeting. I sat next to a fellow who was a vice president. . . . He found my opinions and some technical ideas that I had interesting. He sponsored me to a few other vice presidents.

That was how I got on the list. You actually went to a fishbowl and picked the number where you would sit. So it was just the luck of the draw that I sat next to this guy.

Others connected with mentors and sponsors based on others' perceptions of their strong work:

After my assignment was done, the director called me and said, 'I'm really impressed with your work. I want to try to find you a job'. . . . So he found out that [company] had just moved from New York, and he got me two interviews-one with personnel and one with editorial services. And I was offered both jobs, and took the one at editorial services. I stayed with that group for about 12 years.

ASIAN AND ASIAN AMERICAN WOMEN

Asian women have been a fast-growing part of the US population and its workforce. Most Asian Catalyst respondents identified their or their families' countries of origin as China, the Philippines, Japan, and Korea, while some identified as Southeast Asian. A small number of Asian women respondents cited two or more ethnic backgrounds (e.g., Filipino and Japanese). In this study, women of Chinese descent were the largest subgroup of Asian participants (43%).

Asian women in the Catalyst study were also more likely to be immigrants than other women of color: 16% immigrated before the age of 12, 47% immigrated at age 12 or older, and 34% were born in the USA. Approximately three out of four Asian respondents reported being bilingual (77%), while 23% reported speaking English only.

Asian American women were more likely to have a graduate education than other women of color (59%). However, they were less likely to be within three reporting levels of the CEO level or to have supervisory responsibilities, compared to other women of color. Some reported being valuable to global business by providing connections to underserved markets.

One-quarter of Asian women worked in engineering or research and development, which far exceeded the representation of other women of color in these industries (9%). As reported by the National Center for Education Statistics in *Digest of Education Statistics* (2001), Asian women earned 3.5% of technical degrees (e.g., STEM fields), which exceeded their representation in the USA (2.3%; U.S. Census Bureau, n.d.).

Asian Women: More Acculturated Versus Less Acculturated

In qualitative work, Asian women's values and behavior differed according to whether they were born and raised in the USA or whether they immigrated to the USA. For comparative purposes, the Asian women in the survey portion of the study were split into two groups: "less acculturated" and "more acculturated." In addition to differing on immigration status and second language facility, these two groups also differed in social class/education and professional roles:

- Approximately 80% of the "less acculturated" group had middle- or upper-class or white-collar backgrounds (vs. 56% of "more acculturated" women).
- Some 75% of the "less acculturated" group had graduate education, compared to 49% of the "more acculturated" women.
- Despite greater educational attainment, the "less acculturated" women were less likely to have managerial roles, compared to the "more acculturated" women (28% vs. 55%).
- "More acculturated" women were more likely to feel successful in their careers (81%), compared to "less acculturated" women (55%).

There were no differences between the two acculturation groups in terms of average age, the number of children, average years per job grade, or reporting levels from the CEO. Research has shown that Asian Americans often face discriminatory experiences due to being negatively stereotyped as foreigners (or outsiders)—stereotypes that seemed to increase following the COVID-19 pandemic (Ruiz et al., 2023).

RELATIONSHIPS IN THE WORK ENVIRONMENT

This segment of the early work on women of color addresses the impact of the relationships that women of color have with others at work, including formal and informal relationships.

Networking Strategies Among Women of Color

Productive, informal relationships with others in the work environment have been shown to be key in attaining career success. Research on how women of color use networking strategies to help navigate corporate environments has focused on their relationships with the four or five people they turn to for career advice (Catalyst, 2006). The link between informal network characteristics and rate of corporate advancement, as well as organizational commitment, were analyzed among women of color subgroups in the Catalyst research (2006).

There was a continuum of strategies from "sticking together" (having a network high in those of the same ethnicity or gender and low in colleagues) to "blending in" (having a network high in White individuals, men, or colleagues).

Asian women had the highest number of White individuals and men in their networks, representing a "blending in" strategy. For Asian women, having White individuals and colleagues in their networks positively linked to promotion, while having men in their networks positively related to feelings of commitment to their companies.

Latinas had a high number of White individuals in their networks, representing a "blending in" strategy to some extent. However, on average, more than one-half of their networks were women, representing a "sticking together" strategy. While both of these strategies were linked to Latinas' feelings of organizational commitment, neither strategy was associated with their promotion rates.

African American women had the highest number of other African Americans in their networks, including the highest concentration of women of the same racial/ethnic group, representing a "sticking together" strategy. For African American women, having women, particularly other African American women, in their networks was positively related to their promotion rates, reflecting relatively successful use of the "sticking together" strategy.

These findings for African American women, along with African American women's relatively greater representation at upper corporate levels, compared with Latinas and Asian women, suggested that African American women were able to succeed in corporate environments without being accepted as insiders.

Table 4.1 summarizes the results.

Table 4.1 Networking Strategies Among Women of Color

	Networking Strategy				
	Sticking Together				Blending In
	Women of Same Race/ Ethnicity	Women	Company Colleagues	White Non-Colleagues	Male Non-Colleagues
Asian Women			✓ Promotion	✓ Promotion	✓ Commitment
Latinas		✓	✓ Commitment	✓	
African American Women	✓ Promotion	✓ Promotion	✓ Commitment		

✓ = high percentage of this type of network member (relative to other types of network members)

"Sticking together" = Network high in members of the same race/ethnicity or gender, and low in colleagues

"Blending in" = Network high in men, White individuals, or colleagues

Unique Circumstances Regarding Relationship Development for Women of Color

A Catalyst research project on women of color in the late 2000s focused on client service firms, expanding work on women of color by accounting for structural aspects of organizations. Data collection was limited to in-client service roles given their importance to the bottom line of accounting firms, the influence of senior client service roles, and their historical underrepresentation of women of color (and people of color). The "up-or-out" model of career advancement in these firms creates challenging barriers for anyone but is typically felt more strongly by traditionally marginalized groups without ready access to insider relationships.

Results indicated a client-service focus and firmly entrenched "old boys'" networks, which made inclusion of outsider groups like women of color extremely difficult.

In Figure 4.1, the "Women of Color" portion of the diagram represents instances in which findings for women of color were significantly *more* negative ($p < .10$) than those for both men of color and White women. For example, "stereotyping" indicates that women of color were more likely to cite "managing preconceptions of my race and gender" as a barrier to advancement than were men of color and White women.

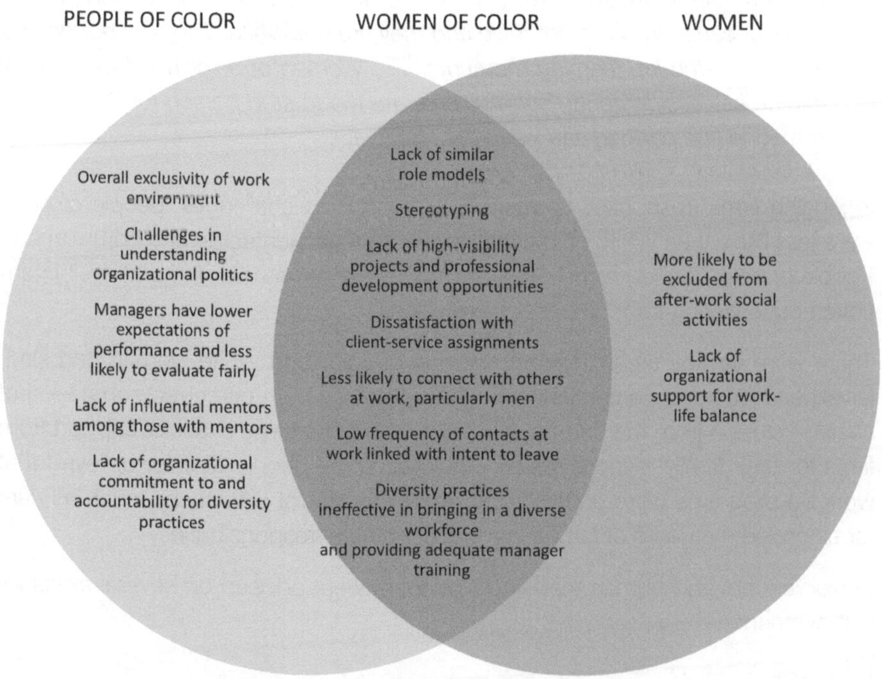

FIGURE 4.1 Workplace Experiences by Gender and Race

Women of color had more in common with men of color than with White women in their attitudes regarding exclusivity of the work environment. Men and women of color were also aligned in their perceptions that practices intended to support inclusion were not as effective as they could be. Overall, both men and women of color felt less included in the accounting firm work environment than did White employees. For example, they were more likely to perceive low expectations from their managers and double standards regarding performance evaluations. In particular, women of color were least likely to believe their managers helped them understand workplace politics. They were also significantly less likely to report that their managers had high expectations for their performance.

Women of color also felt less connected with influential mentors who could help advance their careers. People of color with mentors were more likely to feel that their mentors lacked influence, compared with mentors of their White men colleagues. Perhaps because of this, women of color (along with men of color) felt more challenged than White employees in their understanding of organizational politics. Women of color also reported a lack of high-visibility projects and professional development opportunities, compared to men of color and White employees. Finally, women of color were notably less satisfied than other groups with the ways client service assignments were distributed.

As one man of color stated:

> *We don't see many more women of color at the senior manager and partner levels because they are not male and they are not White. They are not getting the key on-the-job learning moments. . . . Women of color need to not only get the key assignments, but also become the trusted person for the partner, someone [the partner] can leave the client with.*

In judging firms' responses to diversity and inclusion challenges, people of color were less likely than White employees to perceive accountability and commitment. People of color tended to perceive diversity practices at their firms as well-intentioned but suffering from "imperfect execution."

There were several areas in which women of color and White women had similar experiences and perceptions. For example, they both perceived some level of social exclusion from the "old boys'" network and perceived a lack of support from firms for their family responsibilities. However, some people of color believed that work/life programs were particularly insensitive to racial differences, such as care for extended members of families or single mothers' responsibilities.

Senior leaders and human resource managers were advised on several areas for improvement:

- Be more aware of the intersectionality of the identities of women of color, given that the combination of race/ethnicity and gender appears to magnify the effects of race/ethnicity and gender alone. Firms need to move beyond "one-size-fits-all" models in attempting to create inclusive environments for all employees without focusing on any particular group.

- Periodically assess the effectiveness of diversity and inclusion practices to understand whether they are successful. An initial step should be to analyze promotion and retention rates of subgroups at critical career development stages.
- Collect data via employee surveys about perceptions of inclusive and exclusive behaviors in the work environment.
- Eliminate cultural norms that give one group an advantage over others. This can include having leaders committed to making change, communicating frequently, having influential champions model at every level, establishing formal guidelines where appropriate, and using rewards and penalties.

Allyship

Women of color, as well as other historically marginalized groups, may benefit from relationships with those who act as their allies in organizations. Broadly defined, ally work encompasses actions by employees who belong to advantaged social groups that support employees belonging to stereotypically "lower status" social groups (Dang & Joshi, 2023; De Souza & Schmader, 2025). Research has shown that allyship is beneficial to under-represented groups and that men in many workplaces are open to providing allyship to women (Working Mother Research Institute, 2021). Research provides insight into different methods of allyship, including "self ally" work (i.e., developing skills and capabilities among oneself as a potential ally), "relational ally" work (i.e., building positive work relationships with under-represented others in the work environment), and "organizational ally" work (i.e., changing organizational practices to support disadvantaged coworkers; Dang & Joshi, 2023).

Self ally work entails critiquing and scrutinizing thought patterns, emotions, and behavioral responses to disadvantaged group members, as well as developing additional knowledge and skills that can be used to support disadvantaged group members, including women of color. Self-work can be reflected in the opinions and views an employee offers at work, thus contributing to an inclusive organizational culture.

Relational ally work focuses on improving the quality of relationships with socially disadvantaged employees. It is nonreciprocal; advantaged members perceive their objective as providing support rather than receiving it from disadvantaged groups.

Finally, organizational ally work aims to change features of an organization, such as its policies, practices, or norms that directly or indirectly contribute to social disadvantages. It can also include developing alternate organizational practices that potentially enhance workplace experiences and outcomes for socially disadvantaged employees. For example, assessment protocols can be tweaked to be more attuned to communication patterns of employees from different socioeconomic backgrounds.

Relationships With Managers: The Role of Trust

Direct managers play a pivotal role in employees' career progress, having the power to help direct reports grow professionally. In addition to benefitting subordinates' career progress, constructive, trusting manager–subordinate relationships are invaluable to organizations. Trusting relationships can foster positive employee attitudes, task performance, and more effective organizations overall (Dirks & Ferrin, 2002). The impact of trusting relationships extends beyond assigned work to include citizenship behaviors in which employees take actions that go beyond their formal job responsibilities (Dirks & Ferrin, 2002).

Women of color often face greater challenges than White women in forming trusting relationships at work. Negative stereotyping, exclusion from influential networks, and difficulty gaining access to high-visibility assignments can influence how they experience workplaces, further limiting their access to trusting relationships (Giscombe et al., 2011). The study from which these data are drawn focused on White male managers due to their prevalence and power in corporate hierarchies. Data collection included pairing women of color with their White male managers and collecting data from both parties so relationship dynamics could be compared. White women subordinates were used as a comparison group for women of color given work demonstrating White women's greater progress in inclusion versus women of color.

Qualitative analyses revealed two types of trust regarding communication: reliance and disclosure trust. Reliance trust occurs when direct reports can rely on managers to take action on their behalf (e.g., accurately representing their work to others). Results showed that the more that White women relied on their managers to take action on their behalf, the more satisfied they felt with advancement opportunities. In contrast, the perception of women of color regarding their abilities to rely on managers made *no difference* to their satisfaction regarding career advancement.

Disclosure trust occurs when direct reports communicate sensitive or personal information to managers, such as admitting shortcomings or sharing honest feelings and frustrations about work. Women of color rated their level of disclosure as direct reports significantly lower than White women. This reticence appeared to be rooted in apprehension regarding consequences of disclosing and perceived lack of workplace inclusivity:

> *As a woman of color, sometimes you're almost afraid to ask for the feedback, because the inference may be that you're struggling. And so the tendency is to be as self-sufficient as possible, before you go and ask for any kind of feedback.*

White male managers often rated their female direct reports' disclosure *higher* than how women rated their own disclosure, reflecting a disconnect in the working relationship. However, this disconnect was substantially higher when direct reports were women of color (54.2%) than White women (17.2%).

Lack of disclosure among women of color appeared to be so deeply rooted that even when their managers shared insider information with them (e.g., knowledge of corporate politics, unwritten rules, information about people in their networks), women of color did not change their disclosure levels. In contrast, White women direct reports were not only more likely to receive insider information, but their managers' sharing of insider information led to higher levels of trust.

Ideally, for managers to provide support to their direct reports, the direct report must practice a certain level of disclosure. Some managers rely on their direct reports to let them know how and in what ways they require support or assistance. A direct report's disclosure of sensitive information signals that she is open to hearing advice.

At its best, disclosure can transform a manager into a direct report's champion and can create greater career development opportunities, as it did for this Black woman direct report whose White manager provided the following account:

> *When [she] came into the meeting, she was not prepared; she was not really observing or being on point. I asked her, 'How did the meeting go?' She said, 'I was not prepared. I was in the shadow of [my predecessor]. I [had been] with my son who had the flu [the night before]'. That was a milestone. She recognized this as an opportunity for me to coach her. . . . I gave her hints such as, 'Did you stand in front of a mirror and practice presentation skills? Did you practice in front of peers? Every time you step in front of an audience, you are representing [the company]'. Very quickly, she recognized that and leapfrogged past her peers.*

THE PARADOX OF INTERSECTIONAL INVISIBILITY FOR BLACK WOMEN

In exploring the complexities of business organizations, organizational theorists have highlighted the need to understand and embrace the simultaneous presence of contradictory yet interrelated elements within organizational life, which has given rise to paradox theory (Smith & Lewis, 2011). In applying and expanding paradox theory, scholars have turned attention to women of color, specifically Black women, in senior positions: these women experience both "hyper-visibility" and "invisibility" depending on the context. This research provides a valuable contribution to the understanding of race and gender dynamics, providing greater depth and range to these interrelated topics.

As research has shown, Black women are a marginalized group when they hold senior corporate positions. Their stature has been minimized by society and they often face negative stereotypes. In a sense they are "invisible," meaning they are easily overlooked or disregarded. However, when they occupy senior management roles, they become "hyper-visible," because it is unusual to see people of their race and gender in these roles. In effect, they can simultaneously occupy states of hypervisibility *and* invisibility (Purdie-Vaughns & Eibach, 2008; Livingston et al., 2012).

One study illuminated the dynamics underlying the paradox of hypervisibility/invisibility and how women of color are able to manage their careers in these circumstances (Smith et al., 2019). The authors interviewed 59 Black women twice, approximately seven years apart. Participants were selected based on their senior-level positions in various industries, including financial services, consumer products, and healthcare. The authors employed a grounded theory-building approach to examine how Black women executives experience and manage intersectional invisibility. The authors then developed a model explaining the paradoxical effects of executive Black women's "outsider within" status, wherein they experience both opportunities and limitations associated with benign and hostile intersectional invisibility:

- **Intersectional Invisibility**

  The concept of intersectional invisibility was explored in two dimensions: "benign" and "hostile." Benign intersectional invisibility was defined as allowing Black women to deviate from stereotypes and be authentic. "Hostile" intersectional invisibility, on the other hand, subjects Black women to compounded negative stigmas. The study revealed that Black women experience *both* forms of intersectional invisibility and must navigate these paradoxical effects to achieve career success.

- **Agentic Visibility Tactics**

  The study identified several tactics Black women use that allow them to take advantage of the opportunities of "benign" intersectional invisibility or to overcome the constraints of "hostile" intersectional invisibility. These tactics help them manage the opportunities and constraints of intersectional invisibility and to progress in their careers.

- **Leaning into Risk**

  This approach involved Black women taking on challenging roles to gain visibility and to be seen as credible and valuable to their organizations. These assignments also prevented the women from becoming bored and allowed them to demonstrate breakout performance.

- **Use of Bold Autonomy**

  This tactic was defined as women providing "unabashed expressions" about their convictions, making bold statements and standing up for what they felt was right, and using autonomy to execute plans for their careers. It was also used to gain respect and recognition in their organizations, as well as to overcome benign intersectional invisibility.

- **Strategic Deployment of Invisibility**

  This tactic included agentic behaviors to preempt potential mistreatment, devaluation, or stigmatization. At times, this meant avoiding fully authentic displays. It could be prompted by the perception of women of color that stigmas associated with their race and gender posed too large a threat for their authentic displays to overcome. In other words, they would decide when it was appropriate to be "invisible." Participants sometimes referred to invisibility as a choice, and many used it to mine opportunities that others had disregarded as too risky or lacking value.

- **Conscious Relationship Crafting**

  This technique included building one-on-one relationships at all levels. The women used these relationships for career development and professional advancement. This tactic was particularly leveraged in organizations where hostile intersectional invisibility was more pronounced. The conceptual model below (Figure 4.2) summarizes the effects of intersectional invisibility and the coping strategies employed by women of color.

DISMANTLING OF DIVERSITY, EQUITY, AND INCLUSION IN THE USA

At the time of this writing, there are roadblocks for people of color, including women of color and women generally, in business organizations in the USA. One of the main platforms of the US President, Donald Trump, who was elected in 2024, has been to dismantle diversity, equity, and inclusion (DEI) programs across many segments of American society.

DEI programs are intended to foster inclusive environments where "diversity is valued, equity is ensured, and everyone feels a sense of belonging" (Wright, 2025). Trump issued an Executive Order in January 2025, decreeing that DEI programs could no longer be practiced in federal agencies (Ho, 2025). He later issued an order requiring businesses to roll back DEI programs. As a result, many private companies have dismantled their DEI programs or limited their impact.

Trump's attacks on DEI have been quite aggressive. Without evidence, Trump argued that DEI was synonymous with placing unqualified people of color and women in positions in which they were, in effect, incompetent. For example, he

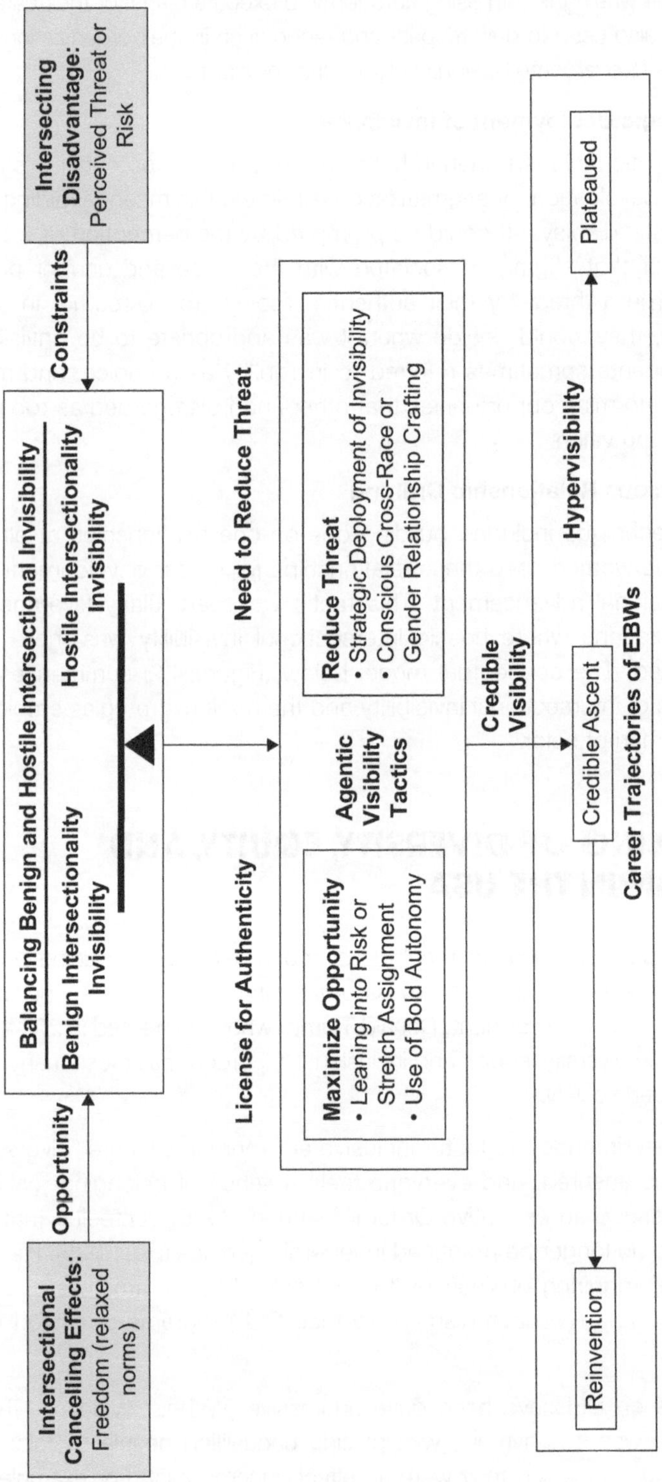

FIGURE 4.2 Effects of and Coping Strategies for Intersectional Invisibility Among Women of Color

incorrectly blamed a plane crash in January 2025 on DEI policies (Zurcher, 2025). A later investigation suggested that Trump's reduction in federal aviation employees might have played a part in the crash (Rashid, 2025).

The larger context of Trump's anti-DEI executive orders is Project 2025, which was created by the Heritage Foundation (Dans & Groves, 2025). Its key aims include restoring "family values" and dismantling the "administrative state." It proposes placing the entire federal bureaucracy under direct presidential control and reducing job protections for government employees. The proposal supports abolishing the Department of Education and ending DEI programs, reflecting a broader crackdown on "woke" ideology (Rashid & Roberts, 2024). In terms of women's rights, although it does not call for a nationwide abortion ban, it suggests withdrawing the abortion pill and emphasizes a "biblically based" definition of marriage and family. The platform is anti-immigration and suggests increased funding for border security and enforcement of immigration laws (Dans & Groves, 2025). The Trump administration is also making voting less accessible to women by attempting to require that voters bring proof of their names at birth. This policy would make voting difficult for married women who have taken their husbands' surnames (Lithwick, 2025).

Trump has also handpicked cabinet members whose qualifications are lower than members of prior administrations (Davis, 2024). Trump apparently prioritizes personal loyalty over qualifications and expertise. Trump's cabinet choices appear to be part of a broader strategy to consolidate power within the executive branch.

The continued existence of DEI efforts in organizations will depend, at least in part, on business leaders' commitments to principles of inclusion. It will remain to be seen whether business leaders believe their organizations are more successful when there is active participation and engagement from a variety of identity groups. Their commitment will clearly have an impact on the working lives of women of color in US organizations.

CHAPTER SUMMARY

This chapter reviews the unique histories of employed women of color in the USA, which greatly vary based on race/ethnicity. Despite their numerous talents and contributions, women of color continue to face challenges in business organizations, such as differential networking and mentoring relationships. This chapter delves into dynamics of relationship development for women of color with others in the workplace, including the paradoxical effects of executive Black women's "outsider within" status.

DISCUSSION QUESTIONS

1. This chapter highlights the intersection of gender and race/ethnicity; what other identities likely intersect as well, and how might they meaningfully shape employees' organizational experiences and roles?
   a. Which additional identity intersections might create unique experiences, such as the "outsider within" experiences of Black women in the USA?
2. How do the workplace experiences of women of color vary by country and global region?
3. Identify at least one other race/ethnicity that is not explicitly discussed in this chapter and research the histories and current experiences of women from this group.
4. Explain how the historical context of a racial/ethnic group shapes modern experiences and representation of its group members in organizations.
   a. Related, explain why the experiences and outcomes of certain women of color might differ from those of other women of color.
5. Contemplate (and perhaps debate) how the current political and social contexts of a region could shape the future representation and experiences of women of color in organizations. Leverage research and data from reputable sources (e.g., peer-reviewed journals and major organizations) to support propositions.

REFERENCES

Carbado, D. W., Crenshaw, K. W., Mays, V. M., & Tomlinson, B. (2013). Intersectionality: Mapping the movements of a theory. *Du Bois Review*, *10*(2), 303–312. https://scholarship.law.columbia.edu/faculty_scholarship/2779

Catalyst. (1999). *Women of color in corporate management: Opportunities and barriers*. Catalyst.

Catalyst. (2002). *Women of color executives: Their voices, their journeys*. Catalyst.

Catalyst. (2006). *Connections that count: The informal networks of women of color in the United States*. Catalyst.

Coaston, J. (May 28, 2019). *The intersectionality wars*. Vox. https://www.vox.com/the-highlight/2019/5/20/18542843/intersectionality-conservatism-law-race-gender-discrimination

Crenshaw, K. (1989). Demarginalizing the intersection of race and sex: A Black feminist critique of antidiscrimination doctrine, feminist theory, and antiracist politics. *University of Chicago Legal Forum*, *1989*(1), Article 8. http://chicagounbound.uchicago.edu/uclf/vol1989/iss1/8

Dang, C. T., & Joshi, A. (2023). On the plurality and politics of ally work: Liberalism and self, relational, and organizational ally work. *Academy of Management Journal*, *66*(5), 1554–1585. https://doi.org/10.5465/amj.2021.0999

Dans, P., & Groves, S. (2025). *Mandate for leadership: The conservative promise*. The Heritage Foundation.

Davis, T. (2024, November 16). *Trump's cabinet of incompetence: A prelude to disaster*. Medium. https://tony-ob-davis.medium.com/trumps-cabinet-of-incompetence-a-prelude-to-disaster-115ecefff153

De Souza, L., & Schmader, T. (2025). When people do allyship: A typology of allyship action. *Personality and Social Psychology Review*, *29*(1), 3–31.

Dirks, K. T., & Ferrin, D. L. (2002). Trust in leadership: Meta-analytic findings and implications for research and practice. *Journal of Applied Psychology*, *87*(4), 611–628.

Evans, S. (2006, Spring). *Women in American politics in the twentieth century*. Gilder Lehrman Institute of American History. https://www.gilderlehrman.org/history-resources/essays/women-american-politics-twentieth-century

Fong, L. Y. S. (1997). Asian-American women: An understudied minority. *The Journal of Sociology & Social Welfare*, *24*(1), Article 7. https://doi.org/10.15453/0191-5096.2399

Giscombe, K., Agin, M., & Deva, V. (2011). *Building trust between managers and women of color direct reports*. Catalyst.

Ho, V. (2025, January 23). Trump revoked an anti-discrimination hiring rule: Here's what it means. *The Washington Post*. https://www.washingtonpost.com/politics/2025/01/23/trump-revoked-equal-employment-opportunity-order/

Hune, S. (2020, May 29). *Asian and Asian American women in the United States before World War II*. Oxford Research Encyclopedia of American History. https://oxfordre.com/americanhistory/view/10.1093/acrefore/9780199329175.001.0001/acrefore-9780199329175-e-585

Hurtado, A. (1998). Sitios y lenguas: Chicanas theorize feminisms. In *Hypatia* (Vol. 13, Issue 2, pp. 134–161). https://doi.org/10.1111/j.1527-2001.1998.tb01230.x

Kelley, S. M. (2023). *American slavers, merchants, mariners, and the transatlantic commerce in captives, 1644–1865*. Yale University Press.

Keyes, L., Small, E., & Nikolova, S. (2020). The complex relationship between colorism and poor health outcomes with African Americans: A systematic review. *Analyses of Social Issues and Public Policy*, *20*(1), 1–22. https://doi.org/10.1111/asap.12223

Lithwick, D. (2025, March 31). Maybe don't take for granted that you'll be able to vote in the midterms. *Slate*. https://slate.com/news-and-politics/2025/03/republicans-save-act-women-voters-midterms.html

Livingston, R. W., Rosette, A. S., & Washington, E. F. (2012). Can an agentic Black woman get ahead? The impact of race and interpersonal dominance on perceptions of female leaders. *Psychological Science*, *23*(4), 354–358.

National Archives, African American History (n.d.). https://www.archives.gov/research/african-americans/migrations

Purdie-Vaughns, V., & Eibach, R. (2008). Intersectional invisibility: The distinctive advantages and disadvantages of multiple subordinate-group identities. *Sex Roles*, *59*, 337–391.

Rashid, H. (2025, January 30). FAA Report on D.C. plane crash is out—and it's an indictment of Trump. *New Republic*. https://newrepublic.com/post/190964/faa-report-dc-plane-crash-staffing-indictment-trump

Rashid, M., & Roberts, W. (2024, October 31). Project 2025's distortion of civil rights law threatens Americans with legalized discrimination. *Center for American Progress*. https://www.americanprogress.org/article/project-2025s-distortion-of-civil-rights-law-threatens-americans-with-legalized-discrimination/

Ruiz, N. G., Im, C., & Tian, Z. (2023, November 30). *Discrimination experiences shape most Asian Americans' lives*. Pew Research Center. https://www.pewresearch.org/race-and-ethnicity/2023/11/30/discrimination-experiences-shape-most-asian-americans-lives/

Smith, A. N., Watkins, M. B., Ladge, J. J., & Carlton, P. (2019). Making the invisible visible: Paradoxical effects of intersectional invisibility on the career experiences of executive Black women. *Academy of Management*, *62*(6), 1705–1734. https://doi.org/10.5465/amj.2017.1513

Smith, W., & Lewis, M. (2011). Toward a theory of paradox: A dynamic equilibrium model of organizing. *Academy of Management Review*, *36*(2), 381–403. https://doi.org/10.5465/amr.2009.0223

U.S. Census Bureau. (n.d.). *State Intercensal Tables: 2000–2010*. https://www.census.gov/data/tables/time-series/demo/popest/intercensal-2000-2010-state.html

U.S. Department of Labor. (2021). *Women's Bureau: An overview, 1920–2021*.

Working Mother Research Institute. (2021, May). *The status of men as allies for multicultural women*. Seramount. https://seramount.com/wp-content/uploads/2021/05/The-Status-of-Men-As-Allies-for-Multicultural-Women.pdf

Wright, N. E. (2025, February 5). DEI (diversity, equity, and inclusion) v. affirmative action: They are not the same. *The National Law Review*, XV(324). https://natlawreview.com/article/dei-diversity-equity-and-inclusion-v-affirmative-action-they-are-not-same

Zurcher, A. (2025, January 31). Combative Trump blames diversity policies after air tragedy. *BBC*. https://www.bbc.com/news/articles/cpvmdm1m7m9o

CHAPTER 5

Workforce Challenges and Opportunities for Aboriginal and Torres Strait Islander Women in Contemporary Australia

Ash Francisco

Since the Australian colonial project began in 1788, government authorities have managed the economic participation of Aboriginal and Torres Strait Islander Australians to the disadvantage of our families, communities, and generations. While Australia was one of the first colonies to franchise women to vote in 1902 with the Commonwealth Franchise Act, women in Australia feel the brunt of negatively gendered politics in the workforce, and this is the case for Aboriginal and Torres Strait Islander women as well. For an understanding of the challenges and opportunities for Aboriginal and Torres Strait Islander women in contemporary Australia, reflection on past experiences and realities are critical.

Australia has been a colonial project since the British invasion and occupation of 1788, relatively late in the game of empires and after key lessons were learned from the Americas and India. We became a federated nation in 1901, yet Aboriginal and Torres Strait Islander people were only recognized as citizens in the Australian Constitution in 1967 through a referendum. The term "colonial project" is used in Australia to denote the ongoing orchestrated oppression of Aboriginal and Torres Strait Islander people by the State (Wolfe, 1999). This "project" is facilitated by the active politicization of Aboriginal and Torres Strait Islander Australia. The vacuous discourse about Aboriginal Australia in federal and state parliament is replicated, reinforced, and facilitation through workplaces and organizations. Aboriginal and Torres Strait Islander affairs is a highly politicalized portfolio and exists within the

DOI: 10.4324/9781003488590-5

contrasting phenomena of being either actively debated or ignored. When Aboriginal and Torres Strait Islander affairs are debated, short-term and non-Aboriginal and Torres Strait Islander-led interventions are discussed at best, and at worst, our existence and agency as Aboriginal and Torres Strait Islander people are questioned in racialized attacks. We are ignored when we call for reparations, truth telling, a treaty (until recently), and a fair go.

Within the context of Australia's ongoing colonial project impacts, both historically and in this moment and within this context, lie gendered histories that have contemporary realities. This chapter discusses this point from an Aboriginal woman's perspective to analyze some of the challenges and opportunities for Aboriginal and Torres Strait Islander women in the workforce.

The current state of participation is considered by the Workplace Gender Equality Agency, with their research indicating that Aboriginal and Torres Strait Islander women have a workforce participation of 51.5% in comparison with 65% of Aboriginal and Torres Strait Islander men (Workplace Gender Equality Agency, n.d.). This research also highlights that Aboriginal and Torres Strait Islander women are more likely to take time out of paid work to care for family in comparison with non-Indigenous Australians and Aboriginal and Torres Strait Islander men. The Australian Bureau of Statistics (2023) details that 61% of Aboriginal and Torres Strait Islander women provide support to someone living outside of their household, and 61% of these women also live in households with dependent children (Australian Bureau of Statistics, 2018). Care responsibilities are a major factor to Aboriginal and Torres Strait Islander women's workforce experiences and participation.

The 2023 constitutional The Voice to Parliament referendum in Australia brought into sharp focus the ongoing legacy of historic injustice and its reformulation into contemporary experience. The referendum asked the Australian population, "A Proposed Law: to alter the Constitution to recognize the First Peoples of Australia by establishing an Aboriginal and Torres Strait Islander Voice. Do you approve this proposed alteration?" This question was posed to amend the Australian constitution as such:

In recognition of Aboriginal and Torres Strait Islander peoples as the First Peoples of Australia:

i. There shall be a body, to be called the Aboriginal and Torres Strait Islander Voice;
ii. The Aboriginal and Torres Strait Islander Voice may **make representations** to the Parliament and the Executive Government of the Commonwealth **on matters relating to Aboriginal and Torres Strait Islander peoples;**
iii. The Parliament shall, subject to this Constitution, have power to make laws with respect to matters relating to the Aboriginal and Torres Strait Islander Voice, including its composition, functions, powers, and procedures.

(State Library of Victoria, n.d.)

The Australian population voted overwhelmingly "no" to the referendum, resulting in a loud "no" to an Aboriginal and Torres Strait Islander voice on the policies and legislation that affect our lives and our place in Australian society.

The result of this "no" vote has been both overt and discreet racism, such as the defunding of Aboriginal and Torres Strait Islander programs and government initiatives for affirmative action, as well as increasing social division. The ongoing legacy and action of the colonial project has had a vast impact on Aboriginal and Torres Strait Islander economic participation and workforces across the country. Yet, there are increasing opportunities to decolonize thinking in leadership and management. This chapter argues that these opportunities would have a large impact on Aboriginal and Torres Strait Islander women's experiences in the workforce.

THE 2023 REFERENDUM'S INSPIRED RACISM AND IMPACT

Diversity, inclusion, and anti-racism frameworks are common forms of action in organizations, yet their existence in a neoliberal reality affect Indigenous people through limited perspectives and understanding of Aboriginal and Torres Strait Islander worldviews (Bargallie, 2021; Bargallie et al., 2024). The neoliberal context is important for understanding the overarching driver of economic power and also as a framework that has negatively tilted the scales for women's participation, the most obvious being the ongoing gender pay gap in Australia, which sits at 78 cents per dollar (Workplace Gender Equality Agency, n.d.), as opposed to the OECD average of 89 cents (Organisation for Economic Co-operation and Development, n.d.). There has been a global trend in 2025 to reduce diversity and inclusion initiatives, even though, as Bargallie et al. (2024) discussed, diversity and inclusion programs take the form of the most basic racial action and expressions of White fragility in lieu of actual systemic change. This is compounded by the active funding of division and social segregation, which have sponsored the progression from casual to overt racism in Australia, while the cultural and social divides between Aboriginal and Torres Strait Islander Australians and the ruling White dominant social class have increased. This is contextualized by Habibis et al. (2016, p. 59): "Whiteness theory stresses that Whiteness is not so much a biophysical phenomenon but rather a multi-layered social construct: an identity more than skin colour." Whiteness theory is important because, as British-born sociologist Ruth Frankenberg (1993) identifies, Whiteness is dominant across three dimensions: as a location of structural advantage or privilege; as a standpoint, the worldview from which those who are White understand themselves and those who are not White; and as a set of unmarked and unnamed cultural practices. The multi-layered social construct of "Whiteness" and in contrast, "otherness," is ingrained in the workplace experience, is ingrained in the value placed on cultural and social capital, and is gendered through constructs of place, identity, and belonging.

THE ONGOING COLONIAL PROJECT IN AUSTRALIA

The Australian workforce exists within the context of the ongoing Australian colonial project: the ongoing, government-orchestrated disadvantage and dispossession of Aboriginal and Torres Strait Islander people through policy, cultural suppression, and historical denialism. This project began with the denial of our existence through the declaration of Australia being *Terra Nullius*, a land of no people, and the resultant theft of land and violence, with all the hallmarks of what we now recognize as genocide.

In the present, 237 years after the beginning of the Australian colonial project, the impact of this violence is realized through the ongoing denial of Aboriginal and Torres Strait Islander Australia, the questioning of culture and identity, and an endemic pattern of lateral violence that plagues Aboriginal family and community life (Mencevska, 2019). Anthropologist Deborah Bird Rose describes this as deep colonizing, or the ways in which Aboriginal and Torres Strait Islander peoples and communities interact with the state and each other (Rose, 2004). The ongoing colonial project impacts the workforce through experiences of inclusion and exclusion. Metz et al. (2022) discuss inclusion and exclusion as being formulated through both the perceptions and realities of a worker's social and human capital in an organization. As Aboriginal and Torres Strait Islander people and communities are so highly politicized, perceptions of our human and social capital are constantly discussed in the public sphere, and therefore, in the workplace. The overt racism experienced by Aboriginal and Torres Strait Islander people in recent years has also impacted Aboriginal and Torres Strait Islander workers, including perceptions of their social and human capital. Habibis et al. (2016) discuss this in their work as the social and cultural divide in Australia and what is experienced as a reduction of trust in Aboriginal and Torres Strait Islander people.

The Gari Yala (Speak the Truth): Gendered Report was a research collaboration between the UTS Jumbunna Institute for Indigenous Education and Research, the Diversity Council Australia, and the Workplace Gender Equality Agency. The report demonstrated that Aboriginal and Torres Strait Islander women experience limited cultural and identity support in the workforce and that Indigenous women carers are the most likely group to experience discrimination in the workforce (Evans, 2021). Importantly, the report indicated that women experience the impact of negative perceptions of their social and human capital impact and value, in addition to upholding cultural values and responsibilities with less support. The report details:

> Aboriginal and Torres Strait Islander women had significantly less support in culturally unsafe situations and had the highest cultural load. These results suggest that trends of women's disadvantage and marginalisation in the workplace are also present in the workplace experiences related to culture and identity.
>
> (Evans, 2021, p. 1)

In this contemporary reality for Aboriginal and Torres Strait Islander women in the workforce is the backdrop of how positive relationship setting is attempted through political governance. This is framed as Aboriginal and Torres Strait Islander self-determination in the Australian political sphere, which impacts communities, workforces, and economies. Yet importantly, recognition of the variation of male "self" and female "self" in self-determination is absent in the colonial project (Nakata, 2020). Given the overarching framework in which policy and legislation are developed and held by the government, yet Aboriginal and Torres Strait Islander affairs have "self-determination," the nuances of lived experience are often missed. The contrasting context of self-determination and a rejection of the Voice to Parliament means that "self-determination" is a hollow concept and relies on non-Indigenous voices to determine what is self-determined. Importantly, nuanced experience by gender is further from being realized with limited consultation and lived experience.

DECOLONIZING THINKING IN THE AUSTRALIAN WORKFORCE

Within the overarching continuum of Aboriginal and Torres Strait Islander women's workforce experiences is the impact of ongoing racism that is rife in Australian society post the Voice Referendum in 2023. In reaction to the referendum, society has drifted toward a further divided community that has adversely chosen to limit its reflexivity to an Aboriginal and Torres Strait Islander standpoint (Taylor & Habibis, 2020). These changes have shaped the workforce experience in violent measure, and they continue to disadvantage Aboriginal and Torres Strait Islanders through actions, rhetoric, and stereotyping from those in positions of power and influence.

As the Commission for Gender Equality in the Public Sector (2025) describes, "First Nations women were less likely to report holding positions as senior managers (overseeing lower-level managers) or supervisors (managing employees who are not managers themselves) than Indigenous men and non-Indigenous men and women." However, the opportunities for Aboriginal and Torres Strait Islander women in the Australian workforce are conceptual, cultural, political, and relational, as Woods et al. (2022) summarized in their discussion of decolonizing business schools in Australia and New Zealand. Of course, so much of the female Aboriginal and Torres Strait Islander experience begins in vocational and tertiary education as a precursor to the workforce. Feelings of exclusion can lead to university turnover. Yet, it is suggested that greater support be given to Aboriginal and Torres Strait Islander students to deal with, and be resistant to, neoliberal values (Durmush et al., 2024). This is especially important for Aboriginal and Torres Strait Islander women due to the increased cultural load described earlier. It also makes sense given the greater representation of Aboriginal and Torres Strait Islander women in higher education in Australia. The Australian Government Department of Education reported in 2019 that there were twice as many female Aboriginal and Torres Strait Islander higher education students as male students and that women made up the majority (66%) of Aboriginal and Torres Strait Islander enrollments in higher degrees, such as doctorates and masters of research (Australian Government Department of Education, 2019).

Beyond preparation for the workforce, a great amount of work has been done to depict the female experience and greater Aboriginal and Torres Strait Islander representation in sectors such as health and the public service. Kamilaroi and Wonnarua academic Debbie Bargallie, in conjunction with colleagues (Bargallie et al., 2024), has detailed the work needed for breaking the racial contract in the Australian Public Service and called for structural reform. Munanjahli and South Sea Island woman associate professor Chelsea Bond, in collaboration with colleagues (Bond et al., 2019), similarly calls for reform for healthcare workers and the consideration of the perpetuation of racial stereotypes and racialized care. Further research that considers the conceptual, cultural, political, and relational elements in different sectors and industries in relation to a woman's workforce reality could aid in increasing women in leadership and management roles and greater workforce participation in general.

CHAPTER SUMMARY

The historical context of contemporary realities for Aboriginal and Torres Strait Islander women in the workforce is significant and profound. These histories influence attitudes, stereotypes, and behaviors of both Aboriginal and Torres Strait Islander and non-Indigenous people, which in turn, affect opportunities and influence boundaries of workforce participation. This has come into sharper focus in recent times due to the significant political activity that has centered on Aboriginal and Torres Strait Islander Australians. The referendum, unfortunately, created the space for negativity and division to take hold across Australia, and its impact is still rippling through workplaces, families, and communities. It has also ensured the continuation of the colonial project, a management of our lives with a rejection of the Aboriginal and Torres Strait Islander Voice to Parliament about Aboriginal and Torres Strait Islander legislation and policy.

This context matters when discussing Aboriginal and Torres Strait Islander women in the workforce because our experiences shape the roles we take, the opportunities we pursue, and the way we balance life, family, culture, and community. The gravitational pull toward the paternalistic continuum in contemporary Australia reverberates through the private and public sectors, through leaders, governance, and politics, and influences the work environment and our perceptions of workforce capacity and engagement. The lack of meaningful change through workforce initiatives, such as diversity and inclusion, which instead speak to the fragility of Whiteness in our organizations and institutions, is an ongoing hindrance to increasing participation.

While the extensive research of sectors with greater Aboriginal and Torres Strait Islanders is a start, much needs to be analyzed across all sectors to further detail the intersectionality between culture, identity, race, and gender. An exploration of Aboriginal and Torres Strait Islander women's increased participation in higher education and the lack of correlations with positions of leadership would further unpack barriers and opportunities. In addition, decolonized thinking across the board—in all workforces, industries, and sectors—would help to fully recognize and comprehend how the ongoing colonial project impacts our people, our workforces, and our participation. Decolonizing thought needs to go further and be applied to workforce barriers and used to inspire opportunities to fully engage the Australian workforce, including Aboriginal and Torres Strait Islander women. The colonial project is a drain on innovation and productivity and an impediment to unlocking the full potential of Aboriginal and Torres Strait Islander women's participation in the Australian workforce.

DISCUSSION QUESTIONS

1. How do historical constructs influence gendered participation in the workforce in your region?
2. What social reform have you witnessed in the last five years? What global trends of social division are apparent in your context? What impact have they had on workforces?
3. Has decolonizing thought been raised in your workplace? If so, how has it been described, and why is it deemed important? How many perspectives within your workforce does a colonial view exclude?

REFERENCES

Australian Bureau of Statistics. (2018, July 9). *Aboriginal and Torres Strait Islander women celebrated*. https://www.abs.gov.au/statistics/people/aboriginal-and-torres-strait-islander-peoples/aboriginal-and-torres-strait-islander-women-celebrated/latest-release

Australian Bureau of Statistics. (2023). *Aboriginal and Torres Strait Islander health performance framework 2021*. https://www.indigenoushpf.gov.au/

Australian Government Department of Education. (2019, August). *Indigenous students in higher degrees by research*. https://www.education.gov.au/download/4830/indigenous-students-higher-degrees-research/7202/document/pdf

Bargallie, D. (2021). *Unmasking the racial contract: Indigenous voices on racism in the Australian public service*. Aboriginal Studies Press.

Bargallie, D., Fernando, N., & Lentin, A. (2024). Breaking the racial silence: Putting racial literacy to work in Australia. *Ethnic and Racial Studies*, *47*(8), 1532–1551. https://doi.org/10.1080/01419870.2023.2206470

Bond, C., Brough, M., Willis, J., Stajic, J., Mukandi, B., Canuto, C., Springer, S., Askew, D., Angus, L., & Lewis, T. (2019). Beyond the pipeline: A critique of the discourse surrounding the development of an Indigenous primary healthcare workforce in Australia. *Australian Journal of Primary Health*, *25*(5), 389–394. https://doi.org/10.1071/PY19044

Commission for Gender Equality in the Public Sector. (2025). Gender and Aboriginal and Torres Strait Islander employees. In *Intersectionality at work: Building a baseline on compounded gender inequality in the Victorian public sector*. Victorian State Government. https://www.genderequalitycommission.vic.gov.au/sites/default/files/2023-10/Intersectionality-At-Work-Report.pdf

Durmush, G., Craven, R. G., Yeung, A. S., Mooney, J., Horwood, M., Vasconcellos, D., Franklin, A., Duncan, C., & Gillane, R. (2024). Enabling Indigenous wellbeing in higher education: Indigenous Australian youth-devised strategies and solutions. *Higher Education*, *87*(6), 1357–1374. https://doi.org/10.1007/s10734-023-01067-z

Evans, O. (2021). *Gari Yala (Speak the Truth): Gendered insights*. WGEA Commissioned Research Report in partnership with the Jumbunna Institute of Education and Research and Diversity Council. https://internationalwim.org/wp-content/uploads/2022/07/gari_yala_genderedinsights2021_output_74e891d02edc4f1b953f5140ae1abda8.pdf

Frankenberg, R. (1993). *The social construction of whiteness: White women, race matters*. University of Minnesota Press.

Habibis, D., Taylor, P., Walter, M., & Elder, C. (2016). Repositioning the racial gaze: Aboriginal perspectives on race, race relations and governance. *Social Inclusion*, *4*(1), 57–67. https://doi.org/10.17645/si.v4i1.492

Mencevska, I. (2019). Truth telling in Australia's historical narrative. *Emerging Scholars in Australian Indigenous Studies*, *5*(1).

Metz, I., Stamper, C. L., & Ng, E. (2022). Feeling included and excluded in organisations: The role of human and social capital. *Journal of Business Research*, *142*, 122–137. https://doi.org/10.1016/j.jbusres.2021.12.045

Nakata, S. (2020). Who is the self in Indigenous self-determination? In L. Rademaker & T. Rowse (Eds.), Indigenous self-determination in Australia: Histories and historiography (pp. 293–310). Australian National University Press.

Organisation for Economic Co-operation and Development. (n.d.). *Gender equality*. Retrieved August 30, 2025 from https://www.oecd.org/en/topics/gender-equality.html

Rose, D. B. (2004). *Reports from a wild country: Ethics of decolonisation*. University of New South Wales Press.

State Library of Victoria. (n.d.). *Indigenous voice to parliament referendum: A guide to resources around the Aboriginal & Torres Strait Islander voice referendum*. Retrieved August 1, 2025, from https://guides.slv.vic.gov.au/c.php?g=961514&p=6982612

Taylor, P. S., & Habibis, D. (2020). Widening the gap: White ignorance, race relations and the consequences for aboriginal people in Australia. *Australian Journal of Social Issues*, *55*(3), 354–371. https://doi.org/10.1002/ajs4.106

Wolfe, P. (1999). *Settler colonialism and the transformation of anthropology: The politics and poetics of an ethnographic event*. Cassell.

Woods, C., Dell, K., & Carroll, B. (2022). Decolonizing the business school: Reconstructing the entrepreneurship classroom through indigenizing pedagogy and learning. *Academy of Management Learning & Education*, *21*(1), 82–103. https://doi.org/10.5465/amle.2020.0366

Workplace Gender Equality Agency. (n.d.). *Gender pay gap data*. Retrieved August 30, 2025 from https://www.wgea.gov.au/pay-and-gender/gender-pay-gap-data

CHAPTER 6

Missteps, Misbehavior, and Mischief

How Gender Stereotypes Bias Reactions to Negative Behavior at Work

Suzette Caleo and Daniel S. Whitman

Imagine two managers—one male and one female—who commit the same missteps: they publicly berate an underperforming employee, slam their hands on the table during moments of frustration, make off-color jokes that alienate colleagues, gossip about team members behind their backs, or manipulate financial reports to meet performance targets. Perhaps they engage in unethical negotiations, taking bribes to ensure contracts, or show blatant favoritism in distributing workloads. Both managers exhibit behaviors that are undeniably problematic. Yet, would they be judged to the same standard, receiving the same level of punishment and the same opportunities for a second chance? Would others attribute their actions to the same causes, calling to mind similar explanations for their behavior?

Organizational scholars have long studied the ways in which individuals "behave badly" at work (Robinson & Bennett, 1995)—whether through organizational injustice (Ambrose et al., 2002), counterproductive work behavior (Gruys & Sackett, 2003), abusive supervision (Tepper, 2000), or incivility (Cortina et al., 2001), among others. Collectively, we refer to these actions as negative work behaviors, or "behavior in the work context that is . . . deemed harmful" (Zhong & Robinson, 2021, p. 1431). Much of the existing research on negative work behaviors focuses on their consequences for organizations, targets, and third-party bystanders. However, researchers have more recently turned their attention to examining consequences for the individuals who engage in those misbehaviors (Zhong & Robinson, 2021). These studies often find that misbehaving individuals incur unfavorable attitudinal and behavioral reactions from others, including a loss of social capital, diminished trust, and negative evaluations (Peng et al., 2014; Tyler et al., 2006).

DOI: 10.4324/9781003488590-6

Emerging evidence, however, suggests that reactions to wrongdoing are not uniform (Polman et al., 2013; Luksyte et al., 2013). For example, studies have begun to demonstrate the role that gender plays in shaping reactions to negative work behaviors (Kim et al., 2022; Motro et al., 2021). This chapter reviews the growing literature on this topic, focusing on how gender stereotypes influence evaluations of individuals who "behave badly" in the workplace. Specifically, we argue that gender stereotypes generate different standards for judging men's and women's misbehaviors and consider the implications of these disparities for evaluations of men and women in the workplace.

GENDER STEREOTYPE CONTENT AND ITS CONNECTION TO NEGATIVE WORK BEHAVIORS

Central to understanding gendered reactions to workplace misbehavior is the content of gender stereotypes. For decades, scholars have documented the degree to which people ascribe distinct stereotypes to men and women (Bem, 1974; Eagly et al., 2020). Despite some slight signs of change, these stereotypes have persisted over time (Eagly et al., 2020). Gender stereotypes tend to fall into two major dimensions: agency and communality. Agency, which is characterized by self-directed goal pursuit, mastery of one's environment, and assertion of control, encompasses traits such as ambition, dominance, and independence (Bakan, 1966; Ma et al., 2022). In contrast, communality focuses on the formation and maintenance of social relationships and includes traits such as warmth, empathy, and morality (Abele et al., 2016). According to gender stereotypes, men are typically associated with agentic attributes and behaviors, whereas women are typically associated with communal attributes and behaviors. These stereotypes are oppositional as well, meaning that men are perceived as low in communality relative to women, and that women are perceived as low in agency relative to men (Heilman et al., 2024).

What do stereotypes about men and women as agentic and communal suggest regarding their perceived likelihood of engaging in negative work behaviors? Evidence suggests that people associate men with misbehaviors more frequently than they do women (Reynolds et al., 2020), a perception that is arguably rooted in the alignment between gender stereotypes of agency and communality and the assumptions, intentions, and behaviors underlying misconduct (Graso & Reynolds, 2024).

Research suggests that many negative work behaviors fulfill psychological needs for agency (Shnabel & Nadler, 2008; Zhong & Robinson, 2021). These behaviors can serve as vehicles for achieving personal goals and exerting control, dominance, or power over others—intentions that are associated with agency. The connection between agency and misbehavior is further supported by research showing that being relentlessly driven to achieve goals can heighten the likelihood of engaging in emotional manipulation (Hyde et al., 2020). Such tendencies align with stereotypes of men as ambitious, dominant, and goal-oriented, reinforcing the association of men with potentially destructive actions that prioritize personal achievement and power over relational harmony. In fact, research on precarious manhood suggests that men may engage in aggression and workplace deviance as a means of demonstrating masculinity (Bosson & Vandello, 2011; Leavitt et al., 2022).

At the same time, misbehaviors often undermine psychological needs for communality (Shnabel & Nadler, 2008; Zhong & Robinson, 2021). Because negative work behaviors result in the erosion of trust and social capital, they can be detrimental to the maintenance of social relationships, conflicting with communal values. Importantly, communality encompasses not only warmth but also morality (Abele et al., 2016), further highlighting its misalignment with many unethical actions. In addition, perceptions of weakness and passivity—more often associated with women—render women more likely to be seen as victims than perpetrators of unethical behavior. Indeed, women are seen as easier to deceive in negotiations than men, reflecting stereotypes of naiveté and gullibility (Kray et al., 2014). These communal stereotypes paint a picture of women that is inconsistent with the idea of behaving badly at work.

Because men are more often associated with agency and women associated with communality, individuals are more likely to perceive men rather than women as actors who engage in misbehaviors. Reynolds et al. (2020) provided evidence of this bias by showing that individuals are more likely to classify perpetrators as male and victims as female. The act of inducing harm implies control and power, characteristics that align with stereotypes about men. Conversely, the communal attributes ascribed to women are at odds with the intentions and actions that drive many negative behaviors. As a result, women are perceived not only as less likely to engage in harmful or unethical actions but also as more likely to be victimized.

Further research supports the notion that gender stereotypes portray men as more likely and women as less likely to engage in misbehaviors. For instance, Prentice and Carranza (2002) found that it is more desirable for women to be wholesome and for men to be rebellious and promiscuous. Similarly, Buss et al. (2020) found that fidelity and purity are viewed as status-enhancing traits for women but not men. Although some traits, such as honesty, appear to be valued equally for both genders (Buss et al., 2020), the broader pattern suggests that stereotypes about men as rebellious and women as virtuous reinforce gendered expectations about misbehavior. These stereotypes are further reflected in everyday language. Idioms such as "boys will be boys" and references to "locker room talk" normalize men's rebellious behaviors, framing them as an extension of masculinity. Together, depictions of men and women presented through stereotypes and language perpetuate assumptions about their perceived propensities to engage in negative work behavior. We argue that these stereotypes not only influence perceptions of men's and women's behaviors but also shape how their actions are judged in the workplace.

PRESCRIPTIVE GENDER STEREOTYPES

We have established that people hold differential stereotypes about men's and women's propensity to misbehave. But how do these stereotypes come to influence how individuals react to men's and women's negative work behaviors? We contend that reactions to misbehaviors will be influenced by prescriptive gender stereotypes. Gender stereotypes have both descriptive and prescriptive properties: they not only depict what men and women *are* and *are not* thought to be like, but they also set prescriptions for what people think they *should* and *should not* be like (Eagly & Karau, 2002; Heilman, 2001). This distinction is critical, as it highlights two distinct mechanisms through which gender discrimination occurs (Heilman et al., 2024). Descriptive gender stereotypes, which characterize what men and women are assumed to be like, are particularly problematic for women in male-dominated domains. In such contexts, women, who are stereotyped as communal and not agentic, tend to be viewed as lacking the attributes necessary for success (Heilman et al., 2024).

Prescriptive gender stereotypes, which are the focus of this chapter, pose a different challenge. By establishing normative expectations for men's and women's behaviors, they create rigid standards: women are expected to exhibit communality (and not agency), and men are expected to exhibit agency (and not communality). Prescriptive gender stereotypes function similarly to injunctive social norms (Cialdini & Trost, 1998; Eagly & Karau, 2002), which are norms that dictate what should or should not be done. A failure to act in alignment with injunctive norms provokes social disapproval (Cialdini & Trost, 1998). Similarly, when individuals deviate from behaviors that are prescribed for their gender, they often face social penalties and backlash, which translate to unfavorable outcomes in work contexts (Rudman & Phelan, 2008).

For women, engaging in behaviors that are deemed stereotypically masculine constitutes a violation of "should nots," or actions that are socially off limits. Thus, when women exhibit agency, they are often subject to social derogation, facing backlash for deviating from prescribed gender norms. Research has demonstrated that women are evaluated more negatively than men when they display dominance (Dupree, 2024; Ma et al., 2022), adopt a bottom-line mentality (Tai et al., 2022), negotiate assertively for themselves (Amanatullah & Morris, 2010), or engage in autocratic leadership (Eagly et al., 1992). Even success in management positions, an achievement thought to require agency, can trigger negative evaluations for women (Dwivedi et al., 2021; Heilman et al., 2004). Beyond agency violations, women also are evaluated less favorably than their male counterparts for failing to perform communal behaviors, such as neglecting to help a coworker (Heilman & Chen, 2005) or failing to support subordinates' work–family balance (Yu et al., 2022).

Although researchers have primarily examined the effects of prescriptive gender stereotypes on women, men who violate gender norms are also subject to negative repercussions. Because stereotypes dictate that they should be agentic and should not be communal, men are socially derided for engaging in stereotypically feminine behaviors or failing to engage in stereotypically masculine behaviors. Specifically, research has shown that men who advocate for others (Bosak et al., 2018), request family leave (Rudman & Mescher, 2013), or fail to complete work-related tasks while on family leave (Parks-Stamm & Tharp, 2023) are evaluated less favorably than their female counterparts. Similarly, men in female-dominated positions are often judged negatively because they are seen as weak and less deserving of respect than women in those positions (Heilman & Wallen, 2010; Moss-Racusin & Johnson, 2016). Thus, although gender stereotypes tend to have more severe consequences for women, men are also penalized for violating prescriptive gender stereotypes.

HOW PRESCRIPTIVE GENDER STEREOTYPES LEAD TO DIFFERENTIAL REACTIONS TO MISBEHAVIORS

As society has made more progress toward gender equality, researchers have observed that women do not always incur penalties for behaving agentically nor do men always incur penalties for behaving communally (Heilman & Chen, 2005; Ma et al., 2022). Specifically, women and men tend to face fewer repercussions when their violations of prescriptive gender stereotypes involve positively valenced behaviors that are broadly socially desirable. By distinguishing between agentic prescriptions (socially desirable agency) and agentic proscriptions (socially undesirable agency), Ma et al. (2022) demonstrated that women are especially vulnerable to negative gender-based judgments when they engage in socially undesirable agentic behaviors (e.g., dominance) compared to socially desirable agentic behaviors (e.g., competence, diligence).

This distinction is particularly relevant to misbehaviors, which fall squarely into the category of socially undesirable actions. Because many negative work behaviors can be characterized as agentic proscriptions, they are especially precarious for women: when women engage in misbehaviors—many of which involve agency and a lack of communality—they violate not only general social norms but also prescriptive gender norms. This dual transgression is likely to amplify the severity of the backlash they experience. Conversely, men may receive more leniency than women for engaging in the same misbehaviors, as such behaviors involve qualities that are viewed as more acceptable for men than for people in general (Prentice & Carranza, 2002). In short, though workplace misbehavior is undesirable for everyone, men's misbehaviors may be perceived as more expected because of gender norms. Women's misbehaviors, in turn, run counter to what is expected of them on the basis of gender norms, thus eliciting a stronger response.

Still, we contend that some negative work behaviors require more agency than others, and that the extent to which misbehavior aligns or conflicts with prescriptive gender stereotypes influences how it will be judged. Misconduct involving extreme agency, such as abusive supervision, may be judged more harshly when exhibited by women, as such behaviors starkly contradict feminine stereotypes. However, misbehaviors that do not strongly align with either agency or communality should elicit similar reactions regardless of gender. Finally, some negative work behaviors may involve lower agency and may even be perceived as feminine or communal in nature. In these cases, men may be judged more harshly than women. In sum, we propose that reactions to misbehavior are influenced not only by the general undesirability of the behavior but also by how closely the behavior aligns or conflicts with prescriptive gender stereotypes. It is those negative behaviors that overlap with the content of gender stereotypes that are most likely to generate ire and negative reactions to the perpetrator.

Reviewing the Evidence: Does Perpetrator Gender Influence Reactions to Different Types of Negative Work Behaviors?

Research on prescriptive gender stereotypes has expanded significantly over the past quarter century (Heilman et al., 2024). However, only recently has there been growing momentum to examine how men and women are judged when engaging in explicitly negative work behaviors. In this section, we review existing findings on reactions to different types of misbehavior based on the perpetrator's gender. As discussed, many of these behaviors involve agency—whether through aggression, exerting control, or pursuing self-interest—and often conflict with communal expectations. However, not all forms of misbehavior are uniformly gender-typed. Some may be perceived as gender-neutral, whereas others may align more closely with communal or stereotypically feminine traits. We structure our discussion according to established categories of negative work behaviors, noting where gendered expectations might shape reactions to those behaviors.

Abusive Supervision

Abusive supervision is defined as the "sustained display of hostile verbal and nonverbal behaviors, excluding physical contact" from supervisors (Tepper, 2000, p. 178). This nonphysical hostility can include actions such as yelling and blaming subordinates, derogating their work, and ostracizing them (Tepper et al., 2008). In recent years, scholars have demonstrated that reactions to abusive supervision are moderated by the gender of the supervisor. Kim et al. (2022) found that female leaders who engage in abusive supervision are rated as less effective than male leaders who engage in abusive supervision, a finding that supports our argument that women are penalized for behaving agentically. In another set of studies, Fiset and Byrne (2025) introduced a specific kind of abusive supervision termed *safety-specific abusive supervision*, arguing that employees may attribute a leader's abusive supervision in a hazardous work environment to a desire to ensure employee safety rather than a malicious intent to harm employees. They found, however, that this was the case for male but not female supervisors. When a woman engaged in safety-specific abusive supervision, her actions were attributed less than a man's abusive supervision to a desire to motivate employees improve. Thus, not only are women penalized to a greater degree than men for engaging in abusive supervision, but they also are less likely to be excused for such misbehaviors.

Incivility

Incivility involves subtle slights and includes condescension, disrespect, and degradation (Cortina et al., 2001); it is disrespectful behavior that otherwise appears mundane. Research suggests that incivility is often selective, meaning that it is more frequently directed toward individuals based on their gender, race, or other marginalized identities (Cortina, 2008). Women are more likely to be targets of workplace incivility than men, and when they experience it from men, they are particularly likely to attribute it to gender bias (Lopez-Alvarez et al., 2024). However, what about incivility that is carried out by women?

Several studies suggest that individuals react more harshly to women than men who engage in incivility. Chen-Xia et al. (2022) found that uncivil behavior is perceived as high in masculinity and low in femininity compared to civil behavior, supporting the idea that incivility is gendered. Furthermore, Motro et al. (2021) found that having an uncivil team member who was a woman had a stronger negative impact on team affect and creativity than having an uncivil male team member. These findings suggest that when women behave uncivilly, they are not only evaluated more negatively, but their incivility may also have broader consequences for the team.

Corporate Misconduct

Corporate misconduct refers to unethical or illegal actions that involve the misrepresentation, omission, or manipulation of information to mislead stakeholders (Zahra et al., 2005). Unlike other negative work behaviors discussed in this chapter, corporate misconduct primarily affects the organization as a whole, often resulting in severe financial and reputational consequences (Karpoff et al., 2008). However, because corporate executives and board directors often oversee decision-making and reporting, responsibility for such misconduct can be attributed to these upper echelon leaders (Arthaud-Day et al., 2006).

How do individuals respond when financial misconduct occurs in an organization led by male versus female leaders? Because corporate misconduct is often motivated by personal gain, overconfidence, self-interest, and competitive pressures (Plöckinger et al., 2016), individuals may react more unfavorably to women who oversee organizations that have engaged in such misconduct. However, existing studies present mixed findings. Using a sample of Chinese organizations, Saeed and Riaz (2022) found that women directors were more likely than men directors to be replaced following financial misconduct, an effect that was strongest in male-dominated industries. In contrast, Naumovska et al. (2020) reported the opposite pattern among firms that were investigated by the Securities and Exchange Commission and the Department of Justice: female directors were less likely to be negatively affected than male directors following a firm's financial misconduct, potentially driven by a growing pressure to increase diversity in leadership positions.

Organizational (In)justice

Organizational justice has been widely studied for its positive effects on employees (Colquitt et al., 2013) and work units (Whitman et al., 2012). It encompasses several dimensions, including distributive justice (fairness in distributing outcomes), procedural justice (fairness of the processes used to make decisions), informational justice (fairness in communication), and interpersonal justice (fairness of interpersonal treatment). Scholars have also examined *organizational injustice*, or the violation of justice rules, recognizing it as distinct from adherence to justice rules (Colquitt et al., 2015).

How do individuals react to men and women who violate organizational justice rules? Research generally suggests that people react more negatively to female managers following unfair situations (Varty et al., 2021). However, the type of justice violation matters. Specifically, women are penalized more than men for violating interpersonal justice rules, but not procedural justice rules. Several studies have shown that female supervisors receive lower performance ratings and lower recommendations for rewards when they are impolite and treat their subordinates disrespectfully (Caleo, 2016; Mu et al., 2024). Further research suggests that this heightened penalty occurs because women who violate interpersonal justice are perceived as excessively agentic (Mu et al., 2024) and because impoliteness is seen as more unacceptable for women than for men (Caleo, 2016).

Research has also examined whether men and women face different consequences for violating distributive justice rules. Caleo (2018) found that men were penalized more than women for distributing pay unequally among employees (equality) in a context where performance-based pay distribution (equity) was expected. This practice arguably constituted a distributive justice violation for both genders; however, men received harsher evaluations and were perceived as less agentic than women. This finding suggests that violating gender norms of agency can intensify negative judgments for men who fail to uphold equity-based distributive justice rules. They also suggest that women may be shielded from criticism when their actions align with communal expectations, even when they violate distributive justice norms. Future research should explore whether other violations of justice rooted in communality are judged differently. For instance, would a supervisor who repeatedly gives underperforming employees second chances face more backlash if they were a man rather than a woman?

Counterproductive Work Behaviors

Counterproductive work behaviors (CWBs) encompass a range of behaviors that detract from the performance of organizations—from theft, destruction of property, and drug and alcohol abuse to inappropriate verbal and physical actions (Gruys & Sackett, 2003). Notably, researchers have varied their conceptualizations of CWBs, sometimes casting a wide net that includes many different types of workplace misconduct (Carpenter et al., 2021). Therefore, several of the negative work behaviors discussed in this chapter, such as abusive supervision and incivility, may fall under the scope of CWBs, depending on the framework used. To maintain clarity, we have used the specific terminology employed by researchers in their respective studies.

Despite this conceptual variety, one set of studies has explicitly examined whether CWBs elicit different reactions for men and women, differentiating between stereotypically masculine and stereotypically feminine CWBs. Botsford Morgan et al. (2018) found that men and women were evaluated differently for engaging in counterproductive work behaviors; however, the pattern that emerged is contrary to what we have proposed here. Specifically, women were penalized to a greater degree than men for engaging in CWBs that were coded as stereotypically feminine (e.g., accessing private medical records without permission, repeatedly missing work, misusing equipment), whereas men were penalized to a greater degree than women for engaging in CWBs that were coded as stereotypically masculine (e.g., sending sexually explicit work emails, threatening or intimidating others, disrespectful and abusive behavior). This finding introduces an interesting complexity to the broader literature on gendered reactions to workplace misconduct. Though we have argued that women typically face greater penalties for agentic misbehaviors that violate both social and gender norms, these studies suggest that punishment may be harsher when individuals engage in CWBs that align with gender stereotypes.

Workplace Gossip

Workplace gossip refers to "an employee communicating to another individual at work about a workplace other who is absent or unaware of the content" (Sun et al., 2023, p. 312). Although numerous studies classify workplace gossip as a negative work behavior, others argue that gossip can also be positive or neutral (Grosser et al., 2010; Robbins & Karan, 2020; Sun et al., 2023). Evidence suggests that employees who engage in negative gossip are judged unfavorably by supervisors (Grosser et al., 2010) and by those who hear the gossip (Kakarika et al., 2024).

Although gossip is stereotypically associated with women (Robbins & Karan, 2020), it remains unclear whether men and women face different consequences for engaging in it. One possibility is that stereotypes about women as gossipers may buffer them from some negative consequences, as the behavior may be perceived as more expected of them. However, workplace gossip, particularly when negative, can erode social harmony and be perceived as a way to exert control over others (Farley et al., 2010). Thus, female gossipers could be viewed less favorably than male gossipers for exhibiting agency and violating communal norms. Research is needed to test these ideas and examine whether individuals react differently to male and female gossipers in the workplace.

Additional Considerations: How Does Perpetrator Gender Shape Reactions to Intent, Emotions, and Responses Surrounding Negative Work Behaviors?

In addition to shaping reactions to different types of misbehavior, research also demonstrates that gender influences how people interpret factors that precede or follow misconduct. This section explores how gender stereotypes shape perceptions and reactions to intent, emotions, and responses surrounding negative work behaviors.

Intentionality and Control

Misbehaviors may vary in the extent to which perpetrators have control over their actions, and this level of control can overlap with perceptions of agency. For example, Mai et al. (2020) differentiated between premeditated and impulsive ethical lapses, arguing that premeditated unethical behavior is agentic in nature. Their findings revealed that unethical behavior that was premeditated rather than impulsive was perceived as less feminine and that women who engaged in premeditated unethical behaviors were punished more severely than men who engaged in the same behaviors. Building on this, we propose that passive forms of misbehavior, such as those in which an individual is swept up or tricked into the misconduct, may result in less severe consequences for women than men. Because women are stereotyped as more naïve or gullible, misbehaviors that occur under such circumstances may be viewed as more acceptable for them.

The Role of Emotions

Scholars have identified negative affect and emotions as instrumental in explaining various negative work behaviors (Scott et al., 2009). Notably, some emotions are more off limits to women relative to men, and one emotion that is particularly relevant to workplace misbehavior is anger. Although anger is not synonymous with misconduct, it has been linked to several negative work behaviors, such as workplace aggression (Hershcovis et al., 2007), counterproductive work behavior (Fox & Spector, 1999), and petty tyranny (Kant et al., 2013). Several studies suggest that women face greater penalties than men for expressing anger. When women display anger in the workplace, they receive lower salaries, are conferred less status, and are more likely to elicit the perception that the anger resulted from internal characteristics rather than situational demands (Brescoll & Uhlmann, 2008; Marshburn et al., 2020). Some research suggests that race moderates these effects, with Black women suffering greater penalties for expressing anger (Motro et al., 2022).

While anger contradicts stereotypical expectations of women as communal, another emotional display—crying—is typically seen as more acceptable for women than for men (Motro & Ellis, 2017). Yet, recent research suggests that women who cry in manipulative ways experience greater backlash than their male counterparts (Pittarello & Motro, 2024). Thus, even emotions that seem more stereotypically aligned with femininity, such as crying, can backfire for women if they are perceived as a tool for manipulation or misconduct.

Responses to Misconduct or Failures

When workplace misconduct occurs, how do individuals react to men and women who engage in damage control through apologies or denials? Emerging research suggests that gender matters (Walfisch et al., 2013), and that reactions to men and women depend on the degree to which the response aligns or conflicts with gender stereotypes. In one set of studies examining apologies following an organizational failure, female CEOs were evaluated more favorably when they engaged in an unqualified apology—accepting full responsibility for a product failure—rather than a qualified apology in which they accepted partial responsibility while also blaming another party (Cowen & Montgomery, 2020). Male CEOs, in contrast, had greater flexibility—they were evaluated no differently regardless of whether they fully or partially accepted responsibility. Similarly, denials issued by male leaders tend to be received more favorably than those issued by female leaders (Montgomery & Cowen, 2024). Evidently, partial apologies and denial responses involve dominance and assertiveness, invoking a violation of prescriptive gender stereotypes for women but not men. As a result, women who downplay or deny wrongdoing may be penalized more harshly.

Intersectionality: An Area for Future Research

Throughout this chapter, we have largely discussed gender as a singular construct. However, social identity does not exist in a vacuum; individuals inhabit multiple intersecting identities that shape the way they are perceived in the workplace. We argue that other social identities, such as race, may influence the patterns of gendered reactions to workplace misbehavior described in this chapter. For example, research in criminal justice and psychology has shown that Black defendants often face greater punishment than their White counterparts (Eberhardt et al., 2006), and the cultural adage "boys will be boys" does not apply in the same way to Black boys, who are frequently denied the same leniency granted to White boys (Goff et al., 2014). Furthermore, evidence suggests that gender discrimination in the workplace varies for Black women relative to White women (Rosette et al., 2016). This presents an important moderator for future research to consider: how do race and gender interact to shape reactions to workplace misbehavior?

Recent work suggests that reactions to workplace misconduct vary by race (Luksyte et al., 2013), and as we have reviewed in this chapter, they also vary by gender. However, much remains unknown about how these two identity dimensions intersect to shape perceptions of negative work behaviors. Thus, future studies should explore how race and gender jointly influence attributions and reactions to workplace misconduct. As we have discussed, we propose that reactions to misconduct are likely shaped by stereotypes; however, it is essential to consider how racial and gender stereotypes operate together to inform judgments.

CHAPTER SUMMARY

In this chapter, we examined a specific subset of prescriptive gender stereotype violations—those involving negative work behaviors. Though much of the existing research on prescriptive gender stereotypes has focused on how men and women are evaluated for engaging in behaviors that are socially desirable in general, we extended this lens to review emerging research on negative work behaviors that are socially undesirable for all. Our review indicates that gender stereotypes shape how men's and women's transgressions are perceived and punished. Across multiple behaviors, research suggests that women often experience harsher backlash for engaging in negative work behaviors that align with agency and conflict with communality. However, not all negative work behaviors are purely agentic, and some misbehaviors may contain communal elements. Understanding how communal misbehaviors are evaluated is an open question that requires more research. Although additional work is needed, our review underscores how gender stereotypes shape not only how success is rewarded but also how misdeeds are punished.

DISCUSSION QUESTIONS

1. How do prescriptive gender stereotypes shape the way negative work behaviors are perceived and punished? Can you think of real-world examples in which men and women were treated differently for engaging in similar misconduct at work?
2. Though many negative work behaviors are associated with agency, some may be more communal in nature. What are some examples of misbehaviors that align with communality rather than agency? Do you think that men would be judged more harshly than women for engaging in these types of behaviors? Why or why not?
3. Some studies on gendered reactions to workplace misconduct have shown mixed results. What factors might explain these inconsistencies across different contexts, industries, or cultural settings?
4. The chapter calls for further research on how race intersects with gender to shape reactions to workplace misconduct. How might race, age, or other identities interact with gender to influence reactions to misbehavior? Can you think of examples where multiple social identities might exacerbate or mitigate the consequences of misconduct?

REFERENCES

Abele, A. E., Hauke, N., Peters, K., Louvet, E., Szymkow, A., & Duan, Y. (2016). Facets of the fundamental content dimensions: Agency with competence and assertiveness—communion with warmth and morality. *Frontiers in Psychology*, *7*, 1810. https://doi.org/10.3389/fpsyg.2016.01810

Amanatullah, E. T., & Morris, M. W. (2010). Negotiating gender roles: Gender differences in assertive negotiating are mediated by women's fear of backlash and attenuated when negotiating on behalf of others. *Journal of Personality and Social Psychology*, *98*(2), 256–267. https://doi.org/10.1037/a0017094

Ambrose, M. L., Seabright, M. A., & Schminke, M. (2002). Sabotage in the workplace: The role of organizational injustice. *Organizational Behavior and Human Decision Processes*, *89*(1), 947–965. https://doi.org/10.1016/S0749-5978(02)00037-7

Arthaud-Day, M. L., Certo, S. T., Dalton, C. M., & Dalton, D. R. (2006). A changing of the guard: Executive and director turnover following corporate financial restatements. *Academy of Management Journal*, *49*(6), 1119–1136.

Bakan, D. (1966). *The duality of human existence: An essay on psychology and religion*. Rand McNally.

Bem, S. L. (1974). The measurement of psychological androgyny. *Journal of Consulting and Clinical Psychology*, *42*(2), 155.

Bosak, J., Kulich, C., Rudman, L., & Kinahan, M. (2018). Be an advocate for others, unless you are a man: Backlash against gender-atypical male job candidates. *Psychology of Men & Masculinity*, *19*(1), 156–165. https://doi.org/10.1037/men0000085

Bosson, J. K., & Vandello, J. A. (2011). Precarious manhood and its links to action and aggression. *Current Directions in Psychological Science*, *20*(2), 82–86. https://doi.org/10.1177/0963721411402669

Botsford Morgan, W., Nelson, J., King, E. B., & Mancini, V. S. (2018). Reactions to men's and women's counterproductive work behavior. *Equality, Diversity and Inclusion: An International Journal*, *37*(6), 582–599. https://doi.org/10.1108/EDI-08-2017-0161

Brescoll, V. L., & Uhlmann, E. L. (2008). Can an angry woman get ahead? Status conferral, gender, and expression of emotion in the workplace. *Psychological Science*, *19*(3), 268–275. https://doi.org/10.1111/j.1467-9280.2008.02079.x

Buss, D. M., Durkee, P. K., Shackelford, T. K., Bowdle, B. F., Schmitt, D. P., Brase, G. L., Choe, J. C., & Trofimova, I. (2020). "Human status criteria: Sex differences and similarities across 14 nations": Correction to Buss et al. (2020). *Journal of Personality and Social Psychology*, *119*(5), 998. https://doi.org/10.1037/pspa0000258

Caleo, S. (2016). Are organizational justice rules gendered? Reactions to men's and women's justice violations. *Journal of Applied Psychology*, *101*(10), 1422–1435. https://doi.org/10.1037/apl0000131

Caleo, S. (2018). When distributive justice and gender stereotypes coincide: Reactions to equity and equality violations. *Journal of Applied Social Psychology*, *48*, 257–268. https://doi.org/10.1111/jasp.12510

Carpenter, N. C., Whitman, D. S., & Amrhein, R. (2021). Unit-level Counterproductive Work Behavior (CWB): A conceptual review and quantitative summary. *Journal of Management*, *47*(6), 1498–1527. https://doi.org/10.1177/0149206320978812

Chen-Xia, X. J., Betancor, V., Chas, A., & Rodriguez-Perez, A. (2022). Gender inequality in incivility: Everyone should be polite, but it is fine for some of us to be impolite. *Frontiers in Psychology*, *13*, 966045. https://doi.org/10.3389/fpsyg.2022.966045

Cialdini, R. B., & Trost, M. R. (1998). Social influence: Social norms, conformity, and compliance. In *The handbook of social psychology*. McGraw-Hill.

Colquitt, J. A., Long, D. M., Rodell, J. B., & Halvorsen-Ganepola, M. D. K. (2015). Adding the "in" to justice: A qualitative and quantitative investigation of the differential effects of justice rule adherence and violation. *Journal of Applied Psychology*, *100*(2), 278–297. https://doi.org/10.1037/a0038131

Colquitt, J. A., Scott, B. A., Rodell, J. B., Long, D. M., Zapata, C. P., Conlon, D. E., & Wesson, M. J. (2013). Justice at the millennium, a decade later: A meta-analytic test of social exchange and affect-based perspectives. *Journal of Applied Psychology*, *98*(2), 199–236. https://doi.org/10.1037/a0031757

Cortina, L. M. (2008). Unseen injustice: Incivility as modern discrimination in organizations. *The Academy of Management Review*, *33*(1), 55–75. https://doi.org/10.2307/20159376

Cortina, L. M., Magley, V. J., Williams, J. H., & Langhout, R. D. (2001). Incivility in the workplace: Incidence and impact. *Journal of Occupational Health Psychology*, *6*(1), 64–80. https://doi.org/10.1037/1076-8998.6.1.64

Cowen, A. P., & Montgomery, N. V. (2020). To be or not to be sorry? How CEO gender impacts the effectiveness of organizational apologies. *Journal of Applied Psychology*, *105*(2), 196–208. https://doi.org/10.1037/apl0000430

Dupree, C. H. (2024). Words of a leader: The importance of intersectionality for understanding women leaders' use of dominant language and how others receive it. *Administrative Science Quarterly*, *69*(2), 271–323. https://doi.org/10.1177/00018392231223142

Dwivedi, P., Misangyi, V. F., & Joshi, A. (2021). "Burnt by the spotlight": How leadership endorsements impact the longevity of female leaders. *Journal of Applied Psychology*, *106*(12), 1885–1906. https://doi.org/10.1037/apl0000871

Eagly, A. H., & Karau, S. J. (2002). Role congruity theory of prejudice toward female leaders. *Psychological Review*, *109*(3), 573–598. https://doi.org/10.1037/0033-295x.109.3.573

Eagly, A. H., Makhijani, M. G., & Klonsky, B. G. (1992). Gender and the evaluation of leaders: A meta-analysis. *Psychological Bulletin*, *111*, 3–22.

Eagly, A. H., Nater, C., Miller, D. I., Kaufmann, M., & Sczesny, S. (2020). Gender stereotypes have changed: A cross-temporal meta-analysis of U.S. public opinion polls from 1946 to 2018. *The American Psychologist*, *75*(3), 301–315. https://doi.org/10.1037/amp0000494

Eberhardt, J. L., Davies, P. G., Purdie-Vaughns, V. J., & Johnson, S. L. (2006). Looking deathworthy: Perceived stereotypicality of black defendants predicts capital-sentencing outcomes. *Psychological Science*, *17*(5), 383–386. http://www.jstor.org/stable/40064553

Farley, S. D., Timme, D. R., & Hart, J. W. (2010). On coffee talk and break-room chatter: Perceptions of women who gossip in the workplace. *Journal of Social Psychology*, *150*(4), 361–368. https://doi.org/10.1080/00224540903365430

Fiset, J., & Byrne, A. (2025). Getting away "Scott" (but not Susan) free: The effects of safety-specific abusive supervision and supervisor gender on follower attributions and safety outcomes. *Journal of Organizational Behavior*, *46*(1), 90–107. https://doi.org/10.1002/job.2837

Fox, S., & Spector, P. E. (1999). A model of work frustration-aggression. *Journal of Organizational Behavior*, *20*, 915–931. https://doi.org/10.1002/(SICI)1099-1379

Goff, P. A., Jackson, M. C., Di Leone, B. A., Culotta, C. M., & DiTomasso, N. A. (2014). The essence of innocence: Consequences of dehumanizing Black children. *Journal of Personality and Social Psychology*, *106*(4), 526–545. https://doi.org/10.1037/a0035663

Graso, M., & Reynolds, T. (2024). A feminine advantage in the domain of harm: A review and path forward. *Biology Letters*, *20*. http://doi.org/10.1098/rsbl.2024.0381

Grosser, T. J., Lopez-Kidwell, V., & Labianca, G. (2010). A social network analysis of positive and negative gossip in organizational life. *Group & Organization Management*, *35*(2), 177–212. https://doi.org/10.1177/1059601109360391

Gruys, M. L., & Sackett, P. R. (2003). Investigating the dimensionality of counterproductive work behavior. *International Journal of Selection and Assessment*, *11*(1), 30–42. https://doi.org/10.1111/1468-2389.00224

Heilman, M. E. (2001). Description and prescription: How gender stereotypes prevent women's ascent up the organizational ladder. *Journal of Social Issues*, *57*(4), 657–674. https://doi.org/10.1111/0022-4537.00234

Heilman, M. E., Caleo, S., & Manzi, M. F. (2024). Women at work: Pathways from gender stereotypes to gender bias and discrimination. *Annual Review of Organizational Psychology and Organizational Behavior*, *11*, 165–192.

Heilman, M. E., & Chen, J. J. (2005). Same behavior, different consequences: Reactions to men's and women's altruistic citizenship behavior. *Journal of Applied Psychology*, *90*(3), 431–441. https://doi.org/10.1037/0021-9010.90.3.431

Heilman, M. E., & Wallen, A. S. (2010). Wimpy and undeserving of respect: Penalties for men's gender-inconsistent success. *Journal of Experimental Social Psychology*, *46*(4), 664–667. https://doi.org/10.1016/j.jesp.2010.01.008

Heilman, M. E., Wallen, A. S., Fuchs, D., & Tamkins, M. M. (2004). Penalties for success: Reactions to women who succeed at male gender-typed tasks. *Journal of Applied Psychology*, *89*(3), 416–427. https://doi.org/10.1037/0021-9010.89.3.416

Hershcovis, M. S., Turner, N., Barling, J., Arnold, K. A., Dupré, K. E., Inness, M., . . . & Sivanathan, N. (2007). Predicting workplace aggression: A meta-analysis. *Journal of Applied Psychology*, *92*(1), 228.

Hyde, J., Grieve, R., Norris, K., & Kemp, N. (2020). The dark side of emotional intelligence: The role of gender and the Dark Triad in emotional manipulation at work. *Australian Journal of Psychology*, *72*(4), 307–317. https://doi.org/10.1111/ajpy.12294

Kakarika, M., Taghavi, S., & González-Gómez, H. V. (2024). Don't shoot the messenger? A morality- and gender-based model of reactions to negative workplace gossip. *Journal of Business Ethics*, *189*, 329–344. https://doi.org/10.1007/s10551-023-05355-7

Kant, L., Skogstad, A., Torsheim, T., & Einarsen, S. (2013). Beware the angry leader: Trait anger and trait anxiety as predictors of petty tyranny. *The Leadership Quarterly*, *24*(1), 106–124. https://doi.org/10.1016/j.leaqua.2012.08.005

Karpoff, J. M., Lee, D. S., & Martin, G. S. (2008). The cost to firms of cooking the books. *Journal of Financial and Quantitative Analysis*, *43*, 581–611.

Kim, J. K., Harold, C. M., & Holtz, B. C. (2022). Evaluations of abusive supervisors: The moderating role of the abuser's gender. *Journal of Organizational Behavior*, *43*(3), 465–482. https://doi.org/10.1002/job.2581

Kray, L. J., Kennedy, J. A., & Van Zant, A. B. (2014). Not competent enough to know the difference? Gender stereotypes about women's ease of being misled predict negotiator deception. *Organizational Behavior and Human Decision Processes*, *125*(2), 61–72. https://doi.org/10.1016/j.obhdp.2014.06.002

Leavitt, K., Zhu, L., Klotz, A., & Kouchaki, M. (2022). Fragile or robust? Differential effects of gender threats in the workplace among men and women. *Organizational Behavior and Human Decision Processes*, *168*, 104112. https://doi.org/10.1016/j.obhdp.2021.104112

Lopez-Alvarez, G., Cardador, M. T., & Restubog, S. L. D. (2024). Do women perceive incivility from men as selective? Examining main effects, coping responses, and boundary conditions. *Human Resource Management*, *63*(3), 517–532. https://doi.org/10.1002/hrm.22213

Luksyte, A., Waite, E., Avery, D. R., & Roy, R. (2013). Held to a different standard: Racial differences in the impact of lateness on advancement opportunity. *Journal of Occupational and Organizational Psychology*, *86*(2), 142–165. https://doi.org/10.1111/joop.12010

Ma, A., Rosette, A. S., & Koval, C. Z. (2022). Reconciling female agentic advantage and disadvantage with the CADDIS measure of agency. *Journal of Applied Psychology*, *107*(12), 2115–2148. https://doi.org/10.1037/apl0000550

Mai, K. M., Ellis, A. P., & Welsh, D. T. (2020). How perpetrator gender influences reactions to premeditated versus impulsive unethical behavior: A role congruity approach. *Journal of Business Ethics*, *166*, 489–503.

Marshburn, C. K., Cochran, K. J., Flynn, E., & Levine, L. J. (2020). Workplace anger costs women irrespective of race. *Frontiers in Psychology*, *11*, 579884. https://doi.org/10.3389/fpsyg.2020.579884

Montgomery, N. V., & Cowen, A. P. (2024). Rumor has it: CEO gender and response to organizational denials. *Journal of Applied Psychology*, *109*(11), 1817–1832. https://doi.org/10.1037/apl0001206

Moss-Racusin, C. A., & Johnson, E. R. (2016). Backlash against male elementary educators. *Journal of Applied Social Psychology*, *46*(7), 379–393. https://doi.org/10.1111/jasp.12366

Motro, D., & Ellis, A. P. (2017). Boys don't cry: Gender and reactions to negative performance feedback. *Journal of Applied Psychology*, *102*(2), 227–235. https://doi.org/10.1037/apl0000175

Motro, D., Evans, J. B., Ellis, A. P. J., & Benson, L. (2022). Race and reactions to women's expressions of anger at work: Examining the effects of the "angry Black woman" stereotype. *Journal of Applied Psychology*, *107*(1), 142–152. https://doi.org/10.1037/apl0000884

Motro, D., Spoelma, T. M., & Ellis, A. P. J. (2021). Incivility and creativity in teams: Examining the role of perpetrator gender. *Journal of Applied Psychology*, *106*(4), 560–581. https://doi.org/10.1037/apl0000757

Mu, F., Shen, W., Bobocel, D. R., & Barron, A. H. (2024). Investigating gendered reactions to manager mistreatment: Testing the presumed role of prescriptivo stereotypes. *Journal of Organizational Behavior*, *45*(5), 720–740. https://doi.org/10.1002/job.2763

Naumovska, I., Wernicke, G., & Zajac, E. (2020). Last to come and last to go? On the complex role of gender and ethnicity in the reputational penalties for directors linked to corporate fraud. *Academy of Management Journal*, *3*, 881–902.

Parks-Stamm, E. J., & Tharp, D. T. (2023). But what did they *do* on leave? Differing evaluations of men and women's completion of work tasks on parental leave. *Journal of Occupational and Organizational Psychology*, *96*, 235–241. https://doi.org/10.1111/joop.12421

Peng, A. C., Schaubroeck, J. M., & Li, Y. (2014). Social exchange implications of own and coworkers' experiences of supervisory abuse. *Academy of Management Journal*, *57*(5), 1385–1405. https://doi.org/10.5465/amj.2012.0080

Pittarello, A., & Motro, D. (2024). Women who cry to manipulate others face more backlash than men. *Journal of Behavioral Decision Making*, *37*(2), e2374. https://doi.org/10.1002/bdm.2374

Plöckinger, M., Aschauer, E., Hiebl, M. R., & Rohatschek, R. (2016). The influence of individual executives on corporate financial reporting: A review and outlook from the perspective of upper echelons theory. *Journal of Accounting Literature*, *37*(1), 55–75.

Polman, E., Pettit, N. C., & Wiesenfeld, B. M. (2013). Effects of wrongdoer status on moral licensing. *Journal of Experimental Social Psychology*, *49*(4), 614–623. https://doi.org/10.1016/j.jesp.2013.03.012

Prentice, D. A., & Carranza, E. (2002). What women should be, shouldn't be, are allowed to be, and don't have to be: The contents of prescriptive gender stereotypes. *Psychology of Women Quarterly*, *26*(4), 269–281. https://doi.org/10.1111/1471-6402.t01-1-00066

Reynolds, T., Howard, C., Sjastad, H., Zhu, L., Okimoto, T. G., Baumeister, R. F., Aquino, K., & Kim, J. (2020). Man up and take it: Gender bias in moral typecasting. *Organizational Behavior and Human Decision Processes*, *161*, 120–141.

Robbins, M. L., & Karan, A. (2020). Who gossips and how in everyday life? *Social Psychological and Personality Science*, *11*(2), 185–195. https://doi.org/10.1177/1948550619837000

Robinson, S. L., & Bennett, R. J. (1995). A typology of deviant workplace behaviors: A multidimensional scaling study. *Academy of Management Journal*, *38*(2), 555–572. https://doi.org/10.2307/256693

Rosette, A. S., Koval, C. Z., Ma, A., & Livingston, R. (2016). Race matters for women leaders: Intersectional effects on agentic deficiencies and penalties. *The Leadership Quarterly*, *27*(3), 429–445. https://doi.org/10.1016/j.leaqua.2016.01.008

Rudman, L. A., & Mescher, K. (2013). Penalizing men who request a family leave: Is flexibility stigma a femininity stigma? *Journal of Social Issues*, *69*(2), 322–340. https://doi.org/10.1111/josi.12017

Rudman, L. A., & Phelan, J. E. (2008). Backlash effects for disconfirming gender stereotypes in organizations. *Research in Organizational Behavior*, *28*, 61–79.

Saeed, A., & Riaz, H. (2022). Women directors turnover following financial misconduct: What's social environment got to do with it? *British Journal of Management*, *34*(2), 805–830. https://doi.org/10.1111/1467-8551.12639

Scott, B. A., Colquitt, J. A., & Paddock, E. L. (2009). An actor-focused model of justice rule adherence and violation: The role of managerial motives and discretion. *Journal of Applied Psychology*, *94*(3), 756.

Shnabel, N., & Nadler, A. (2008). A needs-based model of reconciliation: Satisfying the differential emotional needs of victim and perpetrator as a key to promoting reconciliation. *Journal of Personality and Social Psychology*, *94*(1), 116–132. https://doi.org/10.1037/0022-3514.94.1.116

Sun, T., Schilpzand, P., & Liu, Y. (2023). Workplace gossip: An integrative review of its antecedents, functions, and consequences. *Journal of Organizational Behavior*, *44*(2), 311–334. https://doi.org/10.1002/job.2653

Tai, K., Lee, K., Kim, E., Johnson, T. D., Wang, W., Duffy, M. K., & Kim, S. (2022). Gender, bottom-line mentality, and workplace mistreatment: The roles of gender norm violation and team gender composition. *Journal of Applied Psychology*, *107*(5), 854–865. https://doi.org/10.1037/apl0000936

Tepper, B. J. (2000). Consequences of abusive supervision. *Academy of Management Journal*, *43*(2), 178–190. https://doi.org/10.2307/1556375

Tepper, B. J., Henle, C. A., Lambert, L. S., Giacalone, R. A., & Duffy, M. K. (2008). Abusive supervision and subordinates' organization deviance. *Journal of Applied Psychology*, *93*(4), 721–732. https://doi.org/10.1037/0021-9010.93.4.721

Tyler, J. M., Feldman, R. S., & Reichert, A. (2006). The price of deceptive behavior: Disliking and lying to people who lie to us. *Journal of Experimental Social Psychology*, *42*(1), 69–77. https://doi.org/10.1016/j.jesp.2005.02.003

Varty, C. T., Barclay, L. J., & Brady, D. L. (2021). Beyond adherence to justice rules: How and when manager gender contributes to diminished legitimacy in the aftermath of unfair situations. *Journal of Organizational Behavior*, *42*, 767–784. https://doi.org/10.1002/job.2482

Walfisch, T., Van Dijk, D., & Kark, R. (2013). Impact of status and gender on apology effectiveness. *Journal of Applied Social Psychology*, *43*, 1446–1458. https://doi.org/10.1111/jasp.12101

Whitman, D. S., Caleo, S., Carpenter, N. C., Horner, M. T., & Bernerth, J. B. (2012). Fairness at the collective level: A meta-analytic examination of the consequences and boundary conditions of organizational justice climate. *Journal of Applied Psychology*, *97*(4), 776–791. https://doi.org/10.1037/a0028021

Yu, A., Pichler, S., Russo, M., & Hammer, L. (2022). Family-supportive supervisor behaviors (FSSB) and work-family conflict: The role of stereotype content, supervisor gender, and gender role beliefs. *Journal of Occupational and Organizational Psychology*, *95*, 275–304. https://doi.org/10.1111/joop.12379

Zahra, S. A., Priem, R. L., & Rasheed, A. A. (2005). The antecedents and consequences of top management fraud. *Journal of Management*, *31*(6), 803–828.

Zhong, R., & Robinson, S. L. (2021). What happens to bad actors in organizations? A review of actor-centric outcomes of negative behavior. *Journal of Management*, *47*(6), 1430–1467. https://doi.org/10.1177/0149206320976808

CHAPTER 7

The Role of Gender in Communication

Implications for Leadership

Priyanka Joshi

During my PhD training at the University of Southern California, I conducted experiments to examine how speakers' communication was impacted by the distance of the audience (e.g., Joshi et al., 2016). Incidentally, in these studies, I came across gender differences in the communication patterns of men and women, finding that in general, women used more concrete language than men. I then collected more linguistic data to find that across different paradigms and speech contexts, women communicated more concretely than men. This finding led me to explore why these gender differences in concreteness in communication exist and to examine the consequences of these gender differences in communication.

In this chapter, I leverage my expertise on gender and communication to summarize major findings on the intersections of these topics. Scholars from fields such as management, communication, psychology, sociology, linguistics, and women's studies have been conducting research in this area. Given the breadth and diversity of scholars who have studied gendered patterns in communication styles, and the ways in which these patterns are shaped by the social roles and contexts of communicators, the task of writing a review paper on the topic felt monumental. Over 5,000 papers on the topic of gender and communication have been published in the last five decades. However, a number of clear conclusions can be drawn from the body of work:

- Gender differences in communication persist due to gendered social role expectations and stereotypes.
- Gender differences in communication are context dependent.

DOI: 10.4324/9781003488590-7

- Women tend to be more motivated by relational goals in their communication than men.
- Men tend to be more motivated by instrumental goals in their communication than women.
- Gender differences in communication are consequential and differentially impact men's and women's outcomes in organizations.

GENDERED SOCIAL ROLE EXPECTATIONS

Women and men are more similar than different across various domains of social behavior. This is no surprise, given men and women share 99.9% of DNA structures. Gender differences emerge in certain contexts, and the size of these gender differences depends on the nature of contexts, including who the communication partner is, what the topic of discussion is, and the extent to which gender is salient in the context. When gender differences do occur, women are more relational in their communication and men are more likely to use communication for accomplishing instrumental goals.

According to the biosocial construction theory of gender differences (Wood & Eagly, 2012), differences between men and women can be explained by biological differences in size and function, as well as social structures and processes that further perpetuate gender differences in social behavior. Men's greater strength and the reproductive requirements of women, for example, resulted in gender-based division of labor and social roles. While women's gender roles involved childcare and rearing and work that could be conducted close to home, men's gender roles were associated with hunting, protecting the group from outsiders and taking on work away from home. Because women played a significant role in childbirth and breastfeeding in most societies, women adopted the primary caregiver role for children. The tasks and physical demands associated with pregnancy, breastfeeding, and childcare created a constraint on women's abilities to be away from home for extended periods of time or engage in work that was physically laborious. Thus, women tended to take on roles that allowed them to nurture infants and children while engaging in other work activities. Women engaged in cooperative and collective breeding in small groups, forming close relationships with other women and family members, which benefited the survival and sustenance of their offspring. Men, on the other hand, experienced fewer biological and childcare constraints and were able to take on social roles such as hunting, lumbering, clearing land, and plowing that required strength, speed, and travel away from home.

As societies evolved, including modernization and industrialization, men's roles saw transformation with the ability to take on work for economic gain. As job complexity increased in modern societies, men engaged in activities that involved complex skills, specialized training, and long hours away from home. Men were able to occupy an important role in economic production. However, given their biological role in pregnancy and childcare, women were constrained in their ability to perform roles associated with power and status. Gender segregation and the division of labor not only created differential skills for men and women but also resulted in sustained gender disparities. Men engaged in roles with more opportunity for economic gain, creating greater power and status differences between men's and women's roles. Thus, men's social behavior was directed toward attaining greater status in professional settings, while women's social behavior was directed toward maintaining interpersonal connections and nurturing domestic relationships.

In current society, the roles of men and women are less segregated, with women gainfully employed in many societies. Yet, biological roles and gender segregation in domestic roles continue to sustain gender differences in social behavior. Despite declining birth rates, gains in women's employment, and their access to high-status roles, women continue to play larger roles in childcare and household activities than men (Heilman et al., 2024; Parker et al., 2023; World Bank, 2024). Such gendered role segregation further perpetuates gendered social role expectations such that women are expected to be warm and kind or "communal," and men are expected to be competent, strong, or "agentic."

Socialization of girls and boys follow these gendered role expectations, such that girls are nurtured to be kind, generous, communal, other-oriented, and accommodating, whereas boys are expected to be agentic, action-oriented, competent, strong, brave, and powerful (Cuddy et al., 2008; Fiske, 2010). Girls' and boys' communication are similarly expected to meet these social roles such that girls are encouraged to connect, build relationships, and be accommodating in their communication, while boys are encouraged to assert and establish status. Gendered socialization practices follow social role expectations and gendered patterns of social behavior vary in terms of communal or agentic traits and are observed from an early age (Carli, 2001; Halim et al., 2011; Hsu et al., 2021; Wood & Eagly, 2015).

Studies of gender differences in the play patterns of young children demonstrate that girls' play choices and toy preferences show a greater tendency toward people orientation and nurturance of others, whereas boys' play patterns reflect a preference for non-human objects (Davis & Hines, 2020; Jadva et al., 2010; Raag, 1999; Zosuls & Ruble, 2018). For instance, girls prefer jewelry and kitchen items, while boys prefer vehicles, blocks, and weapons. A recent meta-analysis of studies examining toy preferences concludes that girls and boys show a strong preference for gender-typed play. The range of gender differences in girls preferring feminine-typed toys such as dolls and boys preferring masculine-typed toys such as weapons and vehicles is large. Furthermore, the gender difference in play is not reducing over time, meaning the effect size of gender differences in recent studies is the same as the effect size in older studies (Davis & Hines, 2020). Boys engage in more rough-and-tumble play than girls, and girls' play activities are more likely to be oriented toward real or pretend childcare of infants and pets (Edwards, 1993; McIntyre & Edwards, 2009). Boys' higher gross motor skills than girls and girls' stronger fine motor skills than boys, as well as other biological and hormonal factors, likely play roles in toy choices (Alexander & Hines, 2002; Hines, 2004). In addition, social pressures like peer choices and gendered toy availability play an equally important role in gendered play (Todd et al., 2018). Children who do not conform to social role expectations of their groups are often corrected or penalized (Zucker & Bradley, 1995). In a recent study of toy marketing, Auster and Mansbach (2012) analyzed department store catalogs and demonstrated that marketers continue to market toys as gender differentiated and such gender differentiation in toy advertising has increased in last few decades (Sweet, 2013).

Gender Segregation in Childhood

Girls and boys segregate in terms of gender at a young age (Hoffman & Powlishta, 2001; Maccoby, 1994; Maccoby & Jacklin, 1974; Martin et al., 2013; Mehta & Smith, 2023). Children expect others of the same gender to be similar to them and experience greater similarity when interacting with same gender peers (Martin et al., 2011). By about the age of five years, girls show a strong preference to play with girls and boys show a strong preference to play with boys. Preschool girls and boys spend about 89% of their play time with same-gender peers (Martin et al., 2011). Gender segregation in play increases with age. By adolescence, best friends are almost exclusively of the same gender (Maccoby, 1998; Martin & Fabes, 2001). Such gender segregation in childhood play often paves the way for differential interests and gender-typed behaviors. The more time boys spend with other boys, the greater their preference for gender-typed activities and aggressive behavior and the lower their desire to interact with adults (Martin & Fabes, 2001). The more time girls spend in same-gender groups, the more likely they are to prefer female-typed activities and desire adult contact as well as show greater passivity and lower aggression.

Gender segregation paves the way for gendered patterns of behavior. Studies demonstrate that girls' and boys' social interactions vary in consistent ways (Maccoby, 2002). Girls' groups tend to be smaller than boys' groups (Maccoby, 2002). Girls tend to interact in smaller and more stable dyadic groups. Boys tend to interact in larger and more structured social groups. Hierarchy seems to be more easily established in all-male groups than all-female groups. During play, girls engage in greater collaboration, demonstrate social support, and strive to maintain group harmony. Girls' play themes revolve around social relationships and domestic characters. Boys' play interactions, on the other hand, revolve around competition, conflict, and risk taking. The themes in their play involve danger, heroic actions, destruction, and conflict. Girls tend to know more about their friends than boys do and tend to seek greater intimacy than boys. Thus, girls' and boys' social interaction patterns vary from a young age, with girls showing deeper interpersonal connections than boys and boys demonstrating greater competition than girls.

Gender Segregation in Adulthood

Gendered patterns of social interaction in childhood mimic findings in adult samples. Women often prefer working with people, and men prefer working with things (Su et al., 2009). Women show more interest in social and artistic activities, whereas men demonstrate greater interest in how machines and objects work. In addition, women tend to have a stronger relational gender identity than men. Women are more likely to identify themselves in terms of close others and social roles compared to men (Gabriel & Gardner, 1999). For instance, women are more likely to identify with roles of parents or spouses and mention these identities in their conversations. Furthermore, men identify as more independent than women (Guimond et al., 2006). Women's groups and networks tend to be smaller than men's in both social relationships and work group contexts (Hale, 1999; Ibarra, 1997). In addition, men are more likely to seek positions of status and power than women (Hale, 1999; Ibarra, 1997). Men are more likely to assert dominance, be comfortable with competition, and seek more risks than women. In a meta-analysis, Hsu et al. (2021) found that men tend to be more agentic than women and women tend to be more communal than men, and that these gender differences in agentic and communal traits are more prevalent in societies with greater occupational gender segregation.

Gender differences in social behavior are a byproduct of social role expectations placed upon men and women. Girls are expected to be communal and nurturing while boys are expected to be agentic. In line with these gender expectations, women are expected to use communication as a tool to establish connection and men are expected to use communication as a tool to assert personal goals and drive. These social expectations are then internalized such that women believe that they need to emphasize relationship development and men believe they need to assert independent goals and objectives. Studies have demonstrated that when gender identity is made salient, gender differences in communication are exaggerated, supporting the notion of internalized gender role expectations (Palomares, 2004, 2009). Furthermore, when men and women were requested to write either "as if they were a man" or "as if they were a woman," researchers observed gendered communication styles, such that female guise participants wrote in typically female styles of communication and male guise participants wrote in typically male styles of communication irrespective of their gender (Mulac et al., 2013). Thus, both men and women are aware of gendered communication role expectations and stereotypes and hold consistent beliefs about how men and women communicate. Research on gendered role expectations and stereotypes pave the way for further study in gendered communication.

GENDER DIFFERENCES IN COMMUNAL COMMUNICATION

Communion refers to the sharing of intimate thoughts and feelings and the desire to maintain community by emphasizing commonalities. Women's communication tends to be more communal and directed toward building and maintaining close interpersonal relationships. For instance, women spend more time establishing rapport, engaging in more self-disclosure, intruding less in conversations, and emphasizing similarity between themselves and their conversation partners (e.g., Dindia & Allen, 1992). On the other hand, men are less likely to use these relationship building tools and are less likely to seek similar levels of intimacy and connection in their relationships. Women's use of social media and electronically mediated communication further supports greater communal tendencies, with women spending more time on social media, text messaging, and video calls than men (Kimbrough et al., 2013).

Women are more likely to converse about people than things and are more likely to use constructs related to affiliation and social processes than men. In written communication, women use more affiliation and relational words than men (Newman et al., 2008). In studies of everyday communication, women are more likely to converse about relationship-related topics such as family, romance, and friends. Men are more likely to converse about recreation and external topics (Johnson & Aries, 1983; Sehulster, 2006). Gender differences in communication topics have also been observed in electronic communication. Studies of blogs demonstrate similar patterns of gender differences in conversational topics: women are more likely to write about personal topics and men are more likely to write about external events (Herring et al., 2004). Women are also more likely to write personal journal blogs than men (Nardi et al., 2004) thus suggesting that women are more likely to self-disclose and express personal details in their communication than men.

In studies of children, girls tend to self-disclose more than boys (Rose, 2002). This early tendency is then observed in adult socialization, where gender norms encourage women to self-disclose, but may discourage men from disclosing vulnerabilities. In a meta-analysis of studies on gender differences on self-disclosure (Dindia & Allen, 1992), researchers found that women self-disclose more than men. These differences are stronger when the conversational partner is of the same gender or is a close other such as a friend or family member. Furthermore, people report that women self-disclose more than men, providing support for the idea that communication norms and expectations are gendered, and that women and men are expected to communicate in different ways. In the workplace, self-disclosure plays a more significant role in women's interpersonal trust, such that women show higher levels of trust in coworkers who self-disclose than men, suggesting that self-disclosure plays a more critical role in relationship building for women than men (Qiu et al., 2022).

Lakoff (1973) suggested that women tend to use less powerful language and communicate with less certainty than men. For instance, women are more likely to use tag questions, which are statements followed by a short question. For instance, I could say, "This chapter is interesting, isn't it?" The tag question may communicate my need to establish connection with the reader, or it might communicate my uncertainty about the statement. Small gender differences have been observed in the use of this form of speech. Research indicates that gender differences in powerless communication tend to be small and that there is more overlap in how men and women use tentative speech. In a meta-analysis of studies examining gender differences in tentative language, Leaper and Robnett (2011) found that gender differences are stronger in same-gender interactions than mixed-gender interactions. These effects are stronger when conversations are recorded over a longer period. In general, women use tentative speech to find common ground with their audience and to accommodate audiences that may not share their points of view. For instance, women use tag questions to allow for a lower status conversation partner to contribute to the conversation and to create a sense of partnership and similarity with communication partners.

Gender differences in communal communication are observed in work environments. Weinberg et al. (2019) examined communication differences among men and women employees. They found that women use more feminine styles of communication, characterized by greater self-disclosure, more concrete information, and greater nurturing and encouraging statements than men. Female physicians demonstrate greater partnership behaviors such as psychosocial counseling, positive talk, question asking, and emotion-focused talk than male physicians. Furthermore, female physicians spend two minutes longer with each patient than male physicians (Roter et al., 2002). Thus, when gender differences do emerge in research findings, they provide evidence to suggest that women are more likely to gear their communication to building and maintaining relationships compared to men.

However, gender differences in communal communication are context dependent. Both men and women are more likely to demonstrate relationally focused communication when engaging with women. For instance, speakers are more likely to smile, make eye contact (Hinsz & Tomhave, 1991), and self-disclose when communicating with women than with men (Dindia & Allen, 1992). In addition, gender differences are more salient in close relationships than during communications with strangers. Gender effects are stronger when communication is recorded over a longer time span. Furthermore, gender differences in relational communication tend to be larger in contexts where less restraint is placed on social behavior (Newman et al., 2008).

GENDER DIFFERENCES IN INSTRUMENTAL COMMUNICATION

Instrumental communication is task-oriented and tends to be directed toward establishing and maintaining status. Men tend to discuss topics exterior to themselves, such as sports and recreation, whereas women tend to focus on interior topics such as emotions, family, and relationships (Johnson & Aries, 1983). In a study of blog posts, researchers found that men's blogs are less personal and relate more to external events, compared to women's blogs. Men's blogs also receive greater attention and attract more visitors (Herring et al., 2004; Nardi et al., 2004). In general, men tend to self-disclose less than women, using communication as a tool to accomplish tasks. Men's communication also tends to be more direct than women's communication (Leaper, 2014; Leaper, 2019). Weinberg et al. (2019) showed that in comparison with women, men are more likely to use a communication style characterized by directness, forcefulness, and assertiveness. Men are also less likely to use a communication style characterized by empathy, compassion, and supportiveness. Thus, men seem to use more instrumental communication than women.

Although men report talking less than women, most research in work contexts demonstrates that men speak more than women. In a study of college students, Mulac et al. (1986) recorded student interactions in problem solving situations and found that men spoke more than women in mixed-gender interactions. Men also spoke more in mixed-gender versus same-gender interactions. In a study of US senators, researchers found that male senators spoke more than female senators. Male senators' power was proportional to the amount they spoke, such that more powerful male senators spoke more than less powerful male senators. However, for female senators, power was unrelated to volubility (or the number of words spoken; Brescoll, 2011). Thus, gender differences in volubility cannot be explained by gender differences in power and status. In fact, men and women may differ in the extent to which they seek to establish power in social relationships, regardless of their objective status and power. Additionally, the gender makeup of audiences affects gender differences in volubility. When an audience consists largely of women, women speak more than men (Kriwy et al., 2013).

Men are more likely to intrusively interrupt conversations than women (Anderson & Leaper, 1998). Both men and women interrupt during conversations; however, men's interruptions are more likely to be perceived as intrusive than women's interruptions. Women may interrupt to demonstrate understanding and provide support to the speaker. Furthermore, men are less likely to be interrupted by communication partners than women, allowing them to maintain dominance in communication contexts.

Men are more likely to use competitive banter and putdowns in their speech than women (Tannen, 1994, 1995). A study of online discussion boards shows that women and men have different online styles, and that men's posts are lengthier, more adversarial, and more assertive than women's posts (Herring, 1996a, 1996b). Additionally, men are more likely to self-promote and use putdowns and sarcasm in their posts. In contrast, women are more supportive and demonstrate greater community-building comments, appreciation of others, gratitude, and questions (Herring, 1996a, 1996b). Men's communication behaviors are often perceived as indicative of male dominance and masculinity. When men engage in masculine-typed communication behaviors, women may be particularly prone to feel out of place or unsupported.

Recently, my collaborators and I demonstrated that men use more abstract speech in their communication than women (Joshi et al., 2020). Communication can be seen as lying on a continuum of abstraction ranging from concrete (low in abstraction) to abstract (high in abstraction). Abstract speech is decontextualized, general, and focuses more on the big picture or "why" than concrete speech (Joshi & Wakslak, 2014). Concrete speech is specific, detailed, and focuses on the means or "how" of action. In different contexts, including blog posts, senate speeches, laboratory writing assignments, and entrepreneurial pitches, men frame their ideas more abstractly than women. Furthermore, abstract communication is associated with greater attributions of power and status, such that people who communicate abstractly are more likely to be perceived as leader-like (Palmeira, 2015; Wakslak et al., 2014). Gender differences in communicative abstraction predict entrepreneurial funding, such that men are more likely to receive funding from venture capitalists due to their greater use of abstract communication (Huang et al., 2021). Thus, gender differences are observed not only in what men and women communicate but also in how they frame their communication. Furthermore, these gender differences in communication predict men and women's abilities to obtain organizational rewards.

Gender differences in instrumental communication are context dependent. Previous research and meta-analyses demonstrate that gender differences in instrumental communication range from small to medium, depending on the context (Anderson & Leaper, 1998; Mulac et al., 2001). Some gender differences, such as those associated with hesitant and non-confident speech, have not been consistently replicated (Leaper & Robnett, 2011). Gender differences tend to be exaggerated in same-gender dyads and minimized in mixed-gender groups (Mulac, 1989). When social situations reduce the normative pressures associated with acting in gender conforming ways, gender differences in communication might be minimized. Thus, the gender differences outlined earlier should be interpreted as patterns of behavior that individual men and women may or may not conform to depending on the demands of the situation.

ORGANIZATIONAL IMPLICATIONS OF GENDER DIFFERENCES IN COMMUNICATION

Researchers have examined how social judgments about men and women are impacted by their communication styles. The question of whose communication is better has been of interest. Men's more instrumental styles of communication have been associated with greater leadership emergence. Because organizational cultures tend to be more masculine than feminine, masculine and instrumental communication tends to be valued more than feminine and communal styles of communication. Thus, it is suggested that men's behaviors of directness, self-promotion, and assertiveness are more likely to be perceived as leader-like and hence, men are more likely to be selected in leadership roles. However, when examining leadership *effectiveness*, some researchers find that women's communication is perceived as superior to men's and that it results in greater subordinate wellbeing, participative leadership, and effective team building (Ibarra & Obodaru, 2009; Eagly et al., 2000).

Men's tendency to speak more than women is more predictive of their leadership emergence than their social and communal skills (Riggio et al., 2003). In a meta-analysis, Badura et al. (2018) found that gender differences in leadership emergence continue to persist and can be explained by gender differences in participation within group discussions. Because men who are stereotypically masculine and agentic tend to demonstrate greater verbal participation in groups, they are more likely to be seen as leader-like. However, stereotypes and social expectations play an additive role in explaining gender differences in leadership emergence (Schlamp et al., 2020).

In organizations with masculine cultures, women's more relational styles of speech can be devalued. When women are made aware of the stereotypes associated with their communal communication and their association with lower perceived leadership qualities, they communicate in more masculine ways. However, women who communicate using masculine communication styles involving direct communication and task focus are viewed as lacking warmth and are perceived as less likable (Von Hippel et al., 2011). Thus, even though masculine communication styles are advantageous in leadership emergence contexts, women's use of these styles may have relational costs. Recent research in workplace settings, however, suggests that when women behave in more agentic ways in organizations, they are more likely to emerge as leaders (Lanaj & Hollenbeck, 2015). The prescription for women seeking leadership positions seems to be that they need to communicate assertively while simultaneously focusing on relationship building (Schock et al., 2019). Thus, being assertive and task-oriented while also emphasizing community building and relationality, a characteristic associated with the transformation leadership style, has been recommended for women (Eagly, 2007; Eagly & Revelle, 2022).

While masculine styles of communication predict selection for leadership roles, feminine styles of communication have been associated with greater leadership effectiveness (Eagly & Karau, 2002; Paustian-Underdahl et al., 2014). There has been growing evidence of a feminine advantage in leadership effectiveness, indicating that women's more communal and supportive forms of communication may promote greater leadership effectiveness. In support of this feminine advantage, many communication training programs are now designed to train leaders to develop skills associated with being more employee-centered. However, follow-up studies of managers who have undergone soft skills training indicate that there is very little change in their communication practices after the completion of training (O'Neill et al., 2002). Because most organizations promote masculine cultures in which task orientation and direct communication are prioritized over individual connection, the skills that subordinates value in their managers are not routinely observed. Furthermore, when men act in more feminine ways, they can be penalized and perceived as less likable. For instance, research examining support giving shows that when men provide person-centered supportive feedback, they are perceived as less likable compared to women who provide person-centered supportive feedback, as well as both men and women who provide less person-centered support (Burleson et al., 2005). Thus, men can experience backlash when using more feminine forms of communication.

Stereotypes about how men and women communicate affect others' perceptions of their communication. Because women are expected to communicate in a communal rather than instrumental manner, their communication styles may be seen as unsuitable in leadership emergence contexts. However, relational communication is predictive of leadership effectiveness, and overreliance on instrumental communication qualities when selecting leaders can have a negative impact on the prospect of leadership emergence for women. Thus, it is imperative that organizational leaders develop a keen understanding of how stereotypes about gender and communication shape their selection and promotion decisions.

GUIDELINES FOR EMPLOYEES AND ORGANIZATIONS

- Understand how stereotypes associated with gender and communication affect organizational practices: Organizations may inadvertently reward gender conforming communication patterns and discourage gender nonconforming communication patterns. It is important for organizational leaders to understand the ways that gendered stereotypes about communication negatively impact organizational practices.
- Ensure that leadership selection practices are unbiased: Communication often serves as a window into speakers' thoughts. Yet, communication is also shaped by gendered communication expectations that are salient to the speaker in a context. Hence, it is important that selection and promotion decisions are made after extended evaluations.
- Decision-makers can encourage candidates to demonstrate both communal and agentic communication styles: to examine communication effectiveness, candidates can be explicitly asked to demonstrate their ability to be task-oriented as well as relational-oriented. Instead of relying on candidates to avoid conforming to stereotypes, organizations can explicitly encourage candidates to display a broad range of communication skills.
- Understand the importance of communal and agentic communication within one's context: organizations can benefit by gaining deeper

understandings of employees' perceptions of the importance of communal and agentic communication skills. Understanding when employees value task-oriented versus relational communication will ensure that communication skill trainers emphasize the importance of tailoring communication to one's context.

- Provide specific training opportunities that enable employees to fit their communication style to the context: In most organizational roles, leaders need to use both communal and agentic communication styles. Trainers may assume that agentic communication is natural to most leaders and hence may solely focus on relational communication. However, an eye on a task is as important as connecting with and motivating employees. Thus, trainers need to consider employees' personal communication preferences and gain deeper understandings of organizational contexts to ensure that communication skills learnt during training are in fact effective within the particular organizational context.
- Reward employees for effective communication: It is important that organizations value both communal and agentic communication and ensure that employees are not penalized for speaking in gender non-conforming ways. To promote greater equity, it is important that organizations value and reward communication styles that are stereotypically feminine, which have been historically undervalued.
- In leadership emergence contexts, employees may benefit from using more agentic communication styles: when considering leadership emergence, decision-makers often make quick, heuristic-based decisions about employees' leadership abilities. Because stereotypical characteristics associated with leadership are often masculine (Cheryan & Markus, 2020), employees might benefit from using more instrumental and agentic communication skills.
- Leaders need to gain a deeper understanding of their context to ensure they can use agentic and relational communication styles flexibly: effective communicators can adapt their communication style to the context. Both relational communication and instrumental communication are critical to the functioning of organizations. Regardless of gender, leaders need to communicate about both tasks and relationships and adapt their communication styles to the needs of the context.

CHAPTER SUMMARY

This chapter summarizes research on gendered communication patterns and their consequences for workplace performance. Drawing on a bio-social construction theory of gender differences, the chapter discusses the effects of stereotypical social role expectations and gender socialization patterns on the persistence of gender differences in communication patterns. The chapter explains motivations that often drive women's and men's communication techniques. These patterns of gender differences are context dependent and are more likely to emerge when gender is made salient or when people are rewarded for conforming to gendered expectations. Implications of gender differences in communication on leadership emergence and leadership effectiveness are discussed. Specific strategies are provided for how organizations can promote gender parity and effective communication.

DISCUSSION QUESTIONS

1. In your work-related interactions, have you noticed gender differences in communication?
2. Do gender differences in communication emerge in both older and younger populations? Are gender differences in communication more likely to emerge in same-gender or mixed-gender groups?
3. When you consider managers you have interacted with, what characteristics of their communication do you find particularly predictive of their effectiveness? Are these characteristics more likely to be associated with agency, communality, or both?
4. When men and women haven't spoken in gender conforming ways, have you seen them be penalized?
5. How will you modify your everyday communication at work after reading this chapter?

REFERENCES

Alexander, G. M., & Hines, M. (2002). Sex differences in response to children's toys in nonhuman primates (Cercopithecus aethiops sabaeus). *Evolution and Human Behavior*, *23*(6), 467–479. https://doi.org/10.1016/S1090-5138(02)00107-1

Anderson, K. J., & Leaper, C. (1998). Meta-analyses of gender effects on conversational interruption: Who, what, when, where, and how. *Sex Roles*, *39*(3–4), 225–252. https://doi.org/10.1023/A:1018802521676

Auster, C., & Mansbach, C. (2012). The gender marketing of toys: An analysis of color and type of toy on the Disney store website. *Sex Roles*, *67*(7–8), 375–388. https://doi.org/10.1007/s11199-012-0177-8

Badura, K. L., Grijalva, E., Newman, D. A., Yan, T. T., & Jeon, G. (2018). Gender and leadership emergence: A meta-analysis and explanatory model. *Personnel Psychology*, *71*(3), 335–367. https://doi.org/10.1111/peps.12266

Brescoll, V. L. (2011). Who takes the floor and why: Gender, power, and volubility in organizations. *Administrative Science Quarterly*, *56*(4), 622–641. https://doi.org/10.1177/0001839212439994

Burleson, Brant R., Holmstrom, Amanda J., & Gilstrap, Cristina M. (2005). "Guys can't say that to guys": Four experiments assessing the normative motivation account for deficiencies in the emotional support provided by men. *Communication Monographs*, *72*(4), 468–501. https://doi.org/10.1080/03637750500322636

Carli, L. L. (2001). Gender and social influence. *Journal of Social Issues*, *57*(4), 725. https://doi.org/10.1111/0022-4537.00238

Cheryan, S., & Markus, H. R. (2020). Masculine defaults: Identifying and mitigating hidden cultural biases. *Psychological Review*, *127*(6), 1022–1052. https://doi.org/10.1037/rev0000209

Cuddy, A. J. C., Fiske, S. T., & Glick, P. (2008). Warmth and competence as universal dimensions of social perception: The stereotype content model and the BIAS map. In *Advances in experimental social psychology* (Vol. 40, pp. 61–149). Academic Press. https://doi.org/10.1016/S0065-2601(07)00002-0

Davis, J. T. M., & Hines, M. (2020). How large are gender differences in toy preferences? A systematic review and meta-analysis of toy preference research. *Archives of Sexual Behavior*, *49*(2), 373–394. https://doi.org/10.1007/s10508-019-01624-7

Dindia, K., & Allen, M. (1992). Sex differences in self-disclosure: A meta-analysis. *Psychological Bulletin*, *112*(1), 106–124. https://doi.org/10.1037/0033-2909.112.1.106

Eagly, A. H. (2007). Female leadership advantage and disadvantage: Resolving the contradictions. *Psychology of Women Quarterly*, *31*(1), 1–12. https://doi.org/10.1111/j.1471-6402.2007.00326.x

Eagly, A. H., & Karau, S. J. (2002). Role congruity theory of prejudice toward female leaders. *Psychological Review*, *109*(3), 573–598. https://doi.org/10.1037/0033-295X.109.3.573

Eagly, A. H., & Revelle, W. (2022). Understanding the magnitude of psychological differences between women and men requires seeing the forest and the trees. *Perspectives on Psychological Science*, *17*(5), 1339–1358. https://doi.org/10.1177/17456916211046006

Eagly, A. H., Wood, W., & Diekman, A. B. (2000). Social role theory of sex differences and similarities: A current appraisal. In *The developmental social psychology of gender* (pp. 123–174). Lawrence Erlbaum Associates Publishers.

Edwards, C. (1993). Behavioral sex differences in children of diverse cultures: The case of nurturance to infants. *Department of Psychology: Faculty Publications*. https://digitalcommons.unl.edu/psychfacpub/605

Fiske, S. T. (2010). Venus and mars or down to earth: Stereotypes and realities of gender differences. *Perspectives on Psychological Science*, *5*(6), 688–692.

Gabriel, S., & Gardner, W. L. (1999). Are there "his" and "hers" types of interdependence? The implications of gender differences in collective versus relational interdependence for affect, behavior, and cognition. *Journal of Personality and Social Psychology*, *77*(3), 642–655. https://doi.org/10.1037/0022-3514.77.3.642

Guimond, S., Chatard, A., Martinot, D., Crisp, R. J., & Redersdorff, S. (2006). Social comparison, self-stereotyping, and gender differences in self-construals. *Journal of Personality and Social Psychology*, *90*(2), 221–242. https://doi.org/10.1037/0022-3514.90.2.221

Hale, M. (1999). He says, she says: Gender and worklife. *Public Administration Review*, *59*(5), 410–424. https://doi.org/10.2307/977424

Halim, M. L., Ruble, D. N., & Amodio, D. M. (2011). From pink frilly dresses to "one of the boys": A social-cognitive analysis of gender identity development and gender bias. *Social & Personality Psychology Compass*, *5*(11), 933–949. https://doi.org/10.1111/j.1751-9004.2011.00399.x

Heilman, M. E., Caleo, S., & Manzi, F. (2024). Women at work: Pathways from gender stereotypes to gender bias and discrimination. *Annual Review of Organizational Psychology and Organizational Behavior*, *11*, 165–192. https://doi.org/10.1146/annurev-orgpsych-110721-034105

Herring, S. C. (1996a). Gender and democracy in computer-mediated communication. In R. Kling (Ed.), *Computerization and controversy* (2nd ed., pp. 476–489). Morgan Kaufmann. https://doi.org/10.1016/B978-0-12-415040-9.50121-4

Herring, S. C. (1996b). Posting in a different voice: Gender and ethics in computer-mediated communication. In C. Ess (Ed.), *Philosophical perspectives on computer-mediated communication* (pp. 115–145). State University of New York Press.

Herring, S. C., Kouper, I., Scheidt, L. A., & Wright, E. (2004). *Women and children last: The discursive construction of weblogs*. Into the Blogosphere. https://www.academia.edu/67272676/Women_and_Children_Last_The_Discursive_Construction_of_Weblogs

Hines, M. (2004). Psychosexual development in individuals who have female pseudohermaphroditism. *Child and Adolescent Psychiatric Clinics*, *13*(3), 641–656. https://doi.org/10.1016/j.chc.2004.02.013

Hinsz, V. B., & Tomhave, J. A. (1991). Smile and (half) the world smiles with you, frown and you frown alone. *Personality and Social Psychology Bulletin*, *17*(5), 586–592. https://doi.org/10.1177/0146167291175014

Hoffmann, M. L., & Powlishta, K. K. (2001). Gender segregation in childhood: A test of the interaction style theory. *Journal of Genetic Psychology*, *162*(3), 298. https://doi.org/10.1080/00221320109597485

Hsu, N., Badura, K. L., Newman, D. A., & Speach, M. E. P. (2021). Gender, "masculinity," and "femininity": A meta-analytic review of gender differences in agency and communion. *Psychological Bulletin*, *147*(10), 987–1011. https://doi.org/10.1037/bul0000343

Huang, L., Joshi, P., Wakslak, C., & Wu, A. (2021). Sizing up entrepreneurial potential: Gender differences in communication and investor perceptions of long-term growth and scalability. *Academy of Management Journal*, *64*(3), 716–740. https://doi.org/10.5465/amj.2018.1417

Ibarra, H. (1997). Paving an alternative route: Gender differences in managerial networks. *Social Psychology Quarterly*, *60*(1), 91–102. https://doi.org/10.2307/2787014

Ibarra, H., & Obodaru, O. (2009). Women and the vision thing. *Harvard Business Review*, *87*(1), 62–70.

Jadva, V., Hines, M., & Golombok, S. (2010). Infants' preferences for toys, colors, and shapes: Sex differences and similarities. *Archives of Sexual Behavior*, *39*(6), 1261–1273. https://doi.org/10.1007/s10508-010-9618-z

Johnson, F. L., & Aries, E. J. (1983). Conversational patterns among same-sex pairs of late-adolescent close friends. *Journal of Genetic Psychology*, *142*(2), 225. https://doi.org/10.1080/00221325.1983.10533514

Joshi, P. D., & Wakslak, C. J. (2014). Communicating with the crowd: Speakers use abstract messages when addressing larger audiences. *Journal of Experimental Psychology: General*, *143*(1), 351.

Joshi, P. D., Wakslak, C. J., Appel, G., & Huang, L. (2020). Gender differences in communicative abstraction. *Journal of Personality and Social Psychology*, *118*(3), 417–435. https://doi.org/10.1037/pspa0000177

Joshi, P. D., Wakslak, C. J., Raj, M., & Trope, Y. (2016). Communicating with distant others: The functional use of abstraction. *Social Psychological and Personality Science*, *7*(1), 37–44.

Kimbrough, A. M., Guadagno, R. E., Muscanell, N. L., & Dill, J. (2013). Gender differences in mediated communication: Women connect more than do men. *Computers in Human Behavior*, *29*(3), 896–900. https://doi.org/10.1016/j.chb.2012.12.005

Kriwy, P., Gross, C., & Gottburgsen, A. (2013). Look who's talking: Compositional effects of gender and status on verbal contributions at sociology conferences. *Gender, Work & Organization*, *20*(5), 545–560. https://doi.org/10.1111/j.1468-0432.2012.00603.x

Lakoff, R. (1973). Language and woman's place. *Language in Society*, *2*(1), 45–79. https://doi.org/10.1017/S0047404500000051

Lanaj, K., & Hollenbeck, J. R. (2015). Leadership over-emergence in self-managing teams: The role of gender and countervailing biases. *Academy of Management Journal*, *58*(5), 1476–1494. https://doi.org/10.5465/amj.2013.0303

Leaper, C. (2014). Gender similarities and differences in language. In T. M. Holtgraves (Ed.), *The Oxford handbook of language and social psychology* (pp. 62–82). Oxford University Press. https://doi.org/10.1093/oxfordhb/9780199838639.013.002

Leaper, C. (2019). Young adults' conversational strategies during negotiation and self-disclosure in same-gender and mixed-gender friendships. *Sex Roles*, *81*(9/10), 561–575. https://doi.org/10.1007/s11199-019-1014-0

Leaper, C., & Robnett, R. D. (2011). Women are more likely than men to use tentative language, aren't they? A meta-analysis testing for gender differences and moderators. *Psychology of Women Quarterly*, *35*(1), 129–142. https://doi.org/10.1177/0361684310392728

Maccoby, E. E. (1994). Commentary: Gender segregation in childhood. *New Directions for Child and Adolescent Development*, *1994*(65), 87–97. https://doi.org/10.1002/cd.23219946508

Maccoby, E. E. (1998). *The two sexes: Growing up apart, coming together*. Belknap Press of Harvard University Press.

Maccoby, E. E. (2002). Gender and group process: A developmental perspective. *Current Directions in Psychological Science*, *11*(2), 54. https://doi.org/10.1111/1467-8721.00167

Maccoby, E. E., & Jacklin, C. N. (1974). *The psychology of sex differences*. Stanford University Press.

Martin, C. L., & Fabes, R. A. (2001). The stability and consequences of young children's same-sex peer interactions. *Developmental Psychology*, *37*(3), 431–446. https://doi.org/10.1037/0012-1649.37.3.431

Martin, C. L., Fabes, R. A., Hanish, L., Leonard, S., & Dinella, L. M. (2011). Experienced and expected similarity to same-gender peers: Moving toward a comprehensive model of gender segregation. *Sex Roles*, *65*(5–6), 421–434. https://doi.org/10.1007/s11199-011-0029-y

Martin, C. L., Kornienko, O., Schaefer, D. R., Hanish, L. D., Fabes, R. A., & Goble, P. (2013). The role of sex of peers and gender-typed activities in young children's peer affiliative networks: A longitudinal analysis of selection and influence. *Child Development*, *84*(3), 921–937. https://doi.org/10.1111/cdev.12032

McIntyre, M. H., & Edwards, C. P. (2009). The early development of gender differences. *Annual Review of Anthropology*, *38*, 83–97. https://doi.org/10.1146/annurev-anthro-091908-164338

Mehta, C. M., & Smith, K. (2023). Childhood gender segregation in context: A cultural sociocontextual approach. *Review of General Psychology*, *27*(2), 135–154. https://doi.org/10.1177/10892680221121324

Mulac, A. (1989). Men's and women's talk in same-gender and mixed-gender dyads: Power or polemic? *Journal of Language and Social Psychology*, *8*(3–4), 249–270. https://doi.org/10.1177/0261927X8983006

Mulac, A., Bradac, J., & Gibbons, P. (2001). Empirical support for the gender-as-culture hypothesis. *Human Communication Research*, *27*(1), 121–152. https://doi.org/10.1111/j.1468-2958.2001.tb00778.x

Mulac, A., Giles, H., Bradac, J. J., & Palomares, N. A. (2013). The gender-linked language effect: An empirical test of a general process model. *Language Sciences*, *38*, 22–31. https://doi.org/10.1016/j.langsci.2012.12.004

Mulac, A., Lundell, T. L., & Bradac, J. J. (1986). Male/female language differences and attributional consequences in a public speaking situation: Toward an explanation of the gender-linked language effect. *Communication Monographs*, *53*(2), 115. https://doi.org/10.1080/03637758609376131

Mulac, A., Seibold, D. R., & Farris, J. L. (2000). Female and male managers' and professionals' criticism giving: Differences in language use and effects. *Journal of Language and Social Psychology*, *19*(4), 389–415. https://doi.org/10.1177/0261927X00019004001

Nardi, B. A., Schiano, D. J., Gumbrecht, M., & Swartz, L. (2004). Why we blog. *Communications of the ACM*, *47*(12), 41–46. https://doi.org/10.1145/1035134.1035163

Newman, M. L., Groom, C. J., Handelman, L. D., & Pennebaker, J. W. (2008). Gender differences in language use: An analysis of 14,000 text samples. *Discourse Processes*, *45*(3), 211–236. https://doi.org/10.1080/01638530802073712

O'Neill, K. S., Hansen, C. D., & May, G. L. (2002). The effect of gender on the transfer of interpersonal communication skills training to the workplace: Three theoretical frames. *Human Resource Development Review*, *1*(2), 167–185. https://doi.org/10.1177/15384302001002003

Palmeira, M. (2015). Abstract language signals power, but also lack of action orientation. *Journal of Experimental Social Psychology*, *61*, 59–63. https://doi.org/10.1016/j.jesp.2015.07.003

Palomares, N. A. (2004). Gender schematicity, gender identity salience, and gender-linked language use. *Human Communication Research*, *30*(4), 556–588. https://doi.org/10.1111/j.1468-2958.2004.tb00745.x

Palomares, N. A. (2009). Women are sort of more tentative than men, aren't they? How men and women use tentative language differently, similarly, and counterstereotypically as a function of gender salience. *Communication Research*, *36*(4), 538–560. https://doi.org/10.1177/0093650209333034

Parker, R. F., Aragão, C., Hurst, K., & Kim. (2023, April 13). *In a growing share of U.S. marriages, husbands and wives earn about the same*. Pew Research Center. https://www.pewresearch.org/social-trends/2023/04/13/in-a-growing-share-of-u-s-marriages-husbands-and-wives-earn-about-the-same/

Paustian-Underdahl, S. C., Walker, L. S., & Woehr, D. J. (2014). Gender and perceptions of leadership effectiveness: A meta-analysis of contextual moderators. *Journal of Applied Psychology*, *99*(6), 1129–1145. https://doi.org/10.1037/a0036751

Qiu, J., Kesebir, S., Günaydin, G., Selçuk, E., & Wasti, S. A. (2022). Gender differences in interpersonal trust: Disclosure behavior, benevolence sensitivity and workplace implications. *Organizational Behavior and Human Decision Processes*, *169*, 104119. https://doi.org/10.1016/j.obhdp.2022.104119

Raag, T. (1999). Influences of social expectations of gender, gender stereotypes, and situational constraints on children's toy choices. *Sex Roles*, *41*(11/12), 809–831. https://doi.org/10.1023/A:1018828328713

Riggio, R. E., Riggio, H. R., Salinas, C., & Cole, E. J. (2003). The role of social and emotional communication skills in leader emergence and effectiveness. *Group Dynamics: Theory, Research, and Practice*, *7*(2), 83–103. https://doi.org/10.1037/1089-2699.7.2.83

Rose, A. J. (2002). Co-rumination in the friendships of girls and boys. *Child Development*, *73*(6), 1830–1843. https://doi.org/10.1111/1467-8624.00509

Roter, D. L., Hall, J. A., & Aoki, Y. (2002). Physician gender effects in medical communication: A meta-analytic review. *JAMA*, *288*(6), 756. https://doi.org/10.1001/jama.288.6.756

Schlamp, S., Gerpott, F. H., & Voelpel, S. C. (2020). Same talk, different reaction? Communication, emergent leadership and gender. *Journal of Managerial Psychology*, *36*(1), 51–74. https://doi.org/10.1108/JMP-01-2019-0062

Schock, A.-K., Gruber, F. M., Scherndl, T., & Ortner, T. M. (2019). Tempering agency with communion increases women's leadership emergence in all-women groups: Evidence for role congruity theory in a field setting. *The Leadership Quarterly*, *30*(2), 189–198. https://doi.org/10.1016/j.leaqua.2018.08.003

Sehulster, J. R. (2006). Things we talk about, how frequently, and to whom: Frequency of topics in everyday conversation as a function of gender, age, and marital status. *The American Journal of Psychology*, *119*(3), 407–432. https://doi.org/10.2307/20445351

Su, R., Rounds, J., & Armstrong, P. I. (2009). Men and things, women and people: A meta-analysis of sex differences in interests. *Psychological Bulletin*, *135*(6), 859–884. https://doi.org/10.1037/a0017364

Sweet, E. V. (2013). *Boy builders and pink princesses: Gender, toys, and inequality over the twentieth century* [University of California, Davis]. ProQuest Dissertation Publishing. https://www.proquest.com/openview/eaa5f665af82e76329798e40e2b4fbcf/1?pq-origsite=gscholar&cbl=18750

Tannen, D. (1994). *Gender and discourse*. Oxford University Press.

Tannen, D. (1995, September 1). The power of talk: Who gets heard and why. *Harvard Business Review*, *73*, 138–138.

Todd, B. K., Fischer, R. A., Di Costa, S., Roestorf, A., Harbour, K., Hardiman, P., & Barry, J. A. (2018). Sex differences in children's toy preferences: A systematic review, meta-regression, and meta-analysis. *Infant and Child Development*, *27*(2), e2064. https://doi.org/10.1002/icd.2064

Von Hippel, C., Wiryakusuma, C., Bowden, J., & Shochet, M. (2011). Stereotype threat and female communication styles. *Personality and Social Psychology Bulletin*, *37*(10), 1312–1324. https://doi.org/10.1177/0146167211410439

Wakslak, C. J., Smith, P. K., & Han, A. (2014). Using abstract language signals power. *Journal of Personality and Social Psychology*, *107*(1), 41–55. https://doi.org/10.1037/a0036626

Weinberg, F. J., Treviño, L. J., & Cleveland, A. O. (2019). Gendered communication and career outcomes: A construct validation and prediction of hierarchical advancement and non-hierarchical rewards. *Communication Research*, *46*(4), 456–502. https://doi.org/10.1177/0093650215590605

Wood, W., & Eagly, A. H. (2012). Biosocial construction of sex differences and similarities in behavior. In J. M. Olson & M. P. Zanna (Eds.), *Advances in experimental social psychology* (Vol. 46, pp. 55–123). Academic Press. https://doi.org/10.1016/B978-0-12-394281-4.00002-7

Wood, W., & Eagly, A. (2015). Two traditions of research on gender identity. *Sex Roles*, *73*(11–12), 461–473. https://doi.org/10.1007/s11199-015-0480-2

World Bank. (2024, May 20). *Fertility rate versus female labor force participation*. Our World in Data. https://ourworldindata.org/grapher/fertility-and-female-labor-force-participation?endpointsOnly=0&time=1970.2022&country=~USA

Zosuls, K. M., & Ruble, D. N. (2018). Gender-typed toy preferences among infants and toddlers. In E. S. Weisgram & L. M. Dinella (Eds.), *Gender typing of children's toys: How early play experiences impact development* (pp. 49–72). American Psychological Association. https://doi.org/10.1037/0000077-004

Zucker, K. J., & Bradley, S. J. (1995). *Gender identity disorder and psychosexual problems in children and adolescents*. Guilford Press.

CHAPTER 8

When and Why Should We Care About Gender/Sex in Negotiation?

Shan Sherwan Hussein and Hannah Riley Bowles

Driving with her team to deliver humanitarian aid to a newly liberated area of Ukraine, Sara, a newly hired manager with an international NGO, took advantage of the brief downtime in the van to scroll through her emails. In a chain on her department's budget, she paused to take in some upsetting news: two of her direct staff were being compensated more than she was. Sara thought back to her initial phone call with Human Resources (HR) regarding the terms of her contract. The salary offered fell within a set range, so Sara had believed the compensation was fair. But this was her first expatriate contract, and Sara was unfamiliar with the items being discussed, such as hardship and hazard pay. Now she realized she had conceded more than she should have. If she had pushed for a base salary at the upper end of the range, her hardship and hazard pay would be higher as well, and she would be earning more than those who reported to her. But, since she hadn't, she was in the embarrassing position of earning less than her staff. She had heard somewhere that women don't negotiate as well as men do, and now she felt like living proof. She must be a terrible negotiator.

But as they drove through the devastated landscape, Sara reflected on her years of experience as a humanitarian worker in acute crisis zones. She had negotiated effectively on behalf of thousands of people for services and support. Yet, somehow, she had not recognized these types of problem-solving and conflict management situations as "negotiations." And since childhood, Sara had also negotiated with her family to pursue educational and professional aspirations that deviated from the role expectations of her conservative society and household—including for their blessing and support to work overseas. She had negotiated effectively in

DOI: 10.4324/9781003488590- 8

various realms, and it certainly wasn't the case that she was a bad negotiator just because she was a woman.

The term *negotiation* often evokes images of competitive bargaining over money, such as salary or bonuses for a new job. However, as Sara learned, negotiation actually involves a much broader set of behaviors that most of us engage in on a daily basis—from significant challenges (such as crafting a business deal or managing a heated dispute) to everyday encounters (e.g., who gets to use the car or where to go on a Friday night). In this chapter, we use the term *negotiation* to refer to interpersonal decision making that requires some degree of creative problem-solving or trade-offs to address parties' competing and complementary interests (Raiffa, 1982; Thompson, 2005). In other words, you are negotiating whenever you are working with others to find mutually beneficial solutions to joint decisions on which you don't automatically agree. Specifically, we will focus on the negotiations we engage in day in and day out in pursuit of our career goals—including interactions that we don't typically think about as negotiations, such as asking for much-needed resources or proposing changes to processes that aren't working well.

While research has found that men and women do sometimes achieve differential results in negotiation, these differences depend a great deal on the context—and are much more subtle and varied than the common takeaway that "women don't negotiate aggressively enough." In this chapter, we will explore research showing when gender/sex matters in negotiations[1] and explain how these findings can help people of all genders/sexes advance more deliberately in their careers through negotiation.

WHEN DOES GENDER/SEX MATTER IN NEGOTIATION?

In her hiring negotiation, Sara's lack of understanding of the pay range and standards associated with an expatriate contract clouded her judgment. Her experience highlights the circumstances in which gender/sex is most likely to influence our negotiations. As we will see, gender/sex effects in negotiation are more likely when gender/sex is more relevant and salient, particularly when the context of a negotiation is masculine-stereotypic (e.g., pay negotiations). In addition, gender/sex effects are more likely to emerge when there is a high degree of ambiguity (e.g., lack of objective standards, clarity on pay standards) about how or what to negotiate, as men are more likely than women to have better access to information (Bowles et al., 2022; Sturm, 2009).

Let's compare Sara's contract negotiation to her work negotiations on behalf of survivors of conflict and natural disaster. Evidence from US studies indicates that a stereotype exists that men are more competitive negotiators than women (Kray et al., 2001; Kray & Thompson, 2004), particularly when it comes to negotiating for oneself as opposed to others (Bowles et al., 2005). People expect women to be strong advocates for others, but self-advocating can violate the feminine ideal of putting others' interests ahead of one's own (Amanatullah & Morris, 2010; Amanatullah & Tinsley, 2013). In other words, self-advocating in a competitive bargaining situation activates stereotypes about how men and women will behave as negotiators—particularly, that men will be more assertive and effective (Kray et al., 2001, 2002). In more masculine-stereotypic negotiation situations (e.g., competitive self-advocacy in a male-dominated setting), evidence indicates that men (compared to women) are more likely to initiate negotiations (Kugler et al., 2018) and claim a larger share of the value to be divided (Mazei et al., 2015).[2]

However, when competitive bargaining situations are less masculine stereotypic, these gender/sex effects tend to fade away. For instance, researchers have compared what happens to gender/sex effects when parties are negotiating for higher pay for someone else (as opposed to themselves). Simply switching to other-advocacy from self-advocacy increases women's assertiveness as negotiators (Amanatullah & Morris, 2010; Bowles et al., 2005) and reduces gender/sex effects in negotiation performance (Mazei et al., 2015). Another set of experiments showed that changing the context of competitive bargaining to be less masculine stereotypic had similar effects. Bear and Babcock (2012) manipulated whether pairs of male and female negotiators were playing the role of automobile executives negotiating the price of motorcycle headlamps (a typically male-dominated market) or jewelry dealers negotiating the price of decorative lamp beads (a market that tends to include a balance of male and female buyers and sellers). Holding constant the price negotiation and randomly assigning laboratory study participants to negotiate over headlamps or lamp beads, they found that men outperformed women when playing automobile executives but not when playing jewelry dealers.

Returning to Sara's experiences, it would be hard for her or anyone else to say whether gender/sex influenced her and her negotiating counterparts' behavior or outcomes in any single negotiation. Inferences about gender/sex in negotiation tend to be based on statistically significant patterns in samples of dozens, hundreds, or even thousands of negotiation cases (Bowles et al., 2024). However, Sara's contrasting experiences of failing to bargain the terms of her contract effectively versus negotiating assertively and successfully for greater resources for others in humanitarian contexts fit these more general patterns.

Sara's stories also highlight the importance of not overgeneralizing from experiences in one context. For her, the sting of not negotiating her contract effectively overshadowed her many years of skilled negotiation in much more complex and high-stakes situations of humanitarian assistance. Exposure to subtle stereotypes that men are more assertive negotiators than women can foster "stereotype threat" (Steele, 1997), or anxiety about conforming to a negative stereotype, that undermines women's confidence and performance as negotiators (Kray et al., 2001; Kray & Kennedy, 2017); that is, the fear of "negotiating like a woman" can actually lead women to negotiate less effectively.

Recognizing that gender/sex effects in negotiation shift across situations weakens stereotypic claims about men and women as negotiators (Bowles et al., 2022). Indeed, simple awareness of the potential for stereotype threat can help to counteract it (Johns et al., 2005).

Another important consideration when assessing the likelihood of gender/sex effects emerging in negotiation is the degree of ambiguity about what and how to negotiate. Meta-analyses (i.e., statistical analyses of patterns of results across studies) show that gender/sex differences (male > female) in the propensity to initiate negotiation and in negotiation outcomes decline when the parties have a clearer understanding of negotiating norms (Kugler et al., 2018) and standards (Mazei et al., 2015). Even in masculine-stereotypic negotiation situations, such as self-advocating for higher pay or bargaining as an automobile executive, gender/sex effects dissipate when the parties have known standards from which to negotiate agreement (Bowles et al., 2005). Ambiguity, it seems, opens the door for gender/sex stereotypes or gender/sex-biased standards to influence parties' expectations as they search past experiences and the environment for cues on how to negotiate.

Gaining negotiation experience can also reduce ambiguity and lessen gender/sex effects. Over time, we learn how to behave, where the zone of potential agreement lies, and what appropriate standards for agreement are within that zone. Correspondingly, meta-analytic evidence indicates that gender/sex differences in negotiation outcomes decline when parties are trained or experienced negotiators (Mazei et al., 2015). There is also evidence that the influence of gender/sex stereotypes on negotiation performance can be reduced by encouraging negotiators to think about aspects of their identity that might contribute to their skills as a negotiator (e.g., one's identity as an MBA student; Kray et al., 2001). In sum, both gaining experience and reflecting on one's negotiation strengths may be valuable assets for combating the unwanted influences of gender/sex stereotypes.

Again, Sara's negotiation experiences are illustrative. With better knowledge of this literature, Sara might have recognized that she was entering the negotiation with her employer with a high degree of ambiguity. She was not familiar with negotiating norms nor with the salary ranges of the shiny new contract. Interestingly, around the same time she was negotiating the job in Ukraine, Sara received an offer from a different organization to deploy to Sudan. This second offer could have served as a useful reference point to compare with the Ukraine offer (i.e., no-agreement alternative; Raiffa, 1982; Thompson, 2005). However, Sara did not explore the specific terms of that contract. Her resulting lack of clarity undermined her confidence and goals in the negotiation. By contrast, her years of experience negotiating on behalf of others for humanitarian assistance made her confidently assertive in that context. She very clearly understood the negotiating norms and standards, throwing herself into generating creative solutions to serve people in need.

Notably, the circumstances we have discussed—masculine-stereotyped and ambiguous negotiations—represent only a slice of the world of actual and potential negotiations. Taken together, the research suggests that whether you become a sure-footed negotiator is not determined by your gender/sex or personality. Rather, it depends on whether you have developed the skills and situational understanding needed to assess the zone of possible agreement, to generate solutions that create value for all parties, and to claim value for yourself or those you represent (Thompson, 2005). Moreover, these are skills you can develop through training, observation, and practice (Nadler et al., 2003).

GENDER/SEX IN CAREER NEGOTIATIONS

Much of our understanding of gender/sex in negotiation comes from the study of career negotiations, which can be defined as interpersonal problem-solving with work and life partners to make progress toward professional goals, including management work/family conflicts (Bowles et al., 2019). This focus is likely explained in part by the need for self-advocacy in career negotiations, which (as noted earlier) heightens the potential for gender/sex effects in negotiation performance (Bowles et al., 2005; Mazei et al., 2015). It is also explained by the centrality of the gender/sexed division of labor in our daily lives, which contributes to gender/sex stereotypes. Despite women's gains in education, the occupational gender/sex gap and job segregation by gender/sex persist. Women are entering a wider range of occupations than ever before, but their roles tend to be more communal (i.e., the ability to handle people, compassionate), while men's roles are more agentic (i.e., ambitious, assertive) (Eagly et al., 2020; Eagly & Steffen, 1984).

Much of the research on gender/sex in negotiation has studied pay negotiations, which evoke masculine stereotypes in multiple respects (Bowles et al., 2019, 2022). As noted earlier, pay negotiations trigger expectations of masculine-stereotypic competitive bargaining (Bear, 2011); they also activate associations of men as breadwinners (even though women contribute significantly to household earnings in most families; Pfau-Effinger, 2004). This combination of factors contributes to the common expectation that men, and particularly men from dominant groups (i.e., straight White men in the USA), will be more assertive and effective in their pay negotiations than women (Desai & Gunia, 2023; Hernandez et al., 2019). Though such stereotypes tend to be more robust than men's and women's actual behavior in practice, field evidence suggests that women generally encounter more resistance than men to their pay negotiation attempts (e.g., see Artz et al., 2018; Kray & Kennedy, 2017; cf. Leibbrandt & List, 2015).

When we imagine the typical career negotiation, we might picture a job candidate negotiating their starting salary and benefits with an interviewer or an employee negotiating for a raise and bonus after their performance review. Yet career negotiations encompass a much broader array of interactions. Career negotiation is an essential process for accessing resources and opportunities and for advancing toward one's long-term goals (Bowles & Thomason, 2015). In this chapter, we treat career negotiations as encompassing negotiations over (1) pay, including salary, bonuses, and other types of monetary compensation; (2) work–family conflict, which usually involves negotiating flexible work arrangement in the effort to find a balance between work and family (Rudman & Mescher, 2013); and (3) role, including work assignments and opportunities for responsibility and authority that determine one's career development and advancement (Bowles et al., 2019).

While pay negotiations tend to be masculine-stereotyped, because women are associated more strongly than men with familial caregiving, negotiations for access to family-friendly work practices tend to be feminine-stereotyped (Kelly et al., 2010). Multiple studies indicate that men tend encounter more resistance than women when they attempt to negotiate at work for more flexibility to manage work/family conflicts (Berdahl & Moon, 2013; Rudman & Mescher, 2013; Vandello et al., 2013). Thus, both men and women tend to find it more challenging to negotiate in ways that challenge gender/sexed norms.

Before diving into the dimensions of role negotiation, it is important to highlight that women may face greater expectations than men to take on fewer promotable tasks that serve groups or organizations rather than themselves (Babcock et al., 2017). This office "housework," such as filling in for a colleague or serving on a low-ranking committee (Babcock et al., 2018), appears to be rooted in our early experiences and gender/sex socialization, suggested by the fact that female students in one graduate program volunteered significantly more often than male students to take on the responsibility of booking a room for team meetings (Doğan, 2020). Notably, these groups had minimal previous engagement (i.e., a high level of ambiguity). This ambiguity may have activated gender/sex stereotypes, particularly that male students might be less inclined to take on the logistical role. Being expected to volunteer for or accept low-promotability tasks undermines career advancement by leaving less time for tasks that would enhance and spotlight one's strengths.

Field studies of what managers and professionals negotiate for to advance their careers suggest that problem-solving around work roles (e.g., assignments, developmental opportunities) is more common than negotiations about pay or family-friendly work arrangements (e.g., Bowles et al., 2019; Rousseau, 2005). These studies have uncovered little evidence of systematic gender/sex effects in the domain of role-related negotiations. Whereas negotiations about compensation and access to family-friendly work arrangements correspond to traditional divisions of household labor (i.e., male breadwinner, female caregiver), role negotiations are not as obviously gender/sex stereotyped.

One exception to this may be asking for more time to complete assignments. There is evidence that women are less likely than men to negotiate for time extensions on work products. This may be in part because women worry more than men about burdening or alienating others with delays (Whillans et al., 2021). In addition, men may be more predisposed to negotiations about money and time, which are more likely to activate a masculine-stereotyped, competitive sense of zero-sum conflict (i.e., more for one party is less for the other; Harinck et al., 2000) than negotiations over work roles (e.g., about the contributions one wants to make to one's organization or clients; Bowles et al., 2019).

BE SURE: A FRAMEWORK FOR CAREER SELF-ADVOCACY

Workers, and especially women, often get the message that negotiating for higher pay is the best way to meet their career goals. However, we can enhance our earnings more effectively by negotiating creatively for our professional advancement, concludes research and interviews with individuals ranging from job candidates to executive leaders (Bowles & Williams, 2022). Hannah Riley Bowles (one of the coauthors) developed a four-step SURE framework to help people negotiate "WELL"—across Work, Education, Life, and Leadership goals (Bowles & Williams, 2022). The Be **SURE** framework has four steps: (1) **S**tart with your goals; (2) **U**nderstand what you're negotiating for; (3) **R**educe ambiguity about what, how, and with whom to negotiate; and (4) **E**nhance your negotiation through relationships and your relationships through negotiation. We overview the framework here (Figure 8.1) before discussing how it can help us navigate different phases of negotiation.

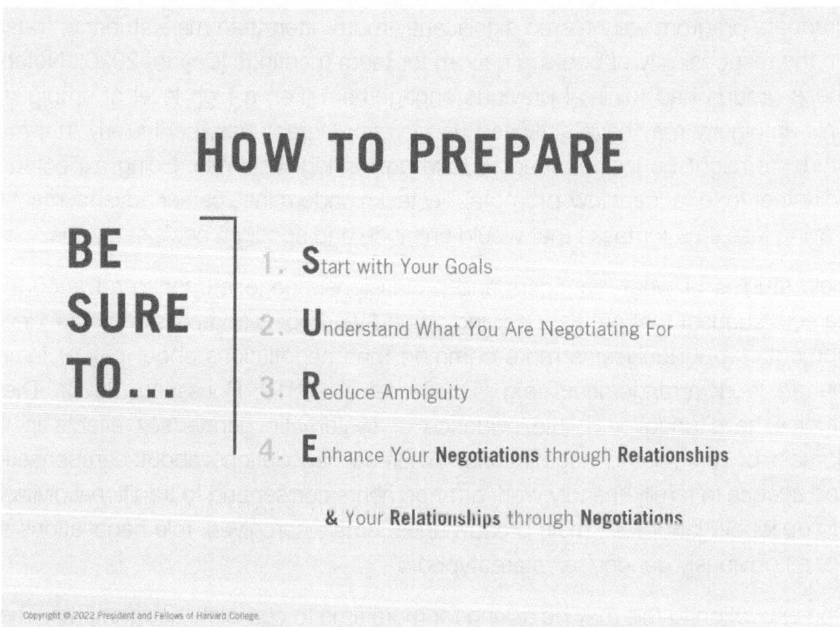

FIGURE 8.1 Prepare to Negotiate WELL

This graphic is adopted from the Be SURE You Are Prepared to Negotiate WELL teaching material (Bowles & Williams, 2022).

Start With Your Goals

To avoid being anchored by your counterpart's expectations, take time to consider your own short-term and long-term aspirations in an upcoming negotiation. Are you negotiating for higher pay, resolution of a work–family conflict, or maybe a new role? Don't let your current situation and perspective limit your long-term goals, and keep in mind that people with specific, challenging goals tend to be better positioned to perform better than those with less specific or no goals (Zetik & Stuhlmacher, 2002a). Think broadly about your career ambitions, including what roles you would like to take on, what responsibilities you would like to adopt, and your targeted compensation. Looking back, Sara lacked a clear goal in her negotiation with the employer.

Understand What You Are Negotiating For

Our career negotiations tend to fall into three general categories: *asking*, *bending*, or *shaping*. Asking involves requesting an opportunity, resource, or reward that is typical for people in your position. This might mean requesting a salary that falls within the range listed in a job advertisement, asking for a promotion at your current workplace, or requesting a hybrid work arrangement that is available to others. When making such requests, it is important to reiterate that the nature of your request is standard. If Sara had negotiated her base salary, this would have been an asking negotiation. Bending refers to the pursuit of special privileges that others in your role wouldn't typically receive, such as being the only one on your team to work remotely or take time off from travel assignments. For bending negotiation, you need to be prepared to justify exceptions. Shaping involves changing standard practice not only for yourself but also for those around you. Examples might include making a proposal to overhaul policies about remote work, expanding operations to a new geographic area, or developing a new service or product line. Shaping negotiations requires you to reach out to various stakeholders and argue convincingly for why your proposed changes are in their and the organization's best interest (Bowles et al., 2019; Bowles & Williams, 2022).

Reduce Ambiguity About What, How, and With Whom to Negotiate

Negotiations are often full of ambiguity, not only about what is negotiable (e.g., salary, remote work) but also about how to negotiate and with whom. Should you ask to move to a different team while you plan to negotiate for a raise? Whom should you speak to first about an opportunity in another department? To reduce such ambiguity, seek out information and advice that will help you answer these what, how, and who questions. In doing so, you will not only set yourself up for more effective negotiations with the right people, but also reduce your anxiety.

In her hiring negotiation, Sara was surrounded by a thick cloud of ambiguity. She did not know with whom to negotiate: someone in HR, her direct supervisor (whom she hadn't even met yet), or her technical supervisor? Nor did she know whether she was permitted to request a higher salary or duty station. If such requests were possible, she was unsure of the appropriate procedure for making them. Sara did have a mentor, who helped her choose between the two different job postings. In retrospect, she could have asked her mentor, who had worked in different conflict zones for decades, for negotiation advice as well.

Enhance Your Negotiation Through Relationships and Your Relationships Through Negotiation

This step involves reaching out to others in and outside your network for information, advice, social support, and advocacy. By gathering information, you can craft an argument that is more legitimate. For example, you might reference industry norms or practices in similar firms. The more legitimate a request seems, the more willing your counterpart will be to fulfill it (Bowles & Babcock, 2013). Prepare to share information about underlying interests that might motivate your counterpart to share information in return (Thompson, 2005). This could allow you to make a compelling case that your goal would be in the best interest of your counterpart as well.

Beyond her mentor, Sara needed to leverage the extensive network of contacts she had established over a decade in the non-profit sector. It would have been ideal if she reached out to them and asked, "How should I approach these offers?" Eventually, Sara became the person to whom others would reach out for information and advice on negotiating their own expatriate contracts. Sara openly shared her lived experience, telling them to go back to the bargaining table to ask for more before signing a contract and guiding them on how to do so.

MITIGATING THE POTENTIAL FOR GENDER/SEX BIASES

As you can see, a broad array of workplace negotiations can help you reach your career (and life) goals. Next, we will consider where gender/sex biases might lurk in the negotiation process—specifically, as you prepare, how you behave at the table, and what outcomes you reach. We will suggest how to defuse gender/sex biases as they emerge with guidance from the Be SURE framework.

Preparing for Negotiation

As explained, one way to decrease the likelihood of gender/sex effects in negotiation is to reduce ambiguity about how and what to negotiate. Much of this work can be done as you prepare to negotiate. Generally speaking, gaining information and advice on how to negotiate effectively and what is potentially negotiable are core to good negotiation preparation (Thompson, 2005). As you begin to identify your goals and understand what you want to negotiate for, it is important to look out for two possible sources of gender/sex biases that might emerge: the social comparisons we make automatically and the composition of our social networks.

Social Comparisons

Psychological research has long established that, when trying to assess themselves and their circumstances, people tend to compare themselves to similar others (Festinger, 1954; Wood, 1989). Such comparisons can aid our negotiation preparation. For example, it can be beneficial to seek out relatable examples of the types of resources and opportunities that similar others (e.g., those of the same professional rank, comparable years of experience) have negotiated for themselves and how they have gone about it. Indeed, the ability to point to such examples could enhance the legitimacy of our negotiation proposals (Thompson, 2005) and thus enhance our relationships through negotiation (Step Four of the Be SURE framework).

At the same time, such comparisons can backfire. One common mistake is to choose people as comparison points based primarily on their similarity to you, to the exclusion of other potentially valuable information. In classic research on the "entitlement effect," scholars sought to understand why women tended to have lower pay expectations than men and an associated willingness to accept lower compensation offers (Major et al., 1984). They discovered that women tended to compare themselves to other women, while men tended to compare themselves to other men (Major & Testa, 1989). In environments where men tended to earn more than women, this propensity for social comparison to similar others led men and women to anchor to different levels of compensation expectations—setting men's sights higher than women's. However, when the researchers exposed men and women to the same information on compensation standards, men and women generally expected the same pay (Major & Testa, 1989). In other words, differences in men's sense of entitlement to high compensation was not related to stable personality traits but rather to their self-comparison to similar others within their social environment.

When seeking to reduce the ambiguity of an upcoming career negotiation by obtaining objective comparison standards (Step Three of the Be SURE framework), it is important to consider whether you are searching broadly enough. Women and other members of historically marginalized groups particularly need to be mindful of the potential limitations of narrow comparisons. Are you focusing on people who are similar to you in some respects but different in other key aspects? One way to challenge our biases is to "consider the alternative" by being open to other possible outcomes beyond the most obvious explanations (Hirt & Markman, 1995). Doing so can help us examine our initial judgments more critically.

Relatedly, experimental evidence suggests that individuals show less gender/sex bias in hiring when they evaluate job candidates jointly (comparing candidates side by side) rather than sequentially (assessing candidates one at a time) (Bohnet et al., 2016). Therefore, being well-informed about and presenting a range of potential comparison standards in your negotiation proposal might not only reduce your own bias but also steer your negotiating counterparts toward thinking more critically about what standards they are using to judge you (e.g., see Belliveau, 2005).

Social Networks

Not only do people tend to compare themselves to similar others, but they also tend to more readily befriend those similar to them (e.g., "birds of a feather flock together"; McPherson et al., 2001). As a result, our social networks tend to reflect our own personal characteristics, such as our gender/sex or race (Currarini et al., 2009; Ibarra, 1993). In situations dominated by a particular demographic type (e.g., venture capital tends to be male-dominated), those from the dominant type (e.g., men compared to women in venture capital) might find it easier to gain access to negotiation-related information and resources because of the structure of social networks (Gompers et al., 2021; see also Ibarra, 1992; Roth, 2009). If most of the people from whom you seek counsel when preparing to negotiate have backgrounds similar to your own, your attempts to reduce ambiguity could lead you in a biased direction.

If gendered/sexed social networks lead to biased career negotiations, what can be done to address them? Some studies of career advancement in male-dominated fields have found that high-potential women are more likely than their male peers to form close professional ties with people outside their immediate work environment in ways that serve their professional interests (Groysberg, 2010; Ibarra, 1997). At the very least, you should aim to be cognizant of the potential for gendered/sexed social networks to influence your search for information and advice. Awareness of your social network can help you access a broader array of data and enhance your relationships through negotiation (Step Four of the Be SURE framework). In particular, reaching out to people with different lived experiences and social connections from your own typically opens doors to novel information and insights that could flush out potential biases in your information sources (Burt et al., 2013).

During the Negotiation

As our negotiations get underway, new sources of gender/sex bias can emerge, both in ourselves and in our counterparts. In fact, ambiguity plays a role in whether we choose to negotiate in the first place. As we saw in Sara's case, ambiguity prevented her from negotiating salary with her prospective employer. Once again, we can overcome this barrier by reducing the ambiguity of the situation (Step Three of the Be SURE framework). In general, people are less inclined to negotiate in situations that are less familiar to them (Reif & Brodbeck, 2017), as well as in those that are counter-stereotypical (as discussed earlier; e.g., Kugler et al., 2018; Reif et al., 2019). Research also shows that both men and women tend to achieve higher wages when they have the autonomy of choice to negotiate rather than when they are informed that they must negotiate (Exley et al., 2019).

Starting with a clear goal is important (Step One of the Be SURE framework), as our opening goals and expectations tend to heavily influence our offers and outcomes (Galinsky et al., 2002; Zetik & Stuhlmacher, 2002a). When gender/sex stereotypes are activated (i.e., saying or thinking that negotiation is a masculine trait), women tend to have less ambitious objectives than men and to depart with less advantageous outcomes (Kray et al., 2001; Major et al., 1984). One set of studies found that when women had a strong sense of a company's negotiating norms, they were less likely to be satisfied with having their first offers accepted in a job negotiation (Kray & Gelfand, 2009).

In general, during negotiation, both under-assertiveness and over-assertiveness can put one at a disadvantage, depending on the situation. We can reduce this disadvantage by adjusting our behavior to the context (Ames & Flynn, 2007). In one study, women were more likely to persist in their negotiations with male "naysayers" (those who refused to make concessions) by using indirect techniques, such as nonverbal cues. By comparison, in negotiations with female naysayers, women tended to persist by using more direct strategies, such as verbal demands and persuasion (Bowles & Flynn, 2010). Thus, persistence in negotiation is not an inherent gender/sex trait but is influenced by the composition of the negotiation dyad. Perhaps because of the gender/sex biases they have faced, women often exhibit a sophisticated ability to adapt their communication strategies to the gender/sex of their counterpart.

Turning to gender/sex bias on the other side of the table, research shows that women are more likely than men to face backlash when advocating for themselves versus others; anticipating such a backlash, women may ask for less than men or make larger concessions than male negotiators (Amanatullah & Morris, 2010). This is largely a systemic problem that needs to be addressed by the organization (Bohnet & Chilazi, 2025). To avoid backlash, women might try adopting other-advocacy language when self-advocating. For instance, "when negotiating her salary, a woman might reframe it as negotiating for money for her family," suggest Amanatullah and Morris (2010). Similarly, when engaged in a "bending" negotiation to shape your work role, you might describe how your proposed changes would benefit the organization (Step Two of the Be SURE framework).

Outcomes of Negotiation

How does our gender/sex affect our negotiated outcomes, including value claiming, value creation, and impasse? Gender/sex is not a firm indicator of a negotiated outcome, which depends on many factors. However, trends related to gender/sex have emerged in some contexts. More generally, taking a broader view of value in negotiation, beyond just economics (Lax & Sebenius, 2006), will help us achieve more in our career negotiations.

Value Claiming

Also known as distributive or "win-lose" negotiation, value claiming involves haggling over resources that are perceived to be fixed and limited (Zetik & Stuhlmacher, 2002b). In the workplace, people often treat pay as a resource that is ripe for value claiming. Artz et al. (2018) found that women were as likely as men to ask for pay increases and promotions at their current workplace, but only women 40 years old and younger achieved the same outcomes as men; older women were not as successful (Artz et al., 2018). In recent years, women's rate of salary negotiation has risen to become equal to or even higher than that of men, yet women continue to earn less than men (Kray et al., 2023). This research put to rest the previous finding that "women don't ask" (Babcock & Laschever, 2003): women today *do* ask, but they receive less than men. To close the pay gap, organizations need to be transparent about what is negotiable. All employees, regardless of gender/sex, need to have access to the same information and to more uniform hiring practices that reduce the amount of individual bias in the system (Shonk, 2025).

Value Creation

Sometimes referred to as integrative or "win-win" negotiation, value creation typically involves adding issues that parties value differently to a negotiation and making trade-offs across them. For example, if an employee desires higher pay, they might negotiate to take on added responsibilities that the employer values. Value creation is a cooperative process of identifying underlying interests and generating values aligned with those interests (Lax & Sebenius, 2006). To create value, both (or all) parties in a negotiation need to be open to engaging in creative thinking and strategies (Gavin, 2019) rather than adopting a purely competitive, win–lose mindset. Notably, an even split of the bargaining zone does not necessarily signal that an integrative agreement has been achieved (Thompson, 2005).

As Step Four of the Be SURE framework stresses, you can strategically leverage the information you gather from your network and relationships to achieve an outcome that creates value for both you and your counterpart. For women in particular, negotiating in ways that transparently take counterparts' interests into account may help reduce the relational risks of self-advocacy (Bowles & Babcock, 2013).

Impasse

There are three main types of impasses: wanted impasses, in which both parties prefer an impasse over an agreement; forced impasse, in which one negotiator wants an impasse while the other wants to reach an agreement; and unwanted impasse, in which neither party desires an impasse and both wish they had reached an agreement (Schweinsberg et al., 2022). Reaching an impasse does not need to signify the end of a negotiation. With resilience, negotiators can recover from setbacks and restart the negotiation process (Spector, 2006). Negotiators might be more likely to reach an impasse when they fail to jointly discuss issues and instead negotiate each issue separately (Thompson, 2005).

Although the negotiation literature encourages individuals to have a strong best alternative to a negotiated agreement, or BATNA (Fisher & Ury, 1981), research shows that in dyadic interactions comprising female–female (FF), male–male (MM), mixed-gender/sex (MF) pairs, the presentation of a strong BATNA by women increased the likelihood of reaching a value-destroying impasse more than the odds of reaching a profitable agreement; by comparison, men were more likely to significantly reap the benefits of a strong alternative (Dannals et al., 2021). This behavior aligns with literature on women's assertiveness, which highlights how it challenges pervasive gender/sex stereotypes. To minimize the risk of backlash, we recommend using the "relational accounts" strategy—that is, legitimating the request while simultaneously aspiring to strengthen the organizational relationship (Bowles, 2013).

GAINING CONFIDENCE THROUGH EXPERIENCE

After her contract mishap, Sara promised herself that she wouldn't make the same mistake again. The next time she considered a contract to work in conflict zones as a freelancer, she was more educated about the different types of contracts and took notice of the fact that the pay rate was daily. She emailed HR and asked for an online meeting. Sara then reached out to her contacts in the hiring organization, who considered the salary being offered and other items and coached her on what she might ask for.

In Sara's meeting with the HR rep, she opened by saying, "I requested this meeting because I made a promise to myself that I would negotiate my contracts." Over the next half hour, they discussed various contract terms, and Sara asked for a higher daily rate. The HR rep took Sara's notes back to the budget holder for the position. A few days later, Sara received an email confirming the daily rate she had asked for, along with the deployment notice period and the rest and recuperation package.

Every negotiator encounters setbacks and moments of doubt and anxiety. Like Sara, with continuous practice, you will gain experience and confidence in recognizing opportunities to meet your own and others' interests through creative, mutually beneficial agreements. We invite you to seize opportunities to apply the Be SURE framework and the research findings we have discussed to your scheduled negotiations—and to negotiations you might not even have considered until now.

CHAPTER SUMMARY

This chapter outlines situations in which gender/sex affects career-related negotiations, including compensation, role advancement, and work–family conflict. The authors discuss how to avoid and mitigate potential gender/sex biases in negotiation as individuals and in organizations. The authors outline a framework for negotiation preparation, "Be SURE," that prepares readers for three important types of career negotiations. Applying the Be SURE Framework, the authors suggest strategies for addressing gender/sex biases as one prepares to negotiate, engage in talks, and formulate outcomes (i.e., reach agreement or walk away).

DISCUSSION QUESTIONS

1. What experiences have you had that you did not recognize as negotiations at the time but do after reading this chapter?
2. Which steps from the Be SURE framework and "Mitigating the Potential for Gender Bias" section do you believe you need to adopt most?
3. What was a primary misnomer you held about negotiations that this chapter corrected?
4. Consider a negotiation you are likely to face in the near future; what new steps will you take before, during, or after the negotiation?
    a. In what ways, if any, does your gender identity (and other identities) shape your strategy?

NOTES

1 Because research on gender/sex in negotiation is largely based on people's self-reports or social interpretations of who is a man and who is a woman, rather than on biological information (Deaux & LaFrance, 1998), we use the term "gender/sex" rather than "sex" in this chapter. Reflective of existing research on gender/sex in negotiation, we focus on documented gender/sex effects associated with people categorized as male/female or men/women. Unfortunately, the negotiation experiences of people with fluid, non-binary, or transgender/sex identities have not yet been widely studied.

2 The research we review is primarily from U.S. and Western European scholars. However, stereotypes about gender/sex and competitiveness vary across culture (e.g., see Shan et al., 2019). For a more comprehensive review, see Bowles et al. (2022, 2024) or the Program on Negotiation at Harvard Law School webinar: https://www.pon.harvard.edu/events/pon-live-when-gender/sex-matters-in-negotiation/

REFERENCES

Amanatullah, E. T., & Morris, M. W. (2010). Negotiating gender/sex roles: Gender/sex differences in assertive negotiating are mediated by women's fear of backlash and attenuated when negotiating on behalf of others. *Journal of Personality and Social Psychology*, *98*(2), 256–267. https://doi.org/10.1037/a0017094

Amanatullah, E. T., & Tinsley, C. H. (2013). Punishing female negotiators for asserting too much . . . or not enough: Exploring why advocacy moderates backlash against assertive female negotiators. *Organizational Behavior & Human Decision Processes*, *120*(1), 110–122. bth. https://doi.org/10.1016/j.obhdp.2012.03.006

Ames, D. R., & Flynn, F. J. (2007). What breaks a leader: The curvilinear relation between assertiveness and leadership. *Journal of Personality and Social Psychology*, *92*(2), 307–324. https://doi.org/10.1037/0022-3514.92.2.307

Artz, B., Goodall, A. H., & Oswald, A. J. (2018). Do women ask? *Industrial Relations*, *57*(4), 611–636. https://doi.org/10.1111/irel.12214

Babcock, L., & Laschever, S. (2003). *Women don't ask: Negotiation and the gender/sex divide*. Princeton University Press.

Babcock, L., Recalde, M. P., & Vesterlund, L. (2018). *Why women volunteer for tasks that don't lead to promotions*, 5.

Babcock, L., Recalde, M. P., Vesterlund, L., & Weingart, L. (2017). Gender/sex differences in accepting and receiving requests for tasks with low promotability. *The American Economic Review*, *107*(3), 714–747.

Bear, J. (2011). "Passing the buck": Incongruence between gender/sex role and topic leads to avoidance of negotiation. *Negotiation and Conflict Management Research*, *4*(1), 47–72.

Bear, J., & Babcock, L. (2012). Negotiation topic as a moderator of gender/sex differences in negotiation. *Psychological Science*, *23*(7), 743–744. https://doi.org/10.1177/0956797612442393

Belliveau, M. A. (2005). Blind ambition? The effects of social networks and institutional sex composition on the job search outcomes of elite coeducational and women's college graduates. *Organization Science*, *16*(2), 134–150. https://doi.org/10.1287/orsc.1050.0119

Berdahl, J. L., & Moon, S. H. (2013). Workplace mistreatment of middle class workers based on sex, parenthood, and caregiving. *Journal of Social Issues*, *69*(2), 341–366. https://doi.org/10.1111/josi.12018

Bohnet, I., & Chilazi, S. (2025). *Make work fair: Data-driven design for real results*. Harper Business, an imprint of HarperCollins Publishers.

Bohnet, I., van Geen, A., & Bazerman, M. (2016). When performance trumps gender/sex bias: Joint vs. separate evaluation. *Management Science*, *62*(5), 1225–1234. https://doi.org/10.1287/mnsc.2015.2186

Bowles, H. R. (2013). Psychological perspectives on gender/sex in negotiation. In M. K. Ryan & N. R. Branscombe (Eds.), *The Sage handbook of gender/sex and psychology* (pp. 465–483). SAGE Publications. https://doi.org/10.4135/9781446269930.n28

Bowles, H. R., & Babcock, L. (2013). How can women escape the compensation negotiation dilemma? Relational accounts are one answer. *Psychology of Women Quarterly*, *37*(1), 80–96. https://doi.org/10.1177/0361684312455524

Bowles, H. R., Babcock, L., & McGinn, K. L. (2005). Constraints and triggers: Situational mechanics of gender/sex in negotiation. *Journal of Personality & Social Psychology*, *89*, 951–965.

Bowles, H. R., & Flynn, F. (2010). Gender/sex and persistence in negotiation: A dyadic perspective. *Academy of Management Journal*, *53*, 769–787.

Bowles, H. R., Mazei, J., & Liu, H. H. (2024). "When" versus "whether" gender/sex/sex differences: Insights from psychological research on negotiation, risk-taking, and leadership. *Perspectives on Psychological Science*, 17456916241231584. https://doi.org/10.1177/17456916241231584

Bowles, H. R., & Thomason, B. (2015). Using research to generate advice for women: Examples from negotiation research. In I. M. Welpe, P. Brosi, L. Ritzenhöfer, & T. Schwarzmüller (Eds.), *Auswahl von Männern und Frauen als Führungskräfte* (pp. 357–366). Springer Fachmedien Wiesbaden. https://doi.org/10.1007/978-3-658-09469-0_31

Bowles, H. R., Thomason, B., & Bear, J. B. (2019). Reconceptualizing what and how women negotiate for career advancement. *Academy of Management Journal*, *62*(6), 1645–1671. psyh. https://doi.org/10.5465/amj.2017.1497

Bowles, H. R., Thomason, B., & Macias-Alonso, I. (2022). When gender/sex matters in organizational negotiations. *Annual Review of Organizational Psychology and Organizational Behavior*, *9*(1), 199–223. https://doi.org/10.1146/annurev-orgpsych-012420-055523

Bowles, H. R., & Williams, Z. (2022, May 6). Briefing sheet: Be SURE you are prepared to negotiate WELL (Case #2230.4). *Harvard Kennedy School*. https://case.hks.harvard.edu/briefing-sheet-be-sure-you-are-prepared-to-negotiate-well/

Burt, R. S., Kilduff, M., & Tasselli, S. (2013). Social network analysis: Foundations and frontiers on advantage. *Annual Review of Psychology*, *64*(1), 527–547. https://doi.org/10.1146/annurev-psych-113011-143828

Currarini, S., Jackson, M. O., & Pin, P. (2009). An economic model of friendship: Homophily, minorities, and segregation. *Econometrica*, *77*(4), 1003–1045.

Dannals, J. E., Zlatev, J. J., Halevy, N., & Neale, M. A. (2021). The dynamics of gender/sex and alternatives in negotiation. *Journal of Applied Psychology*, *106*(11), 1655–1672. bth. https://doi.org/10.1037/apl0000867

Deaux, K., & LaFrance, M. (1998). Gender. In D. T. Gilbert, S. T. Fiske, & G. Lindzey (Eds.), *The handbook of social psychology* (4th ed., pp. 788–827). McGraw-Hill.

Desai, S. D., & Gunia, B. C. (2023). The interplay of gender/sex and perceived sexual orientation at the bargaining table: A social dominance and intersectionalist perspective. *Organizational Behavior and Human Decision Processes*, *179*, 104279.

Doğan, P. (2020). Gender/sex differences in volunteer's dilemma: Evidence from teamwork among graduate students. *Journal of Behavioral and Experimental Economics*, *84*, 101488. https://doi.org/10.1016/j.socec.2019.101488

Eagly, A. H., Nater, C., Miller, D. I., Kaufmann, M., & Sczesny, S. (2020). Gender/sex stereotypes have changed: A cross-temporal meta-analysis of U.S. public opinion polls from 1946 to 2018. *American Psychologist*, *75*(3), 301–315. https://doi.org/10.1037/amp0000494

Eagly, A. H., & Steffen, V. J. (1984). Gender/sex stereotypes stem from the distribution of women and men into social roles. *Journal of Personality and Social Psychology*, *46*, 735–754.

Exley, C. L., Niederle, M., & Vesterlund, L. (2019). Knowing when to ask: The cost of leaning in. *Journal of Political Economy*, *128*(3), 816–854. https://doi.org/10.1086/704616

Festinger, L. (1954). A theory of social comparison processes. *Human Relations*, *7*(2), 117–140. https://doi.org/10.1177/001872675400700202

Fisher, R., & Ury, W. (1981). *Getting to yes: Negotiating agreements without giving in*. Houghton-Mifflin.

Galinsky, A. D., Mussweiler, T., & Medvec, V. H. (2002). Disconnecting outcomes and evaluations: The role of negotiator focus. *Journal of Personality and Social Psychology*, *83*(5), 1131–1140. https://doi.org/10.1037/0022-3514.83.5.1131

Gavin, M. (2019, March 5). 3 ways to create value in a negotiation. *Harvard Business School Online*. Retrieved from https://online.hbs.edu/blog/post/negotiation-tactics-how-to-add-value

Gompers, P. A., Mukharlyamov, V., Weisburst, E., & Xuan, Y. (2021). Gender/sex gaps in venture capital performance. *Journal of Financial and Quantitative Analysis*, 1–29. https://doi.org/10.1017/S0022109020000988

Groysberg, B. (2010). *Chasing stars: The myth of talent and the portability of performance*. Princeton University Press. https://doi.org/10.1515/9781400834389

Harinck, F., De Dreu, C. K. W., & Van Vianen, A. E. M. (2000). The impact of conflict issues on fixed-pie perceptions, problem solving, and integrative outcomes in negotiation. *Organizational Behavior and Human Decision Processes*, *81*(2), 329–358. https://doi.org/10.1006/obhd.1999.2873

Hernandez, M., Avery, D. R., Volpone, S. D., & Kaiser, C. R. (2019). Bargaining while Black: The role of race in salary negotiations. *Journal of Applied Psychology*, *104*(4), 581–592. pdh. https://doi.org/10.1037/apl0000363

Hirt, E. R., & Markman, K. D. (1995). Multiple explanation: A consider-an-alternative strategy for debiasing judgments. *Journal of Personality and Social Psychology*, *69*(6), 1069–1086. https://doi.org/10.1037/0022-3514.69.6.1069

Ibarra, H. (1992). Homophily and differential returns: Sex differences in network structure and access in an advertising firm. *Administrative Science Quarterly*, *37*(3), 422–447. https://doi.org/10.2307/2393451

Ibarra, H. (1993). Personal networks of women and minorities in management: A conceptual framework. *The Academy of Management Review*, *18*(1), 56–87.

Ibarra, H. (1997). Paving an alternative route: Gender/sex differences in managerial networks. *Social Psychology Quarterly*, *60*(1), 91–102. https://doi.org/10.2307/2787014

Johns, M., Schmader, T., & Martens, A. (2005). Knowing is half the battle: Teaching stereotype threat as a means of improving women's math performance. *Psychological Science*, *16*(3), 175–179. https://doi.org/10.1111/j.0956-7976.2005.00799.x

Kelly, E. L., Ammons, S. K., Chermack, K., & Moen, P. (2010). Gender/sexed challenge, gender/sexed response: Confronting the ideal worker norm in a white-collar organization. *Gender & Society*, *24*(3), 281–303. https://doi.org/10.1177/0891243210372073

Kray, L. J., Galinsky, A. D., & Thompson, L. (2002). Reversing the gender/sex gap in negotiations: An exploration of stereotype regeneration. *Organizational Behavior & Human Decision Processes*, *87*(2), 386. https://doi.org/10.1006/obhd.2001.2979

Kray, L. J., & Gelfand, M. J. (2009). Relief versus regret: The effect of gender/sex and negotiating norm ambiguity on reactions to having one's first offer accepted. *Social Cognition*, *27*(3), 418–436. https://doi.org/10.1521/soco.2009.27.3.418

Kray, L. J., & Kennedy, J. A. (2017). Changing the narrative: Women as negotiators—and leaders. *California Management Review*, *60*(1), 70–87. https://doi.org/10.1177/0008125617727744

Kray, L. J., Kennedy, J., & Lee, M. (2023). Now, women do ask: A call to update beliefs about the gender/sex pay gap. *Academy of Management Discoveries*. https://doi.org/10.5465/amd.2022.0021

Kray, L. J., & Thompson, L. (2004). Gender/sex stereotypes and negotiation performance: An examination of theory and research. *Research in Organizational Behavior*, *26*, 103–182. https://doi.org/10.1016/S0191-3085(04)26004-X

Kray, L. J., Thompson, L., & Galinsky, A. (2001). Battle of the sexes: Gender/sex stereotype confirmation and reactance in negotiations. *Journal of Personality & Social Psychology*, *80*(6), 942–958. https://psycnet.apa.org/doi/10.1037/0022-3514.80.6.942

Kugler, K. G., Reif, J. A. M., Kaschner, T., & Brodbeck, F. C. (2018). Gender/sex differences in the initiation of negotiations: A meta-analysis. *Psychological Bulletin*, *144*(2), 198–222. https://doi.org/10.1037/bul0000135

Lax, D. A., & Sebenius, J. K. (2006). *3-D negotiation: Powerful tools to change the game in your most important deals*. Harvard Business Press.

Leibbrandt, A., & List, J. A. (2015). Do women avoid salary negotiations? Evidence from a large-scale natural field experiment. *Management Science*, *61*(9), 2016–2024. https://doi.org/10.1287/mnsc.2014.1994

Major, B., & Testa, M. (1989). Social comparison processes and judgments of entitlement and satisfaction. *Journal of Experimental Social Psychology*, *25*(2), 101–120. https://doi.org/10.1016/0022-1031(89)90007-3

Major, B., Vanderslice, V., & McFarlin, D. B. (1984). Effects of pay expected on pay received: The confirmatory nature of initial expectations. *Journal of Applied Social Psychology*, *14*(5), 399–412. https://doi.org/10.1111/j.1559-1816.1984.tb02247.x

Mazei, J., Hüffmeier, J., Freund, P. A., Stuhlmacher, A. F., Bilke, L., & Hertel, G. (2015). A meta-analysis on gender/sex differences in negotiation outcomes and their moderators. *Psychological Bulletin*, *141*(1), 85–104. https://doi.org/10.1037/a0038184

McPherson, M., Smith-Lovin, L., & Cook, J. M. (2001). Birds of a feather: Homophily in social networks. *Annual Review of Sociology*, *27*(1), 415–444. https://doi.org/10.1146/annurev.soc.27.1.415

Nadler, J., Thompson, L., & Boven, L. V. (2003). Learning negotiation skills: Four models of knowledge creation and transfer. *Management Science*, *49*(4), 529–540. https://doi.org/10.1287/mnsc.49.4.529.14431

Pfau-Effinger, B. (2004). Socio-historical paths of the male breadwinner model—an explanation of cross-national differences1. *The British Journal of Sociology*, *55*(3), 377–399. https://doi.org/10.1111/j.1468-4446.2004.00025.x

Raiffa, H. (1982). *The art and science of negotiation*. Harvard University Press.

Reif, J. A. M., & Brodbeck, F. C. (2017). When do people initiate a negotiation? The role of discrepancy, satisfaction, and ability beliefs. *Negotiation and Conflict Management Research*, *10*(1), 46–66. https://doi.org/10.1111/ncmr.12089

Reif, J. A. M., Kunz, F. A., Kugler, K. G., & Brodbeck, F. C. (2019). Negotiation contexts: How and why they shape women's and men's decision to negotiate. *Negotiation and Conflict Management Research*, *12*(4), 322–342. https://doi.org/10.1111/ncmr.12153

Roth, L. M. (2009). Leveling the playing field: Negotiating opportunities and recognition in gender/sexed jobs. *Negotiation & Conflict Management Research*, *2*(1), 17–30. https://doi.org/10.1111/j.1750-4716.2008.00025.x

Rousseau, D. M. (2005). *I-deals: Idiosyncratic deals employees bargain for themselves*. Routledge.

Rudman, L. A., & Mescher, K. (2013). Penalizing men who request a family leave: Is flexibility stigma a femininity stigma? *Journal of Social Issues*, *69*(2), 322–340. https://doi.org/10.1111/josi.12017

Schweinsberg, M., Thau, S., & Pillutla, M. M. (2022). Negotiation impasses: Types, causes, and resolutions. *Journal of Management*, *48*(1), 49–76. https://doi.org/10.1177/01492063211021657

Shan, W., Keller, J., & Joseph, D. (2019). Are men better negotiators everywhere? A meta-analysis of how gender/sex differences in negotiation performance vary across cultures. *Journal of Organizational Behavior*, *40*(6), 651–675. https://doi.org/10.1002/job.2357

Shonk, K. (2025, May 12). Career negotiations and the pay gap. *Harvard Law School*. Retrieved from https://www.pon.harvard.edu/daily/salary-negotiations/ask-a-negotiation-expert-to-narrow-the-wage-gap-take-a-wider-view-nb/

Spector, B. (2006). Resiliency in negotiation: Bouncing back from impasse. *International Negotiation*, *11*(2), 273–286. https://doi.org/10.1163/157180606778968317

Steele, C. M. (1997). A threat in the air: How stereotypes shape intellectual identity and performance. *American Psychologist*, *52*, 613–629. https://doi.org/10.1037/0003-066x.52.6.613

Sturm, S. (2009). Negotiating workplace equality: A systemic approach. *Negotiation and Conflict Management Research*, *2*, 92–106. https://doi.org/10.1111/j.1750-4716.2008.00030.x

Thompson, L. L. (2005). *The mind and heart of the negotiator* (3rd ed.). Prentice Hall.

Vandello, J. A., Hettinger, V. E., Bosson, J. K., & Siddiqi, J. (2013). When equal isn't really equal: The masculine dilemma of seeking work flexibility. *Journal of Social Issues*, *69*(2), 303–321. https://doi.org/10.1111/josi.12016

Whillans, A. V., Yoon, J., Turek, A., & Donnelly, G. E. (2021). Extension request avoidance predicts greater time stress among women. *Proceedings of the National Academy of Sciences*, *118*(45), e2105622118. https://doi.org/10.1073/pnas.2105622118

Wood, J. V. (1989). Theory and research concerning social comparisons of personal attributes. *Psychological Bulletin*, *106*(2), 231–248. https://doi.org/10.1037/0033-2909.106.2.231

Zetik, D. C., & Stuhlmacher, A. F. (2002a). Goal setting and negotiation performance: A meta-analysis. *Group Processes & Intergroup Relations*, *5*(1), 35–52. https://doi.org/10.1177/1368430202005001537

Zetik, D. C., & Stuhlmacher, A. F. (2002b). Goal setting and negotiation performance: A meta-analysis. *Group Processes & Intergroup Relations*, *5*(1), 35–52. https://doi.org/10.1177/1368430202005001537

CHAPTER 9

Suited for Success?

Women, Networking, and Workplace Success

Brian Rubineau, Richard Tan, and Zhihe Allan Ren

Who succeeds in your organization? While every organization is unique, the processes for organizational success share many commonalities. In very basic terms, to succeed in an organization, one must first gain access to that organization through their hiring process. Once in, one must then achieve enough success to advance within the organization without (or before) exiting the organization. Alliteratively, the process is as follows: access, achieve and advance, and avoid attrition. For each of these three components, networks and networking play very consequential roles. And these networking dynamics tend to be highly gendered in their operation and effects. This chapter examines the evidence and areas of debate for gendered networking processes and effects at each of these three components of organizational success.

The American legal drama TV series, *Suits* (Korsh, 2011–2019), depicting the social dynamics of a high-end New York City law firm, provides some illustrative examples of gendered networking for each of the three components. For the purposes of the show and this chapter, law firm careers tend to follow an up-or-out progress through the stages of Associate (with the sub-stages of Junior Associate, Mid-level Associate, and Senior Associate) to Partner (Gilson & Mnookin, 1989). Partners can also become named Partners, where their name is added to the firm's name. Being a named partner indicates greater prestige and status but is not an up-or-out transition (think Full Professor vs. Full Professor with a named Chair).

ACCESSING JOBS AND ORGANIZATIONS

Changes in who is a named partner in a law firm necessarily changes the name of the firm. In Season 8 of *Suits*, the law firm Zane Specter Litt added two new named

DOI: 10.4324/9781003488590-9

partners to become Zane Specter Litt Wheeler Williams. Of these two names, Alex Williams was brought to the firm as an external hire. How did Alex Williams come to join the firm as a named partner, and why Alex versus someone else?

Alex Williams had earned a reputation as a top lawyer at a competing firm, but Alex was not the only lawyer to whom that description applied. What differentiated Alex was that he was a longtime friend of one of the three named partners of Zane Specter Litt—Harvey Specter. In addition to Alex and Harvey being friends, Harvey owed Alex a favor. Alex's skills and expertise as a lawyer were absolutely necessary for the other named partners to approve his hire, but the qualifications alone were not sufficient. The relationship between Harvey and Alex is what identified and distinguished Alex for the hire. Relationships are critical for accessing jobs in the real world as well.

Outside this fictional setting, personal contacts are still the dominant form of job matching in the labor market (Topa, 2011). Employee referrals are one of the most common forms of recruitment for employers to find applicants (Burks et al., 2015), and personal contacts tend to be the most common way that job seekers identify employers (Gully et al., 2013). Contact networks tend to be highly gender segregated (Brashears, 2008; McPherson et al., 2001; Lawrence & Shah, 2020). This segregation of contact networks means that referrers tend to refer applicants who are socio-demographically similar to themselves, including similar gender categories (Beaman et al., 2018; Fernandez & Sosa, 2005).

Accessing jobs via networks (also known as referring or word-of-mouth recruitment) has long been viewed as a likely contributor to the gender segregation of jobs (Braddock & McPartland, 1987; Drentea, 1998; Reskin, 1993). Scholars have shown that referring can also promote diversity (Rubineau & Fernandez, 2013, 2015). The basic insight is that referring is a kind of reproduction process in which organizational members generate new hires. People tend to refer those who are like themselves in terms of gender as well as other socio-demographic characteristics (Brown et al., 2016; Burks et al., 2015; Hensvik & Skans, 2016). Perhaps surprisingly, this similarity effect is not by itself segregating. Segregating occurs when there are differences in groups in either the number of new hires generated or the extent to which new hires are similar to their referrers (Rubineau & Fernandez, 2015). The group that refers more will increase their representation over time in their organization. Similarly, the group that refers a higher proportion of socially similar new hires will increase their representation over time in their organization. The importance of these differences in referring rates and referring homophily has been leveraged as a tool for organizations' diversity goals.

Many organizations have started using referral programs and bonuses as tools to promote diversity (Kaul, 2021; Rosales et al., 2023). Commonly, these referral bonus programs provide financial incentives for referring hired applicants who help the organization achieve its diversity goals. Programs also promote referring by current employees who are members of underrepresented groups. Research suggests that having underrepresented groups refer more often yields greater diversity gains for the organization than having overrepresented referrers to refer underrepresented applicants (Fernandez & Rubineau, 2019).

There are two known downsides to promoting diversity via referral programs. First, its diversity-promoting effects appear to be most concentrated at the lowest levels of organizations and least effective at the highest echelons. These lopsided effects arise because people tend to refer for openings at their level or lower in their companies–rarely for jobs at higher levels than themselves (Brown et al., 2016; Leicht & Marx, 1997). So, promoting gender diversity via referring results in increases in overall gender diversity, but the glass-ceiling distribution pattern for women in firms is preserved (Fernandez & Rubineau, 2019).

The second downside is applicant quality. Much evidence shows that although employees respond to referral bonuses by referring more job candidates (Friebel et al., 2023; Obukhova & Rubineau, 2022; Pieper et al., 2018; Van Hoye, 2013), many candidates generated by referral bonuses tend to be of lower quality overall (Bond et al., 2018). Obviously, paying more for worse outcomes runs counter to organizational goals. Fortunately, the financial incentive of a referral bonus is not the only way to increase referring behavior. A randomized field experiment in a large organization demonstrated that emails to employees requesting candidate referrals for the firm's job openings also significantly increased referring behavior (Rubineau et al., 2021). So, another effective way of influencing referring behavior is simply to ask employees to refer. This study could not statistically evaluate the quality of the additional job candidates generated by this intervention. However, the study did note that more referral hires came from the treatment group than from the equal-in-size control group. This result strongly suggests that the additional job candidates generated by the email requests were not of lower quality.

Based upon this collection of evidence, it is clear that referral processes are a viable method for promoting women's access to jobs and organizations. Organizations benefit more by providing simple email requests to their current women employees than by changing referral bonus amounts. Efforts to promote gender diversity via referral processes will likely have only lopsided benefits though in which women's representation in firms will increase most at lower levels and increase least at higher levels—where a greater proportion of men exists worldwide (UN Women, 2021). Once women overcome these and other hurdles to access jobs, how do they achieve and advance?

ACHIEVING AND ADVANCING IN ORGANIZATIONS

In the example from *Suits*, Harvey Specter brought in Alex Williams, and the law firm's name changed from Zane Specter Litt to Zane Specter Litt Wheeler Williams. In this change, two names were added. What about Wheeler? Samantha Wheeler was internally promoted to become a named partner. She is an excellent example of organizational achievement and advancement. Her success illustrates two established organizational network processes that operate differently for men and women: workplace support and mentorship.

Workplace Support: Divided or Unified?

The premise of organizations is that we can get more done when working together than separately. Our success in organizations is rarely purely our own. We work with and rely upon others within and outside our organizations to succeed. These support ties tend to be structured differently for men and women in ways that often disadvantage women.

In a classic study, Ibarra (1992) examined two broad sets of support ties in organizations: instrumental support and social support. Instrumental support involves help and advice about getting work done. Social support involves friendship and emotional support within the workplace and beyond. Both forms of support are helpful. Ibarra found that, for men, both sets of support ties predominately stemmed from other men. This finding was not a surprise. In network studies, homophily—the tendency for people's contacts to resemble them on a range of socio-demographic and other factors—is one of the strongest and most consistent findings in social science (McPherson et al., 2001). The surprise was the finding for women. While women's social support ties exhibited the familiar pattern of homophily (i.e., more likely to be other women), the same was not the case for women's instrumental support ties. These were dominated by men. Ibarra explained this finding such that, in most firms, the higher one goes up the authority pyramid, the higher the percentage of men in those positions. This pattern remains true today, more than three decades after Ibarra's work (UN Women, 2021). Instrumental support is usually provided by a peer or someone more senior—rarely someone more junior—than oneself. Therefore, instrumental support groups tend to be dominated by men.

This gendered pattern of workplace support ties has been found in many other network studies decades since Ibarra's study (Allemand et al., 2022; Greguletz et al., 2019; McGuire, 2012; Mickey, 2022). Is it anything more than a quirk or curiosity? How does this give rise to workplace inequality? One simple answer comes from the fact that building and maintaining network ties requires time and energy. This fact, along with the gendered patterns of workplace support ties, puts women at a disadvantage in the workplace. Men's networks of instrumental and social support ties can have more overlap. That is, they can be made up of more of the same people. Women's workplace networks are necessarily more divided. The people who make up men's instrumental support ties can also be their social support ties and vice versa. Investments of time and energy to maintain one network can serve double duty in maintaining the other network as well. Women are less likely to be able to benefit from such overlaps. Women are more likely to need to maintain two distinct networks—instrumental and social support—that are much less likely to have overlapping members. Because of this lower overlap, women's time and energy investments in one network have opportunity costs in terms of neglecting the other network. Men with more overlapping networks do not incur this opportunity cost. This divided time and energy aspect of network maintenance for women means that women's workplace support in both realms tends to be weaker and less robustly useful than men's workplace support. Workplace network support is a realm in which women work even harder than men to get a lower return.

Our example from *Suits* provides a useful illustration of this issue. When considering Alex Williams and Samantha Wheeler, both had strongly supportive senior colleagues. Alex's main source of support was Harvey Specter—both a friend (and poker buddy) and a source of major instrumental support in joining the firm. Samantha's main source of support was Robert Zane—a strong source of instrumental support, but not really a friend or a primary part of Samantha's social support network. Although both characters were promoted to named partner roles, Samantha needed to cultivate social support from those who were not also a source of instrumental support, while Alex could receive both forms of support from Harvey.

Mentors, Sponsors, and Borrowed Social Capital

In addition to the generalized support workers need from their networks, there are often important dyadic workplace relationships in the form of mentors and sponsors that influence worker success (Ayyala et al., 2019; Kammeyer-Mueller & Judge, 2008; Wayne et al., 1999). Here again, gender plays a role.

Mentors are ties who provide guidance, advice, and related support directly to a mentee (Eby et al., 2007). Sponsors are ties who provide advocacy, reputation-building, opportunity identification, and navigation support on behalf of a sponsee (Ayyala et al., 2019). Mentors can be sponsors and vice versa, but they do not always play both roles, and both are important for organizational success. Because of the divided nature of women's workplace networks, they may have more difficulty securing mentors and sponsors than men. These are not the only differences. Some of these differences come when considering the mentors and sponsors themselves.

In a stream of research examining gender and mentoring, Michelle Duguid et al. found that successful women tend to try to avoid mentoring junior women (Duguid, 2011; Duguid et al., 2012). The explanation is that because they are still a rarity among corporate leaders, successful women are in more precarious positions than their male counterparts. The success of a mentor's mentees can reflect the mentor. Investing in mentoring women is riskier for mentors in general, with risks more keenly felt by women mentors. For their own career survival, senior women may be less willing to mentor junior women. While senior men can be helpful mentors for junior women and men alike, there are a range of topics regarding distinctive challenges faced by women about which these men mentors have less experience and knowledge. This imbalance in mentor availability and relevant knowledge is another network-based source of workplace disadvantage for women.

Several studies of workplace sponsors—defined as referrers for referral applicants—found significant gender differences in the effectiveness of sponsors. A study of former judicial clerks being referred by their sponsor judges found men sponsors to be more effective than women sponsors overall (Campbell et al., 2023).

In a study of referral applicant success in a large pharmaceutical firm, the ability of men referrers to get their referral applicants hired was independent of their own individual workplace social capital. However, the ability of women referrers to get their referral applicants hired was directly associated with their own workplace social capital (Rubineau et al., 2019). To be effective sponsors, women need additional capital that sponsoring men do not. This difference also puts the sponsees of women at a disadvantage (Rubineau & Fernandez, 2013, 2015). This sponsorship difference is another dimension of network-based disadvantage for women that is distinct from organizational access dynamics described earlier.

The gendered association between a sponsor's social capital and their sponsee's success points to another gendered network phenomenon: secondhand, or borrowed, social capital. The idea that we can acquire social capital via key contacts or collaborators is well-founded (Hasan & Bagde, 2015; Moore, 2001). Burt (1998) suggested that organizational outsiders like women may need to borrow the workplace social capital of their sponsors and mentors. Several scholars have examined whether the concept of borrowed social capital affects workplace success, with some inconsistent results (Clement et al., 2018; Rhee & Leonardi, 2024).

A detailed examination of gender differences in career success based on borrowed social capital among almost 64,000 debut movie directors found two notable differences (Nguyen, 2024). First, women benefited more from borrowed social capital early in their careers, but those benefits disappeared later in their careers. In contrast, men benefited from borrowed social capital throughout their entire careers. Second, similar to Ibarra's (1992) finding, men's own social capital and borrowed social capital could serve as substitutes for each other, but women did not have this substitution option. That is, for men, the effects of a deficit in either their own social capital or their borrowed social capital could be mitigated through the benefits of the other. In this way, men had two similarly effective network paths to career advancement and success: their own social capital, and the social capital they borrowed from key contacts and collaborators. For women, their own social capital and their borrowed social capital provided distinct benefits that did not serve as substitutes for each other. Women, therefore, must cultivate both their own social capital and borrowed social capital for their career advancement and success, but the benefits are less enduring than those for men.

Success Opportunities for Women via Networks: Mobility

Most research paints a bleak image for women's workplace success via networks. Women appear to be disadvantaged everywhere via network processes at work. But there is one place where women appear to have an advantage: within-firm mobility. Research shows that women are more likely than men to maintain their network ties after experiencing job changes that move them to new work units within the same organization. The preservation of these ties is associated with greater job performance outcomes for mobile women compared to mobile men (Zhang et al., 2024).

New Research: Networks, Gender, and Workplace Climate

While previous sections of this chapter have focused on gender differences in network effects on workplace and career advancement, new research indicates that networks and gender influence workgroup climate in ways that affect workgroup success. Workgroup climate relates to workers' sense of belonging, psychological safety, and a range of other factors associated with workgroup success (Berdahl et al., 2018; Duhigg, 2016; Edmondson, 2018; Nishii, 2013; Sanner & Bunderson, 2015; Woolley et al., 2010).

In a study comparing network-related predictors of success-enhancing workplace climates in a large financial organization, gender homophily in workplace communication networks negatively predicted workplace climate (Rubineau, 2023). Across hundreds of workgroups, the more that coworkers' gender categories influenced workplace communications, the worse the climate of the workgroup. Upon reflection, this finding is not entirely surprising. Consider worker complaints about a workplace that feels too "clique-ish," where workers communicate within segregated groups. Such communication patterns can hinder success, and the effects are worse if those segregated groups are simultaneously highly gender segregated. In another study, the segregation of communication networks across multiple dimensions, including gender, was associated with organizational conflict (Kalantari, 2021). Ideally, gender should play very little role in workplace communication decisions. It makes sense that workgroups with communication patterns divided by gender would be less successful. The surprise from this study was that this negative effect of gender homophily was the single strongest network predictor of workgroup climate. Based on this research, one of the most effective network interventions to improve a workgroup's climate is to promote communication across gender categories.

AVOIDING ATTRITION

What about organizational exit? Networks are known to influence departures from organizations in at least two ways: the first is directly via exit chains and the second is indirectly via the absence of success. Exit chains, also called turnover contagion or group turnover, refer to a phenomenon in which one employee with a network tie with another employee who leaves the firm also becomes more likely to leave the firm (Feng et al., 2024; Porter & Rigby, 2021; Sgourev, 2011). Exit chains are significant and consequential across a range of relationship types, including friendship, referrer–referree, work reliance, and more (Felps et al., 2009; Fernandez et al., 2000; Krackhardt & Porter, 1985, 1986). This research shows that networks play an important role in firm exit. The few studies that tested gender differences reported no significant differences in these workplace network exit chains. Notably, gender differences in the size and structure of workplace networks can spur gender differences in exit likelihoods via these exit chains even when exit chain effects are the same for men and women.

To date, the key pathway for gender differences in network influences on firm exit is via gendered differences in workplace success. The absence of organizational and career success—being passed over for promotion, lack of recognition at work, and the like—are strong predictors of voluntary exit (Klotz et al., 2021; Rubenstein et al., 2018). Returning to our fictional example from *Suits*, the simultaneous addition of both Wheeler and Williams as named partners was necessary. Samantha Wheeler had made it clear that her performance merited her promotion to a named partner and that if that didn't happen, she would leave the firm. The many ways networks are associated with gender differences in workplace success also give rise to gender differences in workplace exit. Nguyen (2024) examined exits from the movie industry by estimating how social capital and borrowed social capital were associated with whether a director made another movie after their debut. In that analysis, success and exit were two sides of the same coin. Similarly, efforts to reduce gender differences in network support and mentoring often have the goal and effect of reducing gender differences in organizational and career attrition (Buckles, 2019; Fried et al., 1996).

CHAPTER SUMMARY

Network contacts, network structure, and networking processes influence workplace outcomes for all workers. These influences are often gendered, working differently for women and men. In most cases, these differences disadvantage women in accessing, achieving and advancing, and avoiding attrition in their workplaces. In at least one case—within-firm mobility—women might be advantaged by network differences. Understanding these differences is critical for individuals, organizations, and policymakers to promote women's workplace success and to remove barriers that would otherwise remain unseen.

DISCUSSION QUESTIONS

1. In accessing workplaces, how do networking processes give rise to a disadvantage for women? Do women and men appear to engage in different networking behaviors at this stage, or is the disadvantage a result of other factors?
2. Men and women alike use networking to access both social and instrumental support in the workplace, but men's networking efforts tend to return greater value and benefits than women's networking investments; why?
3. Both men and women benefit from their own workplace social capital and second-hand or borrowed social capital, but men are described as having an advantage relative to women from these two types of social capital. What explains men's advantage and women's disadvantage?
4. How does networking help explain why women appear to benefit from within-organization workplace mobility more than men?
5. What networking measure is significantly associated with workplace climate?
6. If exit chains operate the same for men and women in the workplace, how can they give rise to gender differences in workplace exit?

REFERENCES

Allemand, I., Bédard, J., Brullebaut, B., & Deschênes, J. (2022). Role of old boys' networks and regulatory approaches in selection processes for female directors. *British Journal of Management*, *33*(2), 784–805.

Ayyala, M. S., Skarupski, K., Bodurtha, J. N., González-Fernández, M., Ishii, L. E., Fivush, B., & Levine, R. B. (2019). Mentorship is not enough: Exploring sponsorship and its role in career advancement in academic medicine. *Academic Medicine*, *94*(1), 94–100.

Beaman, L., Keleher, N., & Magruder, J. (2018). Do job networks disadvantage women? Evidence from a recruitment experiment in Malawi. *Journal of Labor Economics*, *36*(1), 121–157.

Berdahl, J. L., Cooper, M., Glick, P., Livingston, R. W., & Williams, J. C. (2018). Work as a masculinity contest. *Journal of Social Issues*, *74*(3), 422–448.

Bond, B. M., Labuzova, T., & Fernandez, R. M. (2018). At the expense of quality. *Sociological Science*, 380–401.

Braddock, J. H., & McPartland, J. M. (1987). How minorities continue to be excluded from equal employment opportunities: Research on labor market and institutional barriers. *Journal of Social Issues*, *43*(1), 5–39.

Brashears, M. E. (2008). Gender and homophily: Differences in male and female association in Blau space. *Social Science Research*, *37*(2), 400–415.

Brown, M., Setren, E., & Topa, G. (2016). Do informal referrals lead to better matches? Evidence from a firm's employee referral system. *Journal of Labor Economics*, *34*(1), 161–209.

Buckles, K. (2019). Fixing the leaky pipeline: Strategies for making economics work for women at every stage. *Journal of Economic Perspectives*, *33*(1), 43–60.

Burks, S. V., Cowgill, B., Hoffman, M., & Housman, M. (2015). The value of hiring through employee referrals. *The Quarterly Journal of Economics*, *130*(2), 805–839.

Burt, R. S. (1998). The gender of social capital. *Rationality and Society*, *10*(1), 5–46.

Campbell, E. L., Aven, B., & Chow, R. M. (2023). From exception to exceptional: How gender and tenure impact sponsor effectiveness. *Academy of Management Discoveries*, *9*(1), 17–45.

Clement, J., Shipilov, A., & Galunic, C. (2018). Brokerage as a public good: The externalities of network hubs for different formal roles in creative organizations. *Administrative Science Quarterly*, *63*(2), 251–286.

Drentea, P. (1998). Consequences of women's formal and informal job search methods for employment in female-dominated jobs. *Gender & Society*, *12*(3), 321–338.

Duguid, M. (2011). Female tokens in high-prestige work groups: Catalysts or inhibitors of group diversification? *Organizational Behavior and Human Decision Processes*, *116*(1), 104–115.

Duguid, M., Lewin Loyd, D., & Tolbert, P. S. (2012). The impact of categorical status, numeric representation, and work group prestige on preference for demographically similar others: A value threat approach. *Organization Science*, *23*(2), 386–401.

Duhigg, C. (2016, February 25). What Google learned from its quest to build the perfect team. *The New York Times Magazine*, 26. https://www.nytimes.com/2016/02/28/magazine/what-google-learned-from-its-quest-to-build-the-perfect-team.html

Eby, L. T., Rhodes, J. E., & Allen, T. D. (2007). Definition and evolution of mentoring. In T. D. Allen & L. T. Eby (Eds.), *The Blackwell handbook of mentoring: A multiple perspectives approach* (pp. 7–20). Wiley.

Edmondson, A. C. (2018). *The fearless organization: Creating psychological safety in the workplace for learning, innovation, and growth*. John Wiley & Sons.

Felps, W., Mitchell, T. R., Hekman, D. R., Lee, T. W., Holtom, B. C., & Harman, W. S. (2009). Turnover contagion: How coworkers' job embeddedness and job search behaviors influence quitting. *Academy of Management Journal*, *52*(3), 545–561.

Feng, J., Li, J. J., Chen, S., & Rubenstein, A. L. (2024). From a spark to a sweeping fire: An integrative conceptual review of group turnover and a theoretical exploration of its development. *Journal of Applied Psychology*, *109*(1), 13.

Fernandez, R. M., Castilla, E. J., & Moore, P. (2000). Social capital at work: Networks and employment at a phone center. *American Journal of Sociology*, *105*(5), 1288–1356.

Fernandez, R. M., & Rubineau, B. (2019). Network recruitment and the glass ceiling: Evidence from two firms. *RSF: The Russell Sage Foundation Journal of the Social Sciences*, *5*(3), 88–102.

Fernandez, R. M., & Sosa, M. L. (2005). Gendering the job: Networks and recruitment at a call center. *American Journal of Sociology*, *111*(3), 859–904.

Friebel, G., Heinz, M., Hoffman, M., & Zubanov, N. (2023). What do employee referral programs do? Measuring the direct and overall effects of a management practice. *Journal of Political Economy*, *131*(3), 633–686.

Fried, L. P., Francomano, C. A., MacDonald, S. M., Wagner, E. M., Stokes, E. J., Carbone, K. M., Bias, W. B., Newman, M. M., & Stobo, J. D. (1996). Career development for women in academic medicine: Multiple interventions in a department of medicine. *JAMA*, *276*(11), 898–905.

Gilson, R. J., & Mnookin, R. H. (1989). Coming of age in a corporate law firm: The economics of associate career patterns. *Stanford Law Review*, *41*, 567–595.

Greguletz, E., Diehl, M.-R., & Kreutzer, K. (2019). Why women build less effective networks than men: The role of structural exclusion and personal hesitation. *Human Relations*, *72*(7), 1234–1261.

Gully, S. M., Phillips, J. M., & Kim, M. S. (2013). Strategic recruitment: A multilevel perspective. In D. M. Cable, K. Yang, & T. Yu (Eds.), *The Oxford handbook of recruitment* (pp. 161–183). Oxford University Press.

Hasan, S., & Bagde, S. (2015). Peers and network growth: Evidence from a natural experiment. *Management Science*, *61*(10), 2536–2547.

Hensvik, L., & Nordström Skans, O. (2016). Social networks, employee selection, and labor market outcomes. *Journal of Labor Economics*, *34*(4), 825–867.

Ibarra, H. (1992). Homophily and differential returns: Sex differences in network structure and access in an advertising firm. *Administrative Science Quarterly*, *37*(3), 422–447.

Kalantari, M. (2021). Intersectional homophily: A new measure of multi-dimensional homophily in social network. *Academy of Management Proceedings*. https://doi.org/10.5465/AMBPP.2021.14052abstract

Kammeyer-Mueller, J. D., & Judge, T. A. (2008). A quantitative review of mentoring research: Test of a model. *Journal of Vocational Behavior*, *72*(3), 269–283.

Kaul, K. (2021). Refining the referral process: Increasing diversity for technology startups through targeted recruitment, screening and interview strategies. *Strategic HR Review*, *20*(4), 125–129.

Klotz, A. C., Swider, B. W., Shao, Y., & Prengler, M. K. (2021). The paths from insider to outsider: A review of employee exit transitions. *Human Resource Management*, *60*(1), 119–144.

Korsh, A. (Creator). (2011–2019). "Suits." [Television broadcast]: USA Network.

Krackhardt, D., & Porter, L. W. (1985). When friends leave: A structural analysis of the relationship between turnover and stayers' attitudes. *Administrative Science Quarterly*, *30*(2), 242–261.

Krackhardt, D., & Porter, L. W. (1986). The snowball effect: Turnover embedded in communication networks. *Journal of Applied Psychology*, *71*(1), 50–55.

Lawrence, B. S., & Parikh Shah, N. (2020). Homophily: Measures and meaning. *Academy of Management Annals*, *14*(2), 513–597.

Leicht, K. T., & Marx, J. (1997). The consequences of informal job finding for men and women. *Academy of Management Journal*, *40*(4), 967–987.

McGuire, G. M. (2012). Race, gender, and social support: A study of networks in a financial services organization. *Sociological Focus*, *45*(4), 320–337.

McPherson, M., Smith-Lovin, L., & Cook, J. M. (2001). Birds of a feather: Homophily in social networks. *Annual Review of Sociology*, *27*(1), 415–444.

Mickey, E. L. (2022). The organization of networking and gender inequality in the new economy: Evidence from the tech industry. *Work and Occupations*, *49*(4), 383–420.

Moore, P. C. (2001). The transfer of human and social capital: Employee development through assigned peer mentoring. Doctoral dissertation, Stanford University.

Nguyen, N. (2024). Secondhand social capital and the quest for workplace gender equality. Doctoral dissertation, McGill University.

Nishii, L. H. (2013). The benefits of climate for inclusion for gender-diverse groups. *Academy of Management Journal*, *56*(6), 1754–1774.

Obukhova, E., & Rubineau, B. (2022). Market transition and network-based job matching in China: The referrer perspective. *ILR Review*, *75*(1), 200–224.

Pieper, J. R., Greenwald, J. M., & Schlachter, S. D. (2018). Motivating employee referrals: The interactive effects of the referral bonus, perceived risk in referring, and affective commitment. *Human Resource Management*, *57*(5), 1159–1174.

Porter, C. M., & Rigby, J. R. (2021). The turnover contagion process: An integrative review of theoretical and empirical research. *Journal of Organizational Behavior*, *42*(2), 212–228.

Reskin, B. (1993). Sex segregation in the workplace. *Annual Review of Sociology*, *19*(1), 241–270.

Rhee, L., & Leonardi, P. (2024). Borrowing networks for innovation: The role of attention allocation in secondhand brokerage. *Strategic Management Journal*, *45*(7), 1326–1365.

Rosales, R., León, I. A., & León-Fuentes, A. L. (2023). Recommendations for recruitment and retention of a diverse workforce: A report from the field. *Behavior Analysis in Practice*, *16*(1), 346–361.

Rubenstein, A. L., Eberly, M. B., Lee, T. W., & Mitchell, T. R. (2018). Surveying the forest: A meta-analysis, moderator investigation, and future-oriented discussion of the antecedents of voluntary employee turnover. *Personnel Psychology*, *71*(1), 23–65.

Rubineau, B. (2023). *Network correlates of workgroup climate: 3 studies*. Sunbelt, Annual Meeting of the International Network for Social Network Analysis.

Rubineau, B., Duggal, S., Arcario, E., & Billimoria, Y. (2019). *Gender & borrowed social capital*. Sunbelt, Annual Meeting of the International Network for Social Network Analysis.

Rubineau, B., & Fernandez, R. M. (2013). Missing links: Referrer behavior and job segregation. *Management Science*, *59*(11), 2470–2489.

Rubineau, B., & Fernandez, R. M. (2015). Tipping points: The gender segregating and desegregating effects of network recruitment. *Organization Science*, *26*(6), 1646–1664.

Rubineau, B., Duggal, S., Fernandez, R. M., & Arcario, E. (2021). *Influencing referring behavior: An organizational field experiment.* Paper presented at the Annual Meeting of the American Sociological Association.

Sanner, B., & Bunderson, J. S. (2015). When feeling safe isn't enough: Contextualizing models of safety and learning in teams. *Organizational Psychology Review*, *5*(3), 224–243.

Sgourev, S. V. (2011). Leaving in droves: Exit chains in network attrition. *The Sociological Quarterly*, *52*(3), 421–441.

Topa, G. (2011). Labor markets and referrals. In J. Benhabib, A. Bisin, & M. O. Jackson (Eds.), *Handbook of social economics* (pp. 1193–1221). North-Holland. https://doi.org/10.1016/B978-0-444-53707-2.00005-0

UN Women. (2021). *Empowering women at work: Government laws and policies for gender equality*. International Labour Organization. https://www.ilo.org/sites/default/files/wcmsp5/groups/public/@ed_emp/@emp_ent/@multi/documents/publication/wcms_773233.pdf

Van Hoye, G. (2013). Recruiting through employee referrals: An examination of employees' motives. *Human Performance*, *26*(5), 451–464.

Wayne, S. J., Liden, R. C., Kraimer, M. L., & Graf, I. K. (1999). The role of human capital, motivation and supervisor sponsorship in predicting career success. *Journal of Organizational Behavior*, *20*(5), 577–595.

Woolley, A. W., Chabris, C. F., Pentland, A., Hashmi, N., & Malone, T. W. (2010). Evidence for a collective intelligence factor in the performance of human groups. *Science*, *330*(6004), 686–688.

Zhang, E. Y., Aven, B. L., & Kleinbaum, A. M. (2024). License to broker: How mobility eliminates gender gaps in network advantage. *Administrative Science Quarterly*, *69*(2), 227–270.

CHAPTER 10

Sustained Stigma as a Barrier to Work–Life Balance for Women With Criminal Backgrounds

Sabrina D. Volpone, Fred Macoukji, and Marionne Sevilla

Research on how employees balance work and non-work domains has expanded over the past several decades (e.g., Leuhery et al., 2024), reflecting the increasing recognition of the challenges workers face in managing both professional and personal responsibilities (e.g., Vaziri et al., 2022; Wayne, et al., 2022). Early studies primarily examined the experiences of dual-income families, highlighting tensions between job demands and family obligations (e.g., Greenhaus & Beutell, 1985; Hochschild & Machung, 1989). Today, a substantial body of literature demonstrates the effects of work–non-work balance on both employees and organizations, including outcomes such as employee well-being and organizational productivity (e.g., Kossek & Lambert, 2005; Wayne et al., 2020; Wayne et al., 2022).

Although work–life balance is a universal challenge, women experience it in distinctive and often disproportionate ways. For example, research consistently shows that women continue to perform the majority of unpaid domestic and caregiving labor, even when they are employed full-time (Bianchi, 2013; Hochschild & Machung, 1989). This "second shift" places women at heightened risk of role conflict and stress, making balance more difficult to achieve compared to their male counterparts. This persists, despite scholars' progress in identifying strategies for reducing these conflicts, including flexible work arrangements, family leave policies, and employer-provided childcare (e.g., Casper et al., 2025; Golden & Veiga, 2005; Lambert, 2008). These challenges are further intensified by persistent gender wage gaps and occupational segregation, which limit women's access to positions that provide paid leave, flexible schedules, or employer-sponsored childcare (Budig et al., 2010).

DOI: 10.4324/9781003488590-10

Despite this growth, work–life balance scholarship still overlooks many workers outside traditional professional settings. Most research continues to focus on white-collar employees in full-time positions, often in Western contexts, leaving the realities of workers in precarious, part-time, or informal employment largely unexplored (Carreri et al., 2022). As a result, many of the frameworks and interventions proposed in the literature fail to resonate with non-traditional workers (Lewis et al., 2007; von Allmen et al., 2023). To elaborate, women in low-wage and hourly roles face unique vulnerabilities. Indeed, jobs in service, retail, and healthcare often demand rigid schedules, offer limited benefits, and rarely provide the flexibility needed to manage family obligations (Henly & Lambert, 2014). For mothers, the unpredictability of such work can destabilize not only employment but also caregiving arrangements, increasing the risk of work–life imbalance. These inequities became especially visible during the COVID-19 pandemic, when school closures and caregiving needs fell disproportionately on women, leading many to scale back their hours in, or exit, the workforce (Collins et al., 2021).

In recent years, the work–life balance research has expanded to take into consideration the extent to which work–life balance needs to expand to address changes in the modern workforce (e.g., the expansion of remote work during COVID-19; Elbaz et al., 2023; Vyas, 2022). To continue this progress and advance scholarship in this area, scholars must examine populations whose work–life challenges are shaped not only by job demands, but also by systemic inequities and social stigma. One such group is women with criminal records—a population almost invisible in mainstream scholarship. Their experiences illustrate how stigma, gender, and caregiving responsibilities intersect to create barriers that current work–life models are ill-equipped to address. We define criminal record as "a history of arrest, conviction, incarceration or other criminal history" (Caminiti, 2022; Griffith et al., 2019, p. 521).

In this chapter, we begin by describing work–life experiences of women with a criminal record based on discussions in the popular press and in the limited scholarship on the topic. To better understand the origin of these work–life experiences and how they develop, we then take a step back to review key work–life balance experiences that women with criminal backgrounds have while they are incarcerated, as these experiences often undergird the work–life balance experiences that these women face upon re-entry into society. Third, we discuss key work–life balance experiences of women with criminal backgrounds along the human resource management (HRM) lifecycle to shed light on the nuanced work–life considerations of women navigating their criminal backgrounds across the employment experience.

We note that in this chapter, our focus is on work–life balance upon re-entry after incarceration. And while we highlight key events that can happen during incarceration that directly impact work–life experiences upon reentry, we do not discuss the options of work during incarceration; that is, many incarcerated women work but what that work looks like varies depending on the facility and available programs (Richmond, 2014). Available jobs can include institutional jobs (e.g., cleaning, cooking, laundry) or manufacturing tasks (e.g., sewing, electronics assembly, furniture production). Furthermore, some prisons offer vocational training in fields such as cosmetology, culinary arts, or construction. Wages for these jobs are typically extremely low, ranging from a few cents to a few dollars per hour (Brown, 2019). And for women inmates specifically, work opportunities are often fewer and less diverse than for incarcerated men. For example, it has been reported that women face limited job options that reinforce traditional gender roles and may not align with marketable skills needed after release (e.g., van den Broek et al., 2021). As such, while we do not focus on the work experiences of incarcerated women in this chapter, we acknowledge that many inmates are involved in work programs.

THE WORK–LIFE EXPERIENCES OF WOMEN WITH A CRIMINAL RECORD

Although the exact nature of one's criminal record can vary, a number of people of working age have a criminal record, which can impact their employment opportunities, social mobility, and overall reintegration into society (Brame et al., 2014; Shannon et al., 2017). Among these individuals, women represent a substantial and often overlooked demographic. For instance, 205,000 women in the United States (USA) are currently incarcerated in state or federal prisons or local jails, while an additional one million women are on probation or parole (Frost et al., 2006; Lambert, 2019; The Sentencing Project, 2012). Despite constituting only about one-tenth of the overall prison population, women are the fastest-growing segment within the correctional system.

Overall, the criminal justice system in the USA has overlooked the experiences of women (Mallicoat, 2022; Seymour, 2022). This tradition is built on the idea that criminal justice in the USA is gendered (Seymour, 2022); men historically have committed the majority of crimes, and statistics show that more frequent and serious crimes are committed by men, meaning that gender matters (Van Wormer & Bartollas, 2022) in a conversation about incarceration experiences. This gendered experience of crime feeds the way that society responds to those with criminal backgrounds (Mallicoat, 2022). Therefore, we suspect that the work–life balance of people with a criminal background is likely gendered as well. However, given gaps in knowledge around disclosing a criminal history, in the following sections of this chapter, we review literature at the intersection of work–life balance and criminal records in employment contexts for women so that scholars and practitioners can better understand the work–life balance experiences and needs of this population as they reenter society.

Work–Life Balance Experiences During Incarceration

We review key experiences that women with criminal backgrounds have while they are incarcerated that undergird work–life balance experiences after reentry. The challenges of work–life balance for incarcerated women are deeply tied to their roles as caregivers and their health. With the median age for incarcerated women being 34 (Sabol et al., 2007, 2010), many are mothers.

Mental and Physical Health

First, we discuss the mental and physical health experiences of incarcerated women that can impact work–life balance upon release. Regarding mental health, studies have highlighted high rates of mental health issues among incarcerated women, including depression, anxiety, and post-traumatic stress disorder (PTSD) (Bloom & Covington, 2008; Lehrer, 2021; Zhao et al., 2023). Interventions like the "Beyond Violence" program have been tested to address these concerns, showing reductions in PTSD symptoms among participants (Covington, 2022). Regarding physical health, there is a lot of variability in the kind of medical care that any incarcerated person, but especially a pregnant incarcerated person, receives (e.g., Clarke & Adashi, 2011). Research on this topic shows that as a historically male-focused institution, correctional facilities often fail to address the needs of incarcerated women (e.g., reproductive health care, gender-specific substance abuse treatment, appropriate bathroom and recreational facilities (Braithwaite et al., 2005), and protection against sexual victimization while incarcerated (Beck et al., 2013, cf. Clarke & Simon, 2013).

Caregiving

Second, we discuss the caregiving experiences of incarcerated women that can impact work–life balance upon release. Many incarcerated women are mothers. In fact, 2.7 million children in the USA currently have at least one incarcerated parent, and more than 5.7 million have had a parent incarcerated during their childhood (Kaiper-Marquez et al., 2023). There is an emotional toll of separation and difficulties navigating legal systems (e.g., who has custody of children during incarceration) that are important to consider. Research shows that maintaining family connections during incarceration is crucial for the well-being of incarcerated women (Levkovich & Ne'emani, 2022; Morgan et al., 2023) so much so that there are programs (e.g., "Stronger Families") that facilitate communication with children and family members (Stelter et al., 2023). Visitation is only an option/reality for some families (Aiello & McCorkel, 2018; Schubert et al., 2016).

Pregnancy and Delivery

Third, we discuss the pregnancy and delivery experiences of incarcerated women that can impact work–life balance upon release. Pregnancy and childbirth among incarcerated women reveal systemic shortcomings in correctional systems that were primarily designed for men. Approximately 4–7% of women entering prison are pregnant, with an estimated 12,000 pregnant women incarcerated annually in the USA (Clarke & Adashi, 2011; c.f. Clarke & Simon, 2013). However, no government agency consistently tracks these figures. One study, covering 57% of the US prison population, found that 3.8% of newly admitted women were pregnant, resulting in 753 live births, 46 miscarriages, 4 stillbirths, and 11 abortions in a single year (Sufrin et al., 2019).

One issue that can impact work–life balance after release is the fact that there are no national standards for the care of pregnant prisoners, leading to many healthcare concerns for mother and baby (e.g., Wilson et al., 2022). For example, because many incarceration facilities lack on-site care, they require pregnant women to be transported for medical appointments and delivery under procedures that are often modeled on male incarceration standards (e.g., Baldwin & Jones, 2000; Doetzer, 2008). To elaborate, these procedures include the use of shackling during pregnancy and labor, a practice still permitted in many states despite its medical and emotional risks. Shackling increases the likelihood of falls, complicates procedures such as epidurals, inhibits the ability to use necessary birthing positions, and delays emergency medical interventions. Advocacy efforts have led to anti-shackling legislation in some areas, but inconsistent enforcement remains a pressing concern (Sichel, 2008).

Moreover, following childbirth, most incarcerated mothers are separated from their newborns within 24 hours, a traumatic experience that can have long-term emotional and developmental consequences for both mother and child (Beit, 2020; Tracy, 2010). Only a handful of states offer prison nurseries or community-based alternatives (e.g., Indiana's "Wee Ones" program; National Institute for Children's Health Quality, 2020), which allow well-behaved inmates to bond with their babies in nursery wings (e.g., Johnson, 2024; Martin et al., 2024; Tuxhorn, 2022). The vast majority of women, however, must navigate complex arrangements for their infants' care (Pendleton et al., 2022). Studies indicate that around 60–70% of caregivers are relatives, often grandparents, while others involve non-relatives or foster care. These caregiving arrangements are frequently unstable, with more than a quarter of babies experiencing changes in caregivers within the first year due to challenges faced by their temporary guardians. This lack of information about their children's location and welfare can be a source of significant stress that can complicate work–life balance upon release (Shlafer et al., 2019).

Work–Life Balance Experiences During and After Reentry

In the following section, we discuss key work–life balance experiences of women with criminal backgrounds along the human resource management (HRM) lifecycle to shed light on the nuanced work–life considerations of women navigating their criminal backgrounds across the employment experience. Upon release, formerly incarcerated women face numerous challenges balancing their roles and responsibilities. These include securing employment, finding stable housing, and reconnecting with family, particularly children. The struggle to manage these aspects can be overwhelming, especially when compounded by mental health issues and societal stigma. As such, we review research that illuminates the biases and key challenges that female applicants and employees with criminal backgrounds face during imprisonment and after reentry. We organize this section based on the main aspects of the HRM lifecycle.

Recruitment and Selection

First, research suggests that the recruitment and selection stage of the HRM lifecycle is the most significant barrier to employment for those with a criminal record. Overall, extant research shows that people with a criminal record often are devalued during the selection process (Caminiti, 2022; Griffith et al., 2019, p. 521). Having a criminal record is a unique type of concealable identity in that legally, an employer may ask "for more information about a person's criminal history" (EEOC, 2024, p. 1). This correlates with many other concealable identities (e.g., religion, age, military status, genetic information, and marital status) that are protected classes and that employers are prohibited from inquiring about or considering during the hiring process, unless they are directly relevant to the job.

Because having a criminal record is often considered during the employment process (Apel & Sweeten, 2010), applicants/employees are advised to "be prepared to explain" their record to employers (EEOC, 2024, p. 1). This is especially the case for women, as women are almost twice as likely as men to have their criminal background come up during the selection process; that is, jobs in female-dominated sectors (e.g., care work, education, medical support) require more background checks compared to similar jobs in male-dominated sectors (Oppenheim, 2021). As a result, women with criminal records face unique challenges during selection, as they are disproportionately filtered out due to stricter background screening protocols. This underscores the need for more equitable hiring practices and policies that balance public safety with fair access to employment opportunities for individuals with prior convictions. With many parole agreements including a condition of maintaining lawful employment (Stephens, 2024), these challenges during recruitment and selection can threaten work–life balance for women with criminal records in meaningful ways.

Compensation and Benefits

Second, the compensation and benefits aspects of the employment experience can result in bias against applicants and employees with criminal records. Examining bias at this stage of the HRM lifecycle, we consider the types of jobs that those with criminal records are likely to have: jobs that do not come with benefits associated with employment security (e.g., health-care plans, retirement or pension plans, life insurance, sick leave, vacation leave, flexible working hours). We discuss how detrimental that can be for women with families. Although some industries (e.g., construction, food service) have been identified as "criminal-record-friendly" (Vuolo et al., 2022), the jobs available to those with a criminal record in these industries often require only low skill levels, are labor-intensive (e.g., Lageson et al., 2015; Purser, 2012), are often temporary positions (Griffith et al., 2019; Purser, 2012), and do not offer substantial employment benefits. These minimal employment prospects affect both the compensation and benefit opportunities available to those with criminal records, especially women who are taking care of families.

As an example, the re-entry period is a time when women navigate back into their work and life roles, such as adjusting to transitional housing or finding housing and employment, (Keller et al., 2022). Moreover, there are often transition periods when mothers are regaining custody of their children. Systemic barriers often hinder mothers from regaining custody of their children, with the child welfare system sometimes favoring permanent placements over reunification (Muentner et al., 2019). These experiences that impact compensation and benefit considerations are notable in conversations about work–life balance for women with criminal records.

Employee Relations

Third, research suggests that the policies, practices, and procedures associated with the employment relations stage of the HRM lifecycle can also create barriers for women with criminal records as they return to the workforce, particularly due to dual deviance (gender bias and criminal history; Grace, 2022). Stereotypes about criminal history can lead to trust issues, affecting workplace dynamics (HRM International Digest, 2021). Indeed, the stereotypes about women with criminal backgrounds can be different than those men face. Research shows that society responds not only to women's criminal backgrounds but also to their violations of social norms/expectations about how women should behave (Mallicoat, 2022). These norm violations can contribute to a lack of trust toward women with criminal backgrounds and the resulting tense environment can hinder the ability of women with criminal histories to find the social and practical support needed for professional success (HRM International Digest, 2021). Furthermore, tense workplace dynamics make it even more difficult for women with criminal histories to find social and practical support within their organizations (HRM International Digest, 2021), possibly contributing to recidivism. Therefore, there are a number of considerations, including stereotypes about women with criminal records, that can limit work–life balance for women with criminal records after reentering society.

Retention

Fourth, the retention stage of the employment experience can create bias against women applicants and employees with criminal records. Retention challenges often stem from a combination of stigmas and stereotypes associated with criminal histories, such that these employees are perceived as less trustworthy and reliable. Women with criminal records face compounded barriers, as biases tied to both gender and their criminal backgrounds exacerbate challenges in maintaining employment (Levashina et al., 2017; Pachankis, 2007). This dual deviance dynamic affects hiring practices and perpetuates difficulties fostering long-term workplace stability for these employees. Systemic barriers to retention typically include concerns about workplace liability, such as fears of negligent hiring lawsuits. Employers may hesitate to retain individuals with criminal records because of these misconceptions, despite evidence that such employees often demonstrate strong loyalty and lower turnover rates when given genuine opportunities. This loyalty can be attributed to their motivation to rebuild their lives and their affective commitment to organizations that support their reintegration. These misconceptions about women as liabilities are compounded by additional unique stressors that women, compared to men, face when re-entering society (e.g., homelessness, competing family priorities; Dimsdale & Saunders, 2022). In sum, post-incarceration, women face significant challenges in reintegration, particularly in finding employment. These barriers include societal stigma surrounding gender roles and the need to balance work with family responsibilities.

PRACTICAL IMPLICATIONS

Managers and organizations play a critical role in creating and maintaining environments where female applicants and employees with criminal backgrounds can balance work and family. First, one of the most impactful steps they can take is offering flexible work schedules. Many women with criminal backgrounds face challenges such as mandatory check-ins with probation officers, counseling sessions, or court dates. Flexible scheduling allows them to meet these obligations without jeopardizing their employment. Additionally, flexible hours accommodate their family responsibilities, such as childcare or school pickups, making it easier to balance work and personal life. Providing options for remote work, when possible, can also reduce stress and increase productivity.

Second, creating a workplace culture that fosters inclusion and eliminates stigma is equally important. Employers and managers can implement training programs that educate staff about the challenges faced by employees with criminal records and encourage a culture of empathy and support. Mentorship programs within the workplace can provide guidance and encouragement for these women, helping them build confidence and develop skills for career advancement. Furthermore, adopting fair hiring practices and removing questions about criminal records from initial job applications (ban-the-box policies which aim to remove criminal history inquiries from initial job applications; Avery & Lu, 2021) can reduce biases and create a fairer process for hiring. Such initiatives support the need for increased inclusivity in hiring practices, recognizing that the bias faced in employment contexts is consistent across varied backgrounds related to criminal records (e.g., Paetzold et al., 2008; Ray et al., 2016). Overall, such efforts would support current norms: employer attitudes are becoming more progressive toward recruiting and hiring people with convictions.

Third, offering access to resources and benefits that directly address the needs of these employees can make a significant difference. Providing on-site childcare or childcare assistance programs can alleviate one of the most pressing concerns for working mothers. Additionally, partnering with community organizations to offer support services, such as transportation assistance, counseling, and financial planning, can empower these women to succeed both at work and at home. By addressing their unique needs, employers and managers not only help these employees thrive but also contribute to a more inclusive and diverse workforce.

Fourth, organizations should prioritize career development opportunities to ensure long-term success for women employees with criminal backgrounds. Offering tailored training programs, certifications, and tuition reimbursement can provide these women with the skills and qualifications needed to advance within organizations. These initiatives not only enhance their confidence but also signal that the organization values their potential and is invested in their growth. Recognizing and celebrating their achievements through performance reviews, awards, or public acknowledgment can further motivate them to succeed and create a sense of belonging within the workplace.

Fifth, fostering partnerships with local reentry programs and advocacy groups can amplify an organization's impact. These collaborations can provide employers with insights and best practices for supporting employees with criminal records. Additionally, engaging in community initiatives, such as job fairs targeting formerly incarcerated individuals or sponsoring reentry programs, demonstrates a commitment to social responsibility. These efforts can improve an organization's reputation, attract socially conscious consumers, and inspire other businesses to adopt similar practices. By taking a proactive approach, managers and organizations can play a pivotal role in breaking the cycle of incarceration and promoting equity in the workforce.

CHAPTER SUMMARY

In this chapter, we aimed to advance the current state of scholarly and practical conversations noteworthy for women with criminal records as they re-enter society. While direct research on work–life balance for women with criminal backgrounds is scarce, existing studies shed light on the complexities these women face in managing various roles and responsibilities during incarceration and then during reentry after release. Addressing mental health needs, providing vocational and educational opportunities, and supporting family connections are essential components in assisting incarcerated women to achieve a semblance of work–life balance after release.

DISCUSSION QUESTIONS

1. What other occupations can you identify that are largely "invisible" in mainstream research and popular press articles about women in organizations?
   a. Are "invisible" jobs unimportant? Are they more likely to be dangerous or involve "dirty" work?
2. Are there other identities, in addition to gender, that are likely to shape the work experiences (and histories) of women with criminal records? How do these identities intersect?
3. Should community members without criminal records care about the job experiences and outcomes of women with criminal histories? Why or why not?
4. How might the specific jobs of women after incarceration affect their motivation, job attitudes, and life satisfaction? Which facets of work, whether job duties, company culture, or management, might be most influential?

FURTHER READING

Aspinwall, C. (2023). *These states are using fetal personhood to put women behind bars*. https://www.themarshallproject.org/2023/07/25/pregnant-women-prosecutions-alabama-oklahoma

Bushway, S., & Korzenik, J. (2023). 3 myths about hiring people with criminal records. *Harvard Business Review*. https://hbr.org/2023/12/3-myths-about-hiring-people-with-criminal-records

Clarke, J. G., & Simon, R. E. (2013). Shackling and separation: Motherhood in prison. *Virtual Mentor*, *15*(9), 779–785. https://doi.org/10.1001/virtualmentor.2013.15.9.pfor2-1309

Grace, A. (2022). "Get to know me, not the inmate": Women's management of the stigma of criminal records. *The British Journal of Criminology*, *62*(1), 73–89. https://doi.org/10.1093/bjc/azab029

Khan, O. F., & Fazili, A. I. (2016). Work life balance: A conceptual review. *Journal of Strategic Human Resource Management*, *5*(2), 45–52.

Korzennik, J. (2022, October 3). How employers can set formerly incarcerated workers up for success. *Harvard Business Review*. https://hbr.org/2022/10/how-employers-can-set-formerly-incarcerated-workers-up-for-success

Lambert, J. (2019, March 21). *Pregnant behind bars: What we do and don't know about pregnancy and incarceration*. National Public Radio. Retrieved from https://www.npr.

org/sections/health-shots/2019/03/21/705587775/pregnant-behind-bars-what-we-do-and-dont-know-about-pregnancy-and-incarceration

Lee-Johnnson, M. (2020, September 21). Give job applicants with criminal records a fair chance. *Harvard Business Review*. https://hbr.org/2020/09/give-job-applicants-with-criminal-records-a-fair-chance

Oppenheim, M. (2021). *Women "almost twice as likely" to have criminal records disclosed when applying for work*. https://www.the-independent.com/news/uk/home-news/women-criminal-records-disclosed-jobs-stigma-b1813043.html

Sannto, A. (2020). *For most women who give birth in prison, "the separation" soon follows*. https://www.pbs.org/wgbh/frontline/article/for-most-women-who-give-birth-in-prison-the-separation-soon-follows/

Smith, S. S., & Broege, N. C. (2020). Searching for work with a criminal record. *Social Problems*, *67*(2), 208–232. https://doi.org/10.1093/socpro/spz009

Volpone, S. D., Macoukji, F. G., Ragaglia, R., & Lyons, B. J. (2024). Overcoming biases across the human resource management lifecycle for individuals with a criminal record. In N. C. Jones Young & J. N. Griffith (Eds.), *Employing our returning citizens: An employer-centric view* (pp. 123–158). Palgrave Macmillan.

REFERENCES

Aiello, B. L., & McCorkel, J. A. (2018). "It will crush you like a bug": Maternal incarceration, secondary prisonization, and children's visitation. *Punishment & Society*, *20*(3), 351–374.

Apel, R., & Sweeten, G. (2010). The impact of incarceration on employment during the transition to adulthood. *Social Problems*, *57*(3), 448–479.

Avery, B., & Lu, H. (2021, October 1). *Ban the box: U.S. cities, counties, and states adopt fair hiring policies*. National Employment Law Project.

Baldwin, K., & Jones, J. (2000). *Health issues specific to incarcerated women: Information for state title V programs*. The Women's and Children's Health Policy Center, Johns Hopkins School of Public Health. http://www.jhsph.edu/research/centers-and-institutes/womens-and-childrens-health-policy-center/publications/prison.pdf

Beck, A. J., Berzofsky, M., Caspar, R., & Krebs, C. (2013). *Sexual victimization in prisons and jails reported by inmates, 2011–12*. Bureau of Justice Statistics. http://www.bjs.gov/content/pub/pdf/svpjri1112.pdf

Beit, C. (2020). Legal, ethical, and developmental considerations concerning children in prison nursery programs. *Family Court Review*, *58*(4), 1040–1048.

Bianchi, S. M. (2013). The more they change, the more they stay the same?: Understanding family change in the twenty-first century. *Contemporary Sociology*, *3*, 324–331.

Bloom, B., & Covington, S. (2008). Addressing the mental health needs of women offenders. In R. Gido & L. Dalley (Eds.), *Women's mental health issues across the criminal justice system*. Prentice Hall.

Braithwaite, R., Treadwell, H., & Arriola, K. (2005). Health disparities and incarcerated women: A population ignored. *American Journal of Public Health*, *95*(10), 1679–1681.

Brame, R., Bushway, S. D., Paternoster, R., & Turner, M. G. (2014). Demographic patterns of cumulative arrest prevalence by ages 18 and 23. *Crime & Delinquency*, *60*(3), 471–486. https://doi.org/10.1177/0011128713514801

Brown, C. (2019). Incarceration and earnings: Distributional and long-term effects. *Journal of Labor Research*, *40*(1), 58–83.

Budig, M. J., Misra, J., & Böckmann, I. (2010). *The motherhood penalty in cross-national perspective: The importance of work-family policies and cultural attitudes* (LIS Working Paper Series No. 542). Luxembourg Income Study.

Caminiti, S. (2022, July 23). *JPMorgan, Microsoft, and Slack among companies hiring the formerly incarcerated*. CNBC. https://www.cnbc.com/2022/07/23/americans-with-crim-inal-records-are-in-demand-in-the-job-market.html

Carreri, A., Dordoni, A., & Poggio, B. (2022). Work-life balance and beyond: Premises and challenges. In S. Bertolini (Ed.), *Research handbook on work–life balance* (pp. 8–26). Edward Elgar Publishing.

Casper, W. J., Hyde, S. A., Smith, S. G., Amirkamali, F., & Wayne, J. H. (2025). How effective are work-life balance policies? The importance of inclusion. *Annual Review of Organizational Psychology and Organizational Behavior*, *12*.

Clarke, J. G., & Adashi, E. Y. (2011). Perinatal care for incarcerated patients: A 25 year old woman pregnant in jail. *JAMA*, *305*(9), 923–929.

Clarke, J. G., & Simon, R. E. (2013). *Virtual Mentor*, *15*(9), 779–785. https://doi.org/10.1001/virtualmentor.2013.15.9.pfor2-1309

Collins, C., Landivar, L. C., Ruppanner, L., & Scarborough, W. J. (2021). COVID-19 and the gender gap in work hours. *Gender, Work & Organization*, *28*(S1), 101–112. https://doi.org/10.1111/gwao.12506

Covington, S. (2022). Creating a trauma-informed justice system for women. In L. Gelsthorpe & S. Brown (Eds.), *The Wiley handbook on what works with girls and women in conflict with the law: A critical review of theory, practice, and policy*. John Wiley & Sons.

Dimsdale, C., & Saunders, T. (2022). *Women more likely to become homeless after being released from prison than men, analysis shows*. https://inews.co.uk/news/women-more-likely-become-homeless-after-prison-release-men-1630738

Doetzer, G. (2008). Hard labor: The legal implications of shackling female inmates during pregnancy and childbirth. *William & Mary Journal of Women Law*, *14*(2), 363–392.

EEOC. (2024). *Arrest and conviction records: Resources for job seekers, workers and employers*. https://www.eeoc.gov/arrestandconviction

Elbaz, S., Richards, J. B., & Provost Savard, Y. (2023). Teleworking and work–life balance during the COVID-19 pandemic: A scoping review. *Canadian Psychology/Psychologie Canadienne*, *64*(4), 227.

Frost, N. A., Greene, J., & Pranis, K. (2006). *Hard hit: The growth in the imprisonment of women, 1977–2004*. Institute on Women and Criminal Justice, Women's Prison Association. Retrieved from https://www.csdp.org/research/HardHitReport4.pdf

Golden, T. D., & Veiga, J. F. (2005). The impact of extent of telecommuting on job satisfaction: Resolving inconsistent findings. *Journal of Management*, *31*(2), 301–318.

Grace, A. (2022). Get to know me, not the inmate': Women's management of the stigma of criminal records. *The British Journal of Criminology*, *62*, 73–89.

Greenhaus, J. H., & Beutell, N. J. (1985). Sources and conflict between work and family roles. *The Academy of Management Review*, *10*(1), 76–88.

Griffith, J. N., Rade, C. B., & Anazodo, K. S. (2019). Criminal history and employment: An interdisciplinary literature synthesis. *Equality, Diversity and Inclusion*, *38*(5), 505–528.

Henly, J. R., & Lambert, S. J. (2014). Unpredictable work timing in retail jobs: Implications for employee work-life outcomes. *Industrial and Labor Relations Review*, *67*(3), 986–1016.

Hochschild, A. R., & Machung, A. (1989). *The second shift: Working parents and the revolution at home*. Viking.

Human Resource Management (HRM) International Digest. (2021). From the cell, to the community, to employment: Hiring insights on reconciling female identity with an applicant's criminal record. *Human Resource Management International Digest*, *29*(4), 9–11. Emerald.

Johnson, J. (2024). Mothering within a prison nursery—A review of the literature. In I. Masson & N. Booth (Eds.), *The Routledge handbook of women's experiences of criminal justice* (pp. 401–412). Routledge.

Kaiper-Marquez, A., Stickel, T., & Prins, E. (2023). "Daddy made a mistake and needed a time out": Incarcerated parents as moral educators. *Journal of Moral Education*, *52*(2), 244–260.

Keller, E., Jones, L., Kelleher, K., Chisolm, D., & Boch, S. (2022). A time to "make amends and bring pieces together": A phenomenological study of family experiences and considerations when a parent returns home from incarceration. *Health & Social Care in the Community*, *30*(6).

Khan, O. F., & Fazili, A. I. (2016). Work life balance: A conceptual review. *Journal of Strategic Human Resource Management*, *5*(2), 45–52.

Kossek, E. E., & Lambert, S. J. (2005). *Work and life integration: Organizational, cultural, and individual perspectives*. Lawrence Erlbaum Associates Publishers.

Lageson, S. E., Vuolo, M., & Uggen, C. (2015). Legal ambiguity in managerial assessments of criminal records. *Law & Social Inquiry*, *40*(1), 175–204.

Lambert, J. (2019, March 21). *Pregnant behind bars: What we do and don't know about pregnancy and incarceration*. National Public Radio. https://www.npr.org/sections/health-shots/2019/03/21/705587775/pregnant-behind-bars-what-we-do-and-dont-know-about-pregnancy-and-incarceration

Lambert, S. J. (2008). Passing the buck: Labor flexibility practices that transfer risk onto hourly workers. *Human Relations*, *61*(9), 1203–1227.

Lehrer, D. (2021). Trauma-informed care: The importance of understanding the incarcerated women. *Journal of Correctional Health Care*, *27*(2), 121–126.

Leuhery, F., Hasan, S. Z., Mustari, V. H., Widaningsih, R. R. A., & Lubis, F. M. (2024). The evolution of work-life balance: Redefining priorities in human resource management. *Dinasti International Journal of Economics, Finance & Accounting*, *5*(1), 23–34.

Levashina, J., Peck, J. A., & Ficht, L. (2017). Don't select until you check: Expected background checking practices. *Employee Responsibilities and Rights Journal*, *29*, 127–148.

Levkovich, I., & Ne'emani, H. (2022). "Childhood in the shadow of prison bars": How school counselors cope while counseling children of incarcerated parents. *Children & Society*, *36*(6), 1139–1155.

Lewis, S., Gambles, R., & Rapoport, R. (2007). The constraints of a "work-life balance" approach: An international perspective. *The International Journal of Human Resource Management*, *18*(3), 360–373.

Mallicoat, S. L. (2022). *Women, gender, and crime: Core concepts*. Sage Publications.

Martin, B. E., Bates, R., Kelleher, K., & Boch, S. (2024). Incarcerated at birth: An integrative review of prison nurseries in the United States. *The Journal of Perinatal & Neonatal Nursing*, 10–1097.

Morgan, R. A., van Zoonen, W., & ter Hoeven, C. (2023). Lost in the crowd? An investigation into where microwork is conducted and classifying worker types. *European Journal of Industrial Relations*, *29*(3), 301–322. https://doi.org/10.1177/09596801231171997

Muentner, L., Holder, N., Burnson, C., Runion, H., Weymouth, L., & Poehlmann-Tynan, J. (2019). Jailed parents and their young children: Residential instability, homelessness, and behavior problems. *Journal of Child and Family Studies*, *28*(2), 370–386.

National Institute for Children's Health Quality. (2020, June 3). *Indianapolis gives moms and babies in prison a healthy start*. https://nichq.org/blog/indianapolis-gives-moms-and-babies-prison-healthy-start/

Oppenheim, M. (2021). *Women "almost twice as likely" to have criminal records disclosed when applying for work*. https://www.the-independent.com/news/uk/home-news/women-criminal-records-disclosed-jobs-stigma-b1813043.html

Pachankis, J. E. (2007). The psychological implications of concealing a stigma: A cognitive-affective-behavioral model. *Psychological Bulletin*, *133*(2), 328–345.

Paetzold, R. L., Dipboye, R. L., & Elsbach, K. D. (2008). A new look at stigmatization in and of organizations. *Academy of Management Review*, *33*(1), 186–193. https://doi.org/10.2307/20159382

Pendleton, V. E., Schmitgen, E. M., Davis, L., & Shlafer, R. J. (2022). Caregiving arrangements and caregiver well-being when infants are born to mothers in prison. *Journal of Child and Family Studies*, 1–14.

Purser, G. (2012). Still doin' time: Clamoring for work in the day labor industry. *Working USA*, *15*, 397–415.

Ray, B., Grommon, E., Buchanan, V., Brown, B., & Watson, D. P. (2016). Access to recovery and recidivism among former prison inmates. *International Journal of Offender*

Therapy and Comparative Criminology, *60*(2), 191–209. https://doi.org/10.1177/0306624X14557503

Richmond, K. M. (2014). Why work while incarcerated? Inmate perceptions on prison industries employment. *Journal of Offender Rehabilitation*, *53*(4), 231–252.

Sabol, W. J., Minton, T. D., & Harrison, P. M. (2007). *Prison and jail inmates at midyear 2006*. Bureau of Justice Statistics. https://bjs.ojp.gov/library/publications/prison-and-jail-inmates-midyear-2006

Sabol, W., West, H., & Cooper, M. (2010). *Prisoners in 2008*. Bureau of Justice Statistics. http://www.bjs.gov/content/pub/pdf/p08.pdf

Schubert, E. C., Duininck, M., & Shlafer, R. J. (2016). Visiting mom: A pilot evaluation of a prison-based visiting program serving incarcerated mothers and their minor children. *Journal of Offender Rehabilitation*, *55*(4), 213–234.

The Sentencing Project. (2012). *Incarcerated women*. http://www.sentencingproject.org/doc/publications/cc_Incarcerated_Women_Factsheet_Dec2012final.pdf

Seymour, K. (2022). Women in the criminal justice system. In A. Gibbs & F. Gilmour (Eds.), *Women, crime and justice in context* (pp. 57–72). Routledge.

Shannon, S. K. S., Uggen, C., Thompson, M., & Wakefield, S. (2017). The growth, scope, and spatial distribution of people with felony records in the United States, 1948–2010. *Demography*, *54*(5), 1795–1818. https://doi.org/10.1007/s13524-017-0611-1

Shlafer, R. J., Hardeman, R. R., & Carlson, E. A. (2019). Reproductive justice for incarcerated mothers and advocacy for their infants and young children. *Infant Mental Health Journal*, *40*(5), 725–741.

Sichel, D. L. (2008). Giving birth in shackles: A constitutional and human rights violation. *Journal of Gender, Social Policy & Law*, *16*(2), 223–255.

Stelter, R. L., Stump, K. N., Rhodes, J. E., & Kupersmidt, J. B. (2023). A randomized controlled trial of enhanced mentoring program practices for children of incarcerated caregivers: Assessing impacts on youth and match outcomes. *Journal of Community Psychology*, *51*(8), 3216–3242.

Stephens, I. C. (2024). Careers after prison: Preventing recidivism by reforming restrictive licensing regimes. *Texas A&M Law Review*, *12*(1), 375–406.

Sufrin, C., Beal, L., Clarke, J., Jones, R., & Mosher, W. D. (2019). Pregnancy outcomes in U.S. prisons, 2016–2017. *American Journal of Public Health*, *109*(5), 799–805. https://doi.org/10.2105/AJPH.2019.305006

Tracy, C. E. (2010). *Pregnant inmates—the most forgotten of the forgotten*. Law.com. https://www.law.com/article/almID/120244

Tuxhorn, R. (2022). "I've got something to live for now": A study of prison nursery mothers. *Critical Criminology*, *30*(2), 421–441.

van den Broek, D., Black, P., & Nicki. (2021). Doing double time: Women, incarceration and employment discrimination. *Work, Employment and Society*, *35*(5), 968–978.

Van Wormer, K. S., & Bartollas, C. (2022). *Women and the criminal justice system: Gender, race, and class*. Routledge.

Vaziri, H., Wayne, J. H., Casper, W. J., Lapierre, L. M., Greenhaus, J. H., Amirkamali, F., & Li, Y. (2022). A meta-analytic investigation of the personal and work-related antecedents of work–family balance. *Journal of Organizational Behavior*, *43*(4), 662–692.

von Allmen, N., Hirschi, A., Burmeister, A., & Shockley, K. M. (2023). The effectiveness of work–nonwork interventions: A theoretical synthesis and meta-analysis. *Journal of Applied Psychology*, *109*(7), 1115–1131.

Vuolo, M., Schneider, L. E., & LaPlant, E. G. (2022). Employment application criminal record questions and willingness to apply: A mixed method study of self-selection. *American Journal of Sociology*, *128*(2), 552–592.

Vyas, L. (2022). "New normal" at work in a post-COVID world: Work–life balance and labor markets. *Policy and Society*, *41*(1), 155–167.

Wayne, J. H., Michel, J. S., & Matthews, R. A. (2022). Balancing work and family: A theoretical explanation and longitudinal examination of its relation to spillover and role functioning. *Journal of Applied Psychology*, *107*(7), 1094.

Wayne, J. H., Matthews, R., Crawford, W., & Casper, W. J. (2020). Predictors and processes of satisfaction with work-family balance: Examining the role of personal, work, and family resources and conflict and enrichment. *Human Resource Management*, *59*(1), 25–42.

Wayne, J. H., Michel, J. S., & Matthews, R. A. (2022). Balancing work and family: A theoretical explanation and longitudinal examination of its relation to spillover and role functioning. *Journal of Applied Psychology*, *107*(7), 1094–1114.

Wilson, S. H., Marsh, L. N., Zielinski, M., Corbett, A., Siegler, A., & Shlafer, R. (2022). Enhanced perinatal programs for people in prisons: A summary of six states' programs. *Journal of Criminal Justice*, *83*, 101965.

Zhao, Q., Arévalo, S. P., O'Brien, J., & Li, W. (2023). Patterns of interpersonal violence experience and their association with mental health and substance use problems among women with incarceration histories: A multidimensional longitudinal study. *Journal of Family Violence*, *38*(8), 1639–1654.

CHAPTER 11

Masculinity Contest Cultures

Academia as an Exemplar

Jennifer L. Berdahl

A key reason for the stalled gender revolution (England, 2010; England et al., 2020) is the fact that the workplace remains the site of masculinity contests among men (Berdahl et al., 2018). These contests reward displays of physical strength and stamina, putting work first, showing no weakness, and dog-eat-dog competition. These norms not only are toxic for organizations and their employees but also disproportionately harm women and members of other marginalized groups (Berdahl et al., 2018; Glick et al., 2018). "Macho" jobs often come to mind when thinking of masculinity contest culture, such as firefighting (O'Neill & Alonso, 2018), policing (Rawski & Workman-Stark, 2018), banking and finance (Reid et al., 2018), oil rigs (Ely & Meyerson, 2010), and lawyers and venture capitalists (Williams, 2017). However, really any work setting associated with men and masculinity, or stratified by status and authority, tends toward masculinity contest culture (MCC; Berdahl et al., 2018; Glick et al., 2018). Here, I briefly discuss masculinity contest culture in academia, a domain with far-reaching consequences for young lives and careers, societal worldviews, social policy, and technological innovation.

Academia has historically been, and remains, male-dominated. Universities were exclusively male for almost 1,000 years until women were allowed admission to some institutions in the nineteenth century. In my own lifetime, I have seen academia change from a mostly White men's club of tweed blazers and tobacco pipes as a professor's child in the 1960s and 1970s, to faculties that include significant numbers of women and people of color today. Though women began outnumbering men in undergraduate enrollment in the late 1970s and outnumbered men in master's degrees in the early 1980s and doctoral degrees in 2009, men continue to outnumber women in university circles of power: on governing boards, in university

DOI: 10.4324/9781003488590-11

leadership, among full professors, and in the most highly paid fields of science, technology, engineering, mathematics, and business. Power still generally looks and acts masculine at universities. Academia remains rooted in masculine norms, despite its progressive and "woke" reputation. Indeed, attacks on universities for being too liberal, and their public defunding, have coincided with women's gains in academia, such as the "culture wars" against "political correctness" in the 1980s (e.g., Bloom, 1987) and the derision of the "woke university" and diversity, equity, and inclusion (DEI) research and programs after women began earning more PhDs than men in the 2010s. As with other valued and influential spheres once reserved for men, the clap-back against the integration and inclusion of new identities and perspectives in academia has been forceful and fierce.

In this context, it is no wonder that status and voice in the hallowed halls of academia are still earned in large part through the ability to fit and excel within masculine norms. Academia prides itself on being a place of reason, proof, the scientific method, and merit, yet is often defined by a culture that rewards style over substance. Performing masculinity can be a deciding factor in whose voice "wins," gets credit, and is hired or promoted in the increasingly competitive and hierarchical university (Leitheiser et al., 2022). Capturing the masculine style in which opinions are expressed and discoveries are made, Nobel prize-winning scientist Francis Crick famously quipped, "politeness kills science." In a "battle" of ideas, the scales are tipped toward those most willing and able to be ruthless, and to use domination and intimidation tactics, and away from the calm consideration of different viewpoints and forms of evidence.

Later, I discuss how the four dimensions of masculinity contest culture—strength and stamina, putting work first, showing no weakness, and a dog-eat-dog competition—can manifest in academia. To do so, I draw on my experience and observations of different disciplines, departments, and research universities across the USA and Canada over the past three and a half decades.

STRENGTH AND STAMINA

Sometimes referred to as "mine's bigger" competitions, demonstrations of size, strength, and stamina are important for demonstrating manhood and earning status in masculinity contest cultures (Berdahl et al., 2018; Glick et al., 2018). Even though the academic mission of knowledge production and dissemination may seem unrelated to physical stature and strength, having these characteristics can be an advantage in rising through the academic ranks. For example, those promoted to positions of university leadership tend to be relatively tall. One university president I spoke to admitted that his stature probably got him the job over a more qualified, but much shorter, candidate. As another example, in an adversarial relationship between a male associate dean and a faculty member wishing to meet and speak with him, the associate dean said he had no time in his schedule to meet but the physically unfit faculty member could join him on an afternoon run to discuss concerns. In another department, a group of male professors and graduate students met weekly to play basketball, during which time they talked about departmental politics and bonded over deriding female graduate students and assistant professors (according to a male graduate student who'd been invited). These are just a few examples of how physical size and strength can serve as advantages in academia or be used to marginalize less "masculine" others.

Another way strength and stamina is celebrated in academia is through the expectation that academics work so hard they rarely sleep. When I was a graduate student, a junior faculty member at the institution reportedly only slept four hours a night; he was greatly admired for this ability and its implied productivity, and he was regarded as a "rising star" in the field. When I was a junior faculty member at another university, a senior faculty member emphasized how little she slept (and how rarely she went home) as evidence of her research dedication and productivity. As a further demonstration of her strength and stamina, she would ask me to come to her gym to discuss work while she lifted weights. When I was a visiting faculty member at Princeton University, the local coffee shop sold mugs, t-shirts, and even onesies for babies with the logo "sleep is for the weak" (as of this writing, it still does). As a full professor, my department labeled the highest rating for research excellence in a faculty hiring rubric, "When do they sleep?", as if not sleeping equaled research excellence. Even Francis Crick, of the earlier "politeness is the enemy of science" quote, warned against "the temptation to work so hard that there is no time left for serious thinking."

Size and strength are also measured more figuratively in academia. For example, the size and strength of grant funding or institutional prestige are sometimes used as cues to infer the quality and importance of a person's scholarship by those lacking expertise in their field or in lieu of reading their work. This can lead to a "Matthew effect" in science, where outsized visibility is given to articles written by powerful scholars at the expense of equally valid or superior articles written by unknown scholars (Bol et al., 2018; Merton, 1968). The digital age has ushered in even quicker measures of academic size and strength, with Google Scholar, for example, making it easy to count the number and citations of a scholar's publications, fueling a "mine's bigger" competition over metrics within the managerial university (Leitheiser et al., 2022). Like other indicators of size and strength, metrics might be used to evaluate a scholar instead of their work itself. The "mine's bigger" ranking of scholars operates in tandem with university rankings (e.g., US News and World Report), reinforcing dominance hierarchies within and across academic institutions (Stack, 2019). This further motivates universities to focus on metrics over, for example, scholarly originality, creativity, or relevance (Bayanbayeva, 2025; Leitheiser et al., 2022). For example, one of my department chairs stated that faculty salaries should correspond to their citation metrics. Contributing to the "Matthew Effect" of cumulative inequality, metrics are further used to decide whose work to cite, publish, fund, hire, and promote. Letters reviewing candidates for tenure and promotion are often stuffed with metrics and are thin on evaluating the content and contributions of a person's work (Masters-Waage et al., 2024). A reliance on metrics to assess merit is couched as objective and unbiased, yet this reliance rose with the diversity of voices entering academia and, by overshadowing actual assessments of what they have to say, rewards those with the "strength and stamina" to sustain extreme hours and engage in other practices, such as those discussed later, that maximize the quantity over the quality of their output.

PUTTING WORK FIRST

Putting work first in a masculinity contest culture means not letting anything outside of work interfere with work; taking a break or a leave represents an impermissible lack of commitment (Berdahl et al., 2018; Glick et al., 2018; Williams et al., 2016). In the academic MCC, putting work first means demonstrating a willingness to prioritize research productivity above all else. As a graduate student, a full professor in my department used to repeat how he worked a minimum of 70 hours a week when he was in graduate school, suggesting that if we were not willing to work such hours, we would not succeed. Another full professor talked about how, even on vacation with his family, he was behind his computer working on papers most of the time. "It just becomes a habit," he said, and we were expected to develop it. One of my closest friends got married when I was in graduate school, and the wedding was a half-day drive away; I almost didn't go, fearing that missing two days of work (over the weekend) would put me too far behind. As a junior faculty member, I hesitatingly turned down an invitation from a powerful editor to contribute a chapter to a volume he was compiling, explaining that I needed to spend time with my sister that year, who was dying of cancer. I'll never forget how he simply said, "Well, I guess we all have our priorities," and walked away. The message across these experiences was loud and clear: prioritizing friends or family over work, even occasionally or temporarily, was a sign of weakness. It meant you didn't have what it took, that you were, in essence, a non-contender in the game: someone who could not be counted on to give opportunities to, someone who lacked ambition and grit, someone to be devalued and dismissed. The sting of shame that came with the feeling of being unworthy in the eyes of other academics gets internalized, much like the sting of shame a boy feels when he is told to "be a man" (Pleck, 1981).

If "being a man" is putting work first, "being a woman" is putting family first (Aranda & Glick, 2014; Blair-Loy, 2004). Women are viewed as bad women if they don't have children, as bad workers if they do, and as bad mothers if they work (e.g., Berdahl & Moon, 2013). This is especially true in masculinity contest cultures like academia. Munsch (2022) discussed the MCC embedded in the academic tenure clock, designed around male bodies and fatherhood, and the risks that pregnancy and motherhood pose to women's careers. Graduate school and the probationary pre-tenure years for faculty usually last into the mid-30s to early 40s, giving women a choice between having a child(ren) and risking not getting hired or promoted with tenure, or getting hired and promoted and risking not being able to have a child. This dynamic was illustrated in my first tenure-track appointment, as the first woman in my department to get pregnant before tenure. When I told a senior man (who had two children before tenure) that I was pregnant, he told me, "I can't believe you'd risk tenure to have a baby!" When I was eight months pregnant, a senior woman (who had a child after tenure) advised my female peer, in front of me, to "wait to have a baby until *after* tenure." These norms contribute to why men are much more likely than women faculty to have children, to have children before tenure, to get tenure after having children, and to have multiple children (Mason et al., 2019). Norms for women starting families before tenure seem to have improved, but the stigma of caregiving is still there, along with the stereotype that becoming a mother means no longer being a contender in the masculinity contest culture of academia.

SHOW NO WEAKNESS

The norm of showing no weakness means demonstrating nothing but swaggering confidence, never admitting doubt or mistakes, and suppressing any form of personal vulnerability (Berdahl et al., 2018; Glick et al., 2018). Depression, disability, illness, and injury are stigmatized in academia (Munsch, 2022). Yet academics are significantly more likely than the general population to suffer from anxiety and depression (Satinsky et al., 2021; Schindler et al., 2006), consistent with the finding that working in a MCC is associated with poor mental (and physical) health (Glick et al., 2018). People with disabilities are significantly underrepresented in academia and experience substantial barriers and forms of bias (Castro et al., 2024; Lindsay & Fuentes, 2022). I have had colleagues whose disabilities were not accommodated at the university and who were disrespected for having disclosed their need for help. I have heard faculty openly disparaging students who required academic accommodations. During the recent COVID-19 pandemic, it was considered unmanly to wear a mask (Galasso et al., 2020; Haischer et al., 2020) or work from home (Doering & Tilcsik, 2025), both practices that stem from a recognition of our vulnerability to disease; these attitudes played out at universities and other workplaces in debates over masking and returning to in-person work.

Showing no weakness also includes showing no doubt or uncertainty, and in academia, this can manifest as a tendency to not admit that one does not know something, has not read something, or doesn't know the answer to a question. Even in the context of the academic mission of learning and discovery, students and faculty alike are often afraid to ask questions or to reveal they do not know something. They may couch their queries in fanciful language and avoid saying "I do not know" when asked a question. Rather than admitting they do not know the answer, an academic may deliver a "verbal salad" of jargon and unintelligible reasoning with swaggering confidence to cover up their lack of knowledge or understanding, or to try in other ways to project their own feelings of insecurity onto the inquirer. For example, they may answer a question with “it's complex” or “it would take too long to explain,” suggesting the listener would not be able understand. Similarly, questioning assumptions, theories, or results may be met with aggression rather than curiosity and an eagerness to learn more. Showing no weakness in a masculinity contest culture means never being wrong, and this can take the form of trying to prevent others from questioning or challenging one's opinions or scholarship. This does not advance the academic mission of knowledge and discovery, but it does reinforce the dominance of the academic MCC “winners.”

DOG-EAT-DOG

Finally, MCC norms of ruthless competition and stepping on others to get ahead manifest in academia in various ways. Gatekeeping behavior is one. Gatekeeping includes pushing out unwanted voices that might challenge one's theories or results and blocking their advancement through rejection and sabotage. For example, I witnessed a senior faculty member shame a new graduate student in front of her peers and other faculty when the student suggested an alternative explanation for his research results than the one he put forward. One influential scholar at my university accepted every invitation to review an emerging scholar's work that challenged her own to vehemently reject it and try to prevent it from getting published.

Another dog-eat-dog behavior in academia is taking credit for others' ideas, especially when those others can't easily fight back. Faculty at top-tier research institutions are expected to come up with breakthrough ideas and discoveries on a regular basis—not an easy feat. But by recruiting top students, post-docs, and junior colleagues who themselves come up with those breakthroughs, faculty might be able to keep up with expectations. In a position to take advantage, unscrupulous senior scholars take undue, or even full, credit for those ideas; they may even convince themselves they are responsible for them. Though putting their name on a junior person's publication might lead others to attribute the work to the senior scholar, some academics do so even if they contributed little to the ideas or effort involved in the work. In one online forum for academics, a lively discussion took place about whether to put one's name on a publication coming out of a student's doctoral thesis; some argued it would help the student get published and cited, others contended that a doctoral thesis is supposed to be independent work and that taking credit for it would harm the student. A general consensus was that this was something men did more than women, a “masculine” norm within academia. A famous and highly published male academic, for example, was widely known for insisting on being an author on any publication a junior scholar had spoken to him about, even briefly.

Academic fraud is another product of dog-eat-dog norms. Putting forth dishonest work to advance one's own career promotes misinformation and erodes societal trust and investment in research. Academic fraud may include tampering with data, p-hacking (trying out multiple analyses to find one that yields the desired results), post-hoc theorizing (pretending to have predicted a discovery), not reporting studies or results (omitting those not supporting one's hypotheses), and other forms of dishonesty that may help one get published, funded, hired, and promoted at the overall expense of science and society. When I was an assistant professor, such practices were shockingly common; they were considered what it took to get published in a "top" journal. A replication crisis in social psychology resulted from these practices (Ioannidis, 2005; Open Science Collaboration, 2015), and numerous highly published researchers at top universities have been caught engaging in research fraud. The available data suggest that male scientists are more likely than female scientists to commit fraud (Fang et al., 2013), but dog-eat-dog norms encourage everyone wishing to "win" to play along; when women get caught cheating, they are more likely than men to be vilified and scorned.

CHAPTER SUMMARY

I have detailed some of the ways I have noticed masculinity contest culture play out in academic settings. Other academics are likely to notice different ways MCC plays out, especially those whose identities differ from my own, such as men and racialized, queer, or first-generation academics. And doubtless I have conformed to, unwittingly propagated, and even benefitted from some of these MCC norms myself—the fact I have had some success and survived in academia this long would suggest as much. Indeed, I am haunted by the time with family I have missed, the friendships that faded due to neglect, the toll it took at times on my physical, mental, and spiritual health, and the students and colleagues I may have hurt along the way while working in a MCC. I like to think I fought masculinity contest norms more than I followed them, and there have been several painful and discouraging episodes in my career when calling out and fighting MCC nearly cost me my career. I have seen some of the most brilliant students opt out of academia due to the MCC, and some of my most creative and compassionate colleagues have been harassed and marginalized, leading some to give up.

The academic mission of universities is learning and discovery—to seek understanding and knowledge for its own sake and to pursue questions no matter where their answers might lead. Academic research has, among other things, led to insights into human history, our planet, and the universe; it has helped us understand and address societal ills, led to breakthroughs in life-saving medicine and technology, and produced scientific discoveries that inspire awe and innovation. Academia has provided voice to the marginalized and upward mobility to the disadvantaged. At the heart of this mission is academic freedom and equal opportunity. Threats to this mission come from outside the ivory towers, such as political interference and pressure and wealthy and influential donors. Threats also come within, when academic culture rewards dominance over truth and style over substance. Mission-driven interventions that disrupt MCCs in other workplaces (Berdahl et al., 2018) can be drawn upon to disrupt them in academic ones.

DISCUSSION QUESTIONS

1. In what other arenas do masculinity contest cultures tend to exist? Describe how the four MCC features manifest in them.
2. Have you experienced or witnessed MCCs at your university or college? If so, in what ways?
3. Brainstorm a list of all possible outcomes (for individuals, teams, companies) of MCCs. Are all the outcomes negative?
4. When employed at organizations with strong MCCs, do you think women are as likely to engage in MCC behaviors as men?
5. How might other identities shape employee engagement in MCCs, either strengthening or weakening them?
6. The author mentions mission-defined interventions as a way to disrupt MCCs; what exactly might these interventions entail? What would you do to disrupt them?

REFERENCES

Aranda, B., & Glick, P. (2014). Signaling devotion to work over family undermines the motherhood penalty. *Group Processes & Intergroup Relations*, *17*(1), 91–99.

Bayanbayeva, A. (2025). Global university rankings and the dissemination of the Western university model: Balancing global influence and national priorities in Kazakhstan. *Globalisation, Societies and Education*, 1–15. https://doi.org/10.1080/14767724.2025.2515492

Berdahl, J. L., Cooper, M., Glick, P., Livingston, R. W., & Williams, J. C. (2018). Work as a masculinity contest. *Journal of Social Issues*, *74*(3), 422–448.

Berdahl, J. L., Glick, P., & Cooper, M. (2018, November 2). How masculinity contests undermine organizations, and what to do about it. *Harvard Business Review*.

Berdahl, J. L., & Moon, S. H. (2013). Workplace mistreatment of middle class workers based on sex, parenthood, and caregiving. *Journal of Social Issues*, *69*(2), 341–366. https://doi.org/10.1111/josi.12018

Blair-Loy, M. (2004). Work devotion and work time. In C. F. Epstein & A. L. Kalleberg (Eds.), *Fighting for time: Shifting boundaries of work and social life* (pp. 282–316). Russell Sage Foundation.

Bloom, A. (1987). *Closing of the American mind*. Simon and Schuster.

Bol, T., de Vaan, M., & van de Rijt, A. (2018). The Matthew effect in science funding. *PNAS*, *115*(19), 4887–4890. https://doi.org/10.1073/pnas.1719557115

Castro, F., Cerilli, C., Hu, L., Iezzoni, L. I., Varadaraj, V., & Swenor, B. K. (2024). Experiences of researchers with disabilities at academic institutions in the United States. *PloS One*, *19*(8), e0299612.

Doering, L., & Tilcsik, A. (2025). Location matters: Everyday gender discrimination in remote and on-site work. *Organization Science*, *36*(2), 547–571. https://doi.org/10.1287/orsc.2022.16949

Ely, R. J., & Meyerson, D. E. (2010). An organizational approach to undoing gender: The unlikely case of offshore oil platforms. *Research in Organizational Behavior*, *30*, 3–34.

England, P. (2010). The gender revolution: Uneven and stalled. *Gender & Society*, *24*(2), 149–166.

England, P., Levine, A., & Mishel, E. (2020). Progress toward gender equality in the United States has slowed or stalled. *Proceedings of the National Academy of Sciences*, *117*(13), 6990–6997.

Fang, F. C., Bennett, J. W., & Casadevall, A. (2013, January 22). Males are overrepresented among life science researchers committing scientific misconduct. *mBio*, *4*(1), e00640–12. https://doi.org/10.1128/mBio.00640-12. PMID: 23341553; PMCID: PMC3551552.

Galasso, V., Pons, V., Profeta, P., Becher, M., Brouard, S., & Foucault, M. (2020). Gender differences in COVID-19 attitudes and behavior: Panel evidence from eight countries. *Proceedings of the National Academy of Sciences*, *117*(44), 27285–27291.

Glick, P., Berdahl, J. L., & Alonso, N. M. (2018). Development and validation of the masculinity contest culture scale. *Journal of Social Issues*, *74*(3), 449–476.

Haischer, M. H., Beilfuss, R., Hart, M. R., Opielinski, L., Wrucke, D., Zirgaitis, G., . . . & Hunter, S. K. (2020). Who is wearing a mask? Gender-, age-, and location-related differences during the COVID-19 pandemic. *PloS One*, *15*(10), e0240785.

Ioannidis, J. P. A. (2005). Why most published research findings are false. *PLOS Medicine*, *2*(8), e124. https://doi.org/10.1371/journal.pmed.0020124

Leitheiser, S., Vezzoni, R., & Hakkarainen, V. (2022). Painting outside the lines: Transgressing the managerial university, avoiding forced creativity. In A. Franklin (Ed.), *Co-creativity and engaged scholarship*. Palgrave Macmillan, Cham. https://doi.org/10.1007/978-3-030-84248-2_2

Lindsay, S., & Fuentes, K. (2022). It is time to address ableism in academia: A systematic review of the experiences and impact of ableism among faculty and staff. *Disabilities*, *2*(2), 178–203. https://doi.org/10.3390/disabilities2020014

Mason, M. A., Wolfinger, N. H., & Goulden, M. (2019). *Do babies matter? Gender and family in the Ivory Tower*. Rutgers University Press.

Masters-Waage, T., Spitzmueller, C., Edema-Sillo, E., St. Aubin, A., Penn-Marshall, M., Henderson, E., Lindner, P., Werner, C., Rizzuto, T., & Madera, J. (2024). Underrepresented minority faculty in the USA face a double standard in promotion and tenure decisions. *Nature Human Behavior*, *8*, 2107–2118. https://doi.org/10.1038/s41562-024-01977-7

Merton, R. K. (1968). The Matthew effect in science. *Science*, *159*(3810), 56–63. https://doi.org/10.1126/science.159.3810.56. PMID 17737466. S2CID 3526819.

Munsch, C. L. (2022). Strength, stamina, and structural violence in the social sciences. *The Journal of Men's Studies*, *30*(3), 402–424. https://doi.org/10.1177/10608265221108205

O'Neill, O., & Alonso, N. (2018, March 23). Emergency responders and the dangers of "masculinity contests." *Harvard Business Review*.

Open Science Collaboration. (2015). Estimating the reproducibility of psychological science. *Science*, 349, aac4716. https://doi.org/10.1126/science.aac4716

Pleck, J. H. (1981). *The myth of masculinity*. MIT Press.

Rawski, S. L., & Workman-Stark, A. L. (2018). Masculinity contest cultures in policing organizations and recommendations for training interventions. *Journal of Social Issues*, *74*, 607–627.

Reid, E. M., O'Neill, O. A., & Blair-Loy, M. (2018). Masculinity in male-dominated occupations: How teams, time, and tasks shape masculinity contests. *Journal of Social Issues*, *74*(3), 579–606.

Satinsky, E. N., Kimura, T., Kiang, M. V., Abebe, R., Cunningham, S., Lee, H., Lin, X., Liu, C., Rudan, I., Sen, S., Tomlinson, M., Yaver, M., & Tsai, A. C. (2021). Systematic review and meta-analysis of depression, anxiety, and suicidal ideation among Ph.D. students. *Scientific Reports*, *11*, 14370. https://doi.org/10.1038/s41598-021-93687-7

Schindler, B. A., Novack, D. H., Cohen, D. G., Yager, J., Wang, D., Shaheen, N., Guze, P., Wilkerson, L., & Drossman, D. A. (2006). The impact of the changing health care environment on the health and well-being of faculty at four medical schools. *Academic Medicine*, *81*(1), 27–34.

Stack, M. (2019). Academic stars and university rankings in higher education: Impacts on policy and practice. *Policy Reviews in Higher Education*, *4*(1), 4–24. https://doi.org/10.1080/23322969.2019.1667859

Williams, J. C. (2017, July 12). Why sexual harassment is more of a problem in venture capital. *Harvard Business Review*.

Williams, J. C., Berdahl, J. L., & Vandello, J. A. (2016). Beyond work-life "integration". *Annual Review of Psychology*, *67*, 515–539. https://doi.org/10.1146/annurev-psych-122414-033710

CHAPTER 12

Moving Forward

What Works—and What Doesn't—to Advance Women at Work

Siri Chilazi

When Maria Klawe arrived on the campus of Harvey Mudd College as its first female president in 2006, she was determined to increase the presence of women in computer science (CS). Contrary to many women's advancement initiatives, though, her vision of how to make progress centered not on changing women but rather on changing the systems, policies, and practices of the school.

Klawe and her team began with a thorough analysis of why women made up only 10% of computer science majors at Harvey Mudd (even worse than the national average of 21%; National Girls Collaborative Project, 2024). Upon discovering that female students did not feel comfortable in the computing culture or believe they would do well in CS, the department redesigned its introductory course and shifted classroom norms to promote more collaboration between students. It also created paid internships to boost students' confidence in doing the work of a computer scientist while exposing first-year women to role models through a paid trip to the Grace Hopper Celebration of Women in Computing Conference. At the same time, Klawe appointed women to chair several of Harvey Mudd's academic departments and directed financial support toward departmental efforts to attract and hire more women faculty and change the imagery associated with CS on campus (Klawe, 2013).

The results speak for themselves. Within four years, the proportion of women CS students had quadrupled. In 2018, a whopping 56% of graduating computer science degree recipients were women (Klawe, 2013). And in 2025, the overall student body was 51% women, while the faculty was 39% women (Harvey Mudd College, 2025).

Harvey Mudd College's inspiring story shows that gender equality is an attainable goal when we use the right approaches. In this final chapter, we answer the

DOI: 10.4324/9781003488590-12

question of where to go from here by distinguishing between evidence-based methods whose effectiveness has been established through rigorous research and popular but unsupported strategies for women's advancement in organizations. We begin by reviewing strategies focused on individuals and then move to strategies at the organizational level before charting a path forward.

INDIVIDUAL-LEVEL APPROACHES: MYTH VERSUS REALITY

Many popular approaches to advance women and gender equity in the workplace focus on helping people play the existing game, rather than on redesigning the playing field. They often aim to change how we think and feel instead of how we act. And their focus is on changing or de-biasing individuals instead of systems. The most common of these approaches include diversity and unconscious bias trainings, often targeted at people of all genders; women-centric trainings and programs, designed to upskill or otherwise tangibly help women; and popular advice for women on how to succeed at work, which turns out to influence not only women's but also men's perceptions of what works to make progress.

All of these approaches frame the challenge of women's advancement as being about individuals—with important consequences. If we assume we are solving a people problem, we naturally assume we will need a people solution. One of the many unconscious biases scholars have identified, the fundamental attribution error, leads us to overemphasize individual, personality-based explanations for behaviors while discounting situational and systemic explanations (Ross, 1977). So instead of seeing a biased promotion process as the issue, we blame the individuals who "haven't quite proven themselves yet" or "don't have the executive presence required at the next level." The danger with this focus is that research shows it can shift attention away from crucial system changes because the individual and systemic frames often compete (Chater & Loewenstein, 2023).

Here, we dive into the evidence behind these individual-focused approaches and propose a way forward to maximize their usefulness in advancing women at work.

Diversity and Unconscious Bias Training

The first workplace diversity trainings were introduced in the 1960s as a consequence of the Civil Rights Movement in the USA (Dobbin & Kalev, 2022). In recent years, these efforts have become increasingly prevalent and have often taken the shape of unconscious bias trainings, especially after leading tech companies including Google and Facebook made their internal unconscious bias trainings publicly available in the mid-2010s (Bock & Welle, 2014; Pepitone, 2015). The underlying idea of these trainings is that by educating people about their biases and signaling an organizational commitment to diversity and equity, we can get individuals to make different decisions.

Yet, despite their popularity, the evidence linking diversity and unconscious bias trainings to behavior change is incredibly thin. While some workshops, simulations, and courses have succeeded in increasing people's awareness of bias and even their motivation to tackle it (Cundiff et al., 2018; Devine et al., 2012; Devine et al., 2017; Forscher et al., 2017), in most cases, this has not translated into action (Bezrukova et al., 2016). The latest meta-analysis—a statistical analysis that combines results from multiple scientific studies to evaluate the effectiveness of an intervention—that examined different methods to reduce prejudice in hundreds of studies over the last two decades found little support for the hypothesis that changes in unconscious bias awareness result in sustainable behavior change (Paluck et al., 2021).

Indeed, one of the few studies that has examined behavior change as an outcome of diversity training in a global organization found that a one-hour online module did not impact behaviors among men or White employees, even though attitudes toward women in the workplace improved (Chang et al., 2019). A larger, correlational analysis of more than 40 years of data from over 800 American companies showed no relationship between the existence of diversity training and the likelihood that women or people of color made it into management (with the exception of Latinas, whose chances of becoming managers were lower when diversity training was provided). In three-quarters of cases, training programs included legal content, which was associated with a *decrease* in the proportion of White women, Black women and men, and Asian American women and men in management (Dobbin & Kalev, 2022). These findings align with other studies that have documented backlash and increased discrimination as a result of trainings: humans generally dislike being told how to think and what to do (Kaiser et al., 2013; Legauit et al., 2013).

Part of the problem with traditional trainings is that their design doesn't incorporate the latest evidence of what works to change behavior. A recent review of 70 academic studies found that the most effective interventions to reduce workplace discrimination targeted actual behaviors through accountability or social norms, for example, so as to minimize the manifestation of bias (Costa, 2024). However, typical trainings are generic, rather than tailored to specific decisions (such as hiring or promotion), and delivered at pre-determined times, such as during onboarding or once a year (Chang et al., 2023). The content generally aims to de-bias individuals through mindset change—which research has shown to be extremely difficult, if not impossible—rather than by providing concrete guidance on how to behave differently.

However, new evidence is emerging that behaviorally designed diversity training—that is, training that incorporates insights from behavioral science—*can* work to change measurable outcomes. In a field experiment with over 3,000 managers hiring for more than 10,000 open positions in a global telecommunications and engineering firm, some managers were invited to watch a seven-minute diversity training video before gaining access to submitted applications while others continued business as usual. Importantly, the video was timely and featured the company's own employees, including two senior executives, discussing the importance of workplace diversity and explicitly affirming that the company valued diversity and inclusion in hiring. As a result, women were 12% more likely to be shortlisted for a job opening by a manager who had been assigned the diversity training compared to a manager who had not. Similarly, non-national applicants (candidates whose nationality differed from the country of the job opening) were 13% more likely to be shortlisted and 20% more likely to be hired (Arslan et al., 2025).

The bottom line is that the evidence to date should make us skeptical about the ability of most individually-focused trainings to shift behaviors and yield meaningful progress for women at work. Given that unconscious bias is an aspect of how humans process information, we simply cannot train ourselves out of it. However, timely, targeted, and context-specific nudges that make fairness salient during moments that matter are a more promising approach.

Women-Centric Trainings and Programs

Like general diversity trainings, programs targeted specifically at women—such as leadership development workshops, mentoring programs, negotiation trainings, affinity groups, and networking events—have been around for more than half a century (Ely et al., 2011). In 2023, according to the World Economic Forum's *Future of Jobs* report, 79% of more than 800 surveyed companies in 45 countries had DEI programs in place specifically targeted at women (World Economic Forum, 2023). However, the effectiveness of these programs is difficult to assess because many are not formally evaluated, and those that are often base evaluations on participants' self-reported satisfaction rather than more concrete organizational outcomes, such as women's promotion rates (Debebe et al., 2016). While anecdotal examples of successful programs abound (Allen & Aweh, 2021), and some rigorous studies documenting positive effects of women's leadership programs exist (Alwazzan & Al-Angari, 2020), a recent global review of women's leadership program evaluations found the programs' impact on individuals and organizations "inconclusive" and challenged "the premise that individual level strategies can affect organizational and cultural change" (Gardiner et al., 2023).

Perhaps the central challenge of women-centric programs is that they can reinforce gender stereotypes and send the message that women, rather than the biased systems they inhabit, need fixing. Extensive research has shown that in nearly all skills and traits, including those traditionally associated with leadership (e.g., ambition; Thomas et al., 2024), average gender differences between women and men pale in comparison with variation among women (and among men). Stereotypes tend to exaggerate any slightly distinctive characteristics of a group, leading us to erroneously believe that differences are larger than they are (Eyal & Epley, 2017). Thus, approaches that make such stereotypes even more salient by focusing on "bringing women up to par with men" may end up being counterproductive.

Moreover, having women—but not men—spend valuable time on training programs can inadvertently exacerbate gender gaps in the workplace as men continue to do promotable work while women take time from their daily tasks and receive messages that it is their job to fix systemic inequities (Babcock et al., 2022). Worse, these programs can become a performative check-the-box for organizations to signal that they care about women's advancement without having to change anything about how they operate. As the authors of a *Harvard Business Review* article on women's leadership development programs (WLDPs) conclude: "WLDPs can have significant value, but companies must use these programs as an opportunity to assess and improve the workplace itself" (Johnson et al., 2023).

Popular Advice for Women

Anne-Marie Slaughter, a then-former senior State Department official, made waves with a 2012 article arguing that due to systemic inequities, women still couldn't have it all: to thrive as high-powered leaders while also being deeply engaged with their families (Slaughter, 2012). A few months later, Facebook's then Chief Operating Officer, Sheryl Sandberg, contributed to the conversation with her book, *Lean In*, which argued that while external (societal) barriers to gender equality were real, individual women should focus on the "barriers that exist within ourselves" to gain power. The paradigm of leaning in encouraged women who wanted to make it to the top to build their self-confidence, become more ambitious, raise their hands more, and dive in instead of pulling back when new opportunities arose (Sandberg, 2013).

While *Lean In* was a vernacular-shaping moment in the conversation about women's advancement, the underlying advice was not new. For decades, women had been instructed to change how they behaved, spoke, dressed, thought, and felt in order to make gains in workplaces that were not designed to enable their success. To close the gender pay gap, women were exhorted to negotiate more and better (though they sometimes faced backlash for doing so; Bowles & Babcock, 2013). To have their ideas taken seriously, they were advised to be more assertive (though many found that following this advice backfired, as they were socially penalized and found less likeable; Heilman et al., 2024). And to avoid triggering gendered stereotypes about work and family, women were warned not to draw attention to their lives outside of work. Yet, research continues to show that systemic barriers are a major contributor to gender inequity at work. For example, the same performance ratings translate into faster advancement and greater rewards for men than women (Castilla, 2008), and men tend to get more credit than women for the same effort (Sarsons et al., 2021).

Messaging focused on women's empowerment turns out to influence both women's and men's perceptions of gender (in)equality in important ways. In a series of experiments, when exposed to *Lean In* messages that emphasized women's potential to overcome gendered challenges through self-improvement, people were more likely to endorse solutions that required women to change themselves (Kim et al., 2018). When messages, instead, focused on organizational barriers to women's advancement, people were more likely to endorse solutions that required organizations to change their systems. The researchers summarize: "When society points to how women *can* change—they can dream bigger, talk louder—it also points to who and what *should* change" (Kim et al., 2018).

While concrete advice on how to succeed in the workplace can be beneficial for everyone, popular advice aimed at women that emphasizes individual-level empowerment can contribute to harmful beliefs about the causes and remedies of gender inequity. It is time we move beyond a focus on fixing women and fix biased workplace systems instead.

Moving Forward: Connecting Individual and System Change

To accelerate women's advancement at work, connecting individual action to systemic change can be a powerful approach. Consider the example of Miranda (a pseudonym), a high performer and one of very few Latina senior managers at a technology firm, who started facing scrutiny of her personal life during virtual meetings in the COVID-19 pandemic. Colleagues would make sometimes friendly, sometimes hostile remarks about her children appearing in the background during meetings, which led Miranda to worry about how her work would be perceived and evaluated by others. To advocate for herself individually, Miranda raised the issue with her manager while emphasizing her business results and performance against agreed-upon metrics. But she didn't stop there. In order to leverage her situation to create a fairer workplace for everyone, Miranda suggested a broad review of performance evaluations in the remote work environment, proposing concrete and evidence-based solutions such as soliciting feedback in response to specific rather than open-ended questions and requiring behavioral examples to back up evaluators' comments (Mackenzie et al., 2019). As a result, Miranda ended up leading a task force that redesigned the company's performance evaluation system. In the process, she transitioned from advocating on her own behalf and "leaning in" to helping her company de-bias an assessment process for the benefit of everyone (Chilazi et al., 2022).

There is, of course, room (and a need) for women to lean into opportunities and ensure that they are navigating the workplace strategically. Trainings and programs can help with this to some extent. But what the evidence suggests they cannot do is redesign fundamentally biased systems. For this, we need organizational approaches to level the playing field.

ORGANIZATION-LEVEL APPROACHES: MYTH VERSUS REALITY

Employers have been engaged in efforts to integrate women into their workforces for more than half a century, but the early 2020s saw a veritable boom of DEI-related activity after the tragic killing of George Floyd and the racial reckoning it spawned, as well as massive workplace shifts caused by the COVID-19 pandemic. More money than ever was spent on programming; more consultants and DEI professionals than ever were hired; and companies made an unprecedented number of public statements and commitments related to diversity. While well-meaning, many of these efforts focused more on signaling intentions and "talking the talk" rather than changing underlying organizational processes and systems in order to "walk the walk."

Rigorous academic research spanning dozens of years has identified a host of practices that are highly effective at closing gender gaps in the workplace. In other words, the good news is that we know what works and what the "best evidence" suggests we should do. The bad news is that many companies are still stuck copying competitors' "best practices" and investing resources in popular but unproven efforts.

Here, we review the efficacy of some of the most popular organizational methods—systems, processes, policies, and other practices—to advance women in organizations, and distinguish empirically supported methods from those that garner attention and profit but are not backed up by evidence.

De-Biasing Organizational Processes

Research has shown that one of the most promising ways to advance women at work is to redesign existing organizational processes that govern how work gets done every day, such as how we attract, screen, interview, hire, support, evaluate, promote, and reward employees (Bohnet, 2016). These processes contain built-in biases because they were designed by biased humans. Moreover, behavioral science has shown that these processes and policies influence people's behavior in profound ways. Fortunately, they are much easier to change than dozens, hundreds, or thousands of individual minds. Put differently, we do not need to de-bias people to get them to make decisions that are less biased and more fair; people's actions change when the systems surrounding them change. By leveraging "behavioral design" to create smarter and less biased processes, we can help ourselves live up to our best intentions and perform even better than we could if left to our own devices (Bohnet & Chilazi, 2025).

Consider the traditional resume format where candidates tend to list their work history by dates (e.g., "July 2015–June 2018: Assistant Manager, Operations"). This format makes career gaps—time off for the purpose of childcare, elder care, a sabbatical, or any other reason—particularly salient to employers, and research shows that employers tend to penalize candidates with gaps in their work history (despite the lack of evidence that career gaps have any bearing on an employee's skills). A field experiment in the United Kingdom with more than 9,000 employers tested a revised resume format where experience was listed by amount of time rather than specific dates (e.g., "3 years: Assistant Manager, Operations"). The new format, which allowed recruiters to see beyond career gaps and focus on employees' talents, increased the likelihood that both women and men were invited to an interview by 15% (Kristal et al., 2023).

When it comes to promotions, most organizations use an opt-in process that requires either the employee or their manager to proactively propose the person for consideration. However, women have been shown to be less likely to put themselves forward this way, in part because of (well-founded) fears of social backlash. An evidence-based process redesign to level the playing field is moving to an opt-out promotion system, whereby after a certain pre-determined amount of time in a given role, all employees are automatically considered for promotion unless they withdraw their name from consideration. Changing the default from opt-in to opt-out has been shown to eliminate gender differences in the propensity to compete (He et al., 2021).

As part of performance evaluations, many organizations ask employees to first assess themselves, and those self-ratings are then shared with managers as a starting point for their assessments. Since research has shown that women are likely to evaluate themselves more harshly than men, these lower self-ratings can disproportionately hurt women's evaluations if they become an anchor point from which managers adjust slightly up or down (Abraham, 2023). A natural experiment in a multinational financial services company showed that when managers did not have access to employees' self-ratings one year due to a system glitch, women of color—who typically gave themselves the lowest ratings and ended up with the lowest manager ratings—who were newly hired (such that managers could not rely on past years' ratings) were evaluated on par with men. Once it learned this, the company decided to stop sharing employees' self-evaluations with managers (Bohnet et al., 2025). Other large companies, including IBM, have come to the same conclusion (PerformYard, 2021).

These examples underscore the fact that no organizational design is neutral. While all of the aforementioned redesigns were, on their face, gender-neutral, by debiasing hiring, promotions, and performance evaluations, respectively, they disproportionately benefited those who had been most negatively impacted by bias: women (as well as people with career breaks and people with lower tendencies to self-promote).

Workplace Flexibility

Workplace flexibility can take many forms, including remote and hybrid work, part-time work, and flexible hours. All of these have been shown to increase productivity, improve employee satisfaction, and promote better work–life balance (Bloom et al., 2015; Kelly et al., 2014). Flexible work is especially in demand among women and parents of all genders, as well as those with longer commutes, and is more popular among employees than employers (Barrero et al., 2023). An analysis of women's labor force participation in the USA during and after the COVID-19 pandemic revealed that the availability of remote work made it possible for some mothers who would have otherwise exited the workforce to stay in it (Goldin, 2022)—in fact, the labor force participation of US women aged 25–54 hit its all-time peak at around 78% in 2024 (U.S. Bureau of Labor Statistics, 2025).

While there is no one-size-fits-all approach to implementing flexibility, the ability to have more control over one's time and place of work is a critical enabler of women's advancement in the workplace. As organizational behavior scholar Kathleen McGinn explained,

> Organizations are going to have to deal with the fact that the 'ideal worker' is gone. Increasingly, neither men nor women want their lives to revolve entirely around work. Organizations can't just keep expecting their employees to sacrifice everything for their jobs; they're going to have to figure that out.
>
> (Baskin, 2023)

Indeed, many organizations have. Technology company Dropbox made remote work the default for all employees in 2020, setting core work hours with overlap across time zones and developing a toolkit to help teams operate effectively in the new environment; two years later, 93% of employees felt the approach was working (Dropbox, 2020; Markell-Goldstein, 2023). One Florida location of fast-food chain Chick-fil-A provided scheduling flexibility by allowing employees to work all of their weekly full-time hours in three days; a quarter of employees opted in and the results revealed higher retention, lower absenteeism, and more applications from prospective candidates who were drawn to the policy (Murphy, 2022). At an Italian multiutility company, employees were allowed to choose their hours and work location once a week (they were required to be onsite the rest of the time); both women and men spent more time on household and care activities and reported increased life satisfaction and less stress (Angelici & Profeta, 2024).

Beyond location and hours, one essential component of organizational flexibility policies is gender-neutral, non-transferable, and paid parental leave. Leave should be offered equally to all employees because policies that specify a "primary" and "secondary" caregiver (with different leave allocations for each) reinforce gendered stereotypes of women as carers and men as earners, and also perpetuate gender inequality at home as "secondary" caregivers have less opportunity to be involved in childcare and housework. Leave should be non-transferable because research has shown that men are more likely to take it when they have a use-it-or-lose-it allocation (Patnaik, 2019). Finally, leave should be paid to ensure all parents can access it, as happened in San Francisco when a city ordinance augmented wage replacement rates: men's leave-taking increased four-fold compared to women's (Dow et al., 2017).

The lack of flexible work options has historically prevented employees, especially women, from contributing to the workplace to the fullest. Fortunately, organizations are increasingly choosing to redesign work arrangements to level the playing field for all.

Data-Driven Approaches to Managing Diversity

When the European Central Bank (ECB) set out to increase the number of women among its senior managers, it turned to goals as an evidence-based tool to help it deliver. The ECB met its 30% target in 2019 and discovered that the women promoted under the goal had better salary trajectories than their male peers. The goal not only helped ECB advance more women on par with men but also allowed it to place better talent in important leadership roles (Hospido et al., 2022).

The same data-driven approaches that organizations use to manage their "core business" are not always applied to promoting gender equality. However, abundant research shows that tracking relevant data, setting stretching yet realistic goals, implementing appropriate incentives, and creating accountability through transparency work to change behaviors and improve outcomes in a variety of contexts (Chilazi & Bohnet, 2020). Across studies, accountability has emerged as one of the most potent ways for organizations to reduce discriminatory outcomes (Costa, 2024). This can involve, for example, assigning specific individuals or groups (such as a task force) the responsibility for achieving results; instituting scorecards that track performance on agreed-upon metrics against targets; or having leaders regularly check with their direct reports regarding progress. This data and accountability-driven approach is how global consumer goods company Unilever attained gender parity in managerial roles globally (Chilazi et al., 2021).

Mentorship and Sponsorship

At the individual level, mentorship and sponsorship are critical enablers of employees' career success. While mentorship is advice, guidance, and support that can be provided by anyone, sponsorship is concrete career advancement advocacy and opportunities provided by someone with power (and the willingness to use it on the sponsee's behalf). As the adage goes, and as evidence suggests, women tend to be over-mentored and under-sponsored—and women of color tend to have the hardest time accessing effective sponsorship (Ibarra, 2019).

At the organizational level, research indicates that formalized mentorship and/or sponsorship can be an important accelerator of women's advancement. In over 800 large and midsize US firms, the presence of mentorship programs correlated with sizeable increases of Black women (18% increase over five years), Hispanic women (24%), Hispanic men (9%), Asian women (24%), and Asian men (18%) in management (Dobbin & Kalev, 2016). The challenge with formal programs is that they cannot mandate senior leaders to want to use their own political and social capital to advance their protégés. Thus, providing opportunities for authentic relationships to evolve naturally between junior and senior employees is an important part of the puzzle, and one where proven practices are only emerging (Ibarra, 2022).

One promising and complementary approach to formal mentor/sponsorship is micro-sponsorship: small, everyday actions of support, recognition, validation, and/or advocacy that people can provide to each other without any specialized training or programs (Roberts et al., 2023). Affirming another person's idea in a meeting; giving credit to everyone who was part of a project team; interrupting an interrupter to ensure everyone can have their voice heard; and forwarding an opportunity to someone who may not have received it are all examples of micro-sponsorship. While not a formal organizational intervention, fostering a culture of micro-sponsorship can be a powerful way to ensure that women's contributions are accurately seen and valued.

Employee Resource Groups and Related Programming

Despite their enormous popularity in organizations, employee resource groups (ERG) or affinity groups have not been studied on a large scale, and the limited evidence of their effectiveness is mixed (Welbourne et al., 2017). By their nature, ERGs are designed to bring people together for programmatic activities (such as networking, speaking, or social events) around a specific identity or, in some cases, interest. In a 2022 survey, nearly 25,000 employees across the USA rated ERGs highest on community building but lower on dimensions including leadership connection and career advancement (Catalino et al., 2022). From a representation standpoint, the presence of ERGs was associated with increases of White women and Latino men (but decreases in White and Black men) in management across more than 800 US companies (Dobbin & Kalev, 2022).

However, ERGs—such as women's networks—are often touted by companies as one way to advance gender equality, and on this score, their track records are slimmer. Preliminary evidence found that in one high-tech company in Silicon Valley, the women and Black ERGs' "efforts at contesting gender and racial inequality were undermined" (Seegars, 2021), and that among nearly 400 American ERG members surveyed online, contrary to expectations, ERG membership failed to yield positive social outcomes (Beaver, 2018). More broadly, programmatic or "add-on" efforts such as social outings, lunch-and-learns, or celebrations like International Women's Day rarely change the underlying processes, practices, norms, and daily behaviors that remain key sources of gender inequity in organizations (Zheng, 2025). Women's advancement would be more tangibly served by, say, conducting a company-wide compensation audit and equalizing pay instead of having employees attend a speaker event on the history of Equal Pay sponsored by the women's network. As trailblazing diversity consultant Elsie Y. Cross remarked, "[Practices that are] little more than activities—ethnic dinners, celebrations of all kinds of holidays, or other kinds of 'cultural issues'. . . . How can such initiatives get to the heart of the matter?" (Cross, 2000).

At the end of the day, ERGs and other programmatic efforts are typically introduced to manage the symptoms of underlying gender inequities, such as women feeling isolation and lack of belonging when they are underrepresented. Anecdotally, they succeed at making role models more visible and support more available. But these programs are designed to help women navigate the existing system more successfully instead of changing the system so that women can thrive on par with men. Therefore, on their own, ERGs and other programs are unlikely to move the needle enough.

Moving Forward: Focus on Leveling the Playing Field

In contrast to individual-level interventions that aim to change the game by changing the players, effective organizational interventions instead change the playing field on which the game is played. Put differently, the organizational practices to advance women with the best evidence behind them tackle the underlying biased structures, processes, and policies that generate gender inequity to begin with. In general, formality and structure—in processes, evaluations, and policies, including in their application—reduce biased behaviors and outcomes, whereas ambiguity and informality exacerbate gender inequities (Costa, 2024). Tackling organizational structures entails making small tweaks to how day-to-day work gets done and thereby embedding fairness into everything organizations do. The good news is it doesn't have to be complicated or costly—and we know what works.

Law firm Reed Smith is a case study in how it can be done. As recently retired director of global diversity, John Iino, explained, "Our hearts and minds were always in the right place. But things really changed when it went from a 'should do' to being part of the process." Among many other efforts, beginning in 2017, the firm implemented granular scorecards that monitored the gender, race, and sexual orientation of all lawyers by office, practice group, and client team, allowing it to identify barriers to gender equality. Armed with data, the firm then analyzed the organizational processes driving the numbers. For example, succession planning emerged as a hot spot of potential bias, so Reed Smith redesigned the nomination process:

senior leaders were now asked to name three individuals as potential successors every year. Time use was another area of focus since billable hours were critical to advancement and recognition. These efforts translated into measurable results: between 2018 and 2023, the share of women among office managing partners nearly doubled from 22 to 41%, and in 2023, women made up over 40% of partner promotions (Reed Smith, 2023). Such progress was possible because the company's leaders realized that they had to embed efforts to advance gender equality into their everyday work of hiring and promoting lawyers, serving clients, and setting business goals. Instead of relying on individuals' good intentions, they made fairness a systemic practice.

MOVING FORWARD: ACCELERATING PROGRESS FOR WOMEN AT WORK

Women have made remarkable progress toward full equality in the workplace and in society over the last century. While most of the overt barriers have been dismantled—women can vote; job advertisements seeking "men only" are no longer legal; and women can obtain credit in their own name the same way as men—more subtle, unconscious barriers remain. Even in environments that seemingly offer equal opportunities, the pernicious effects of biased systems, processes, and policies continue to generate an unlevel playing field for women.

Because the problem is systemic, the solutions need to be, too. In light of the evidence, we need to continue the shift from individual solutions toward systemic approaches that center on redesigning biased processes instead of fixing women. However, because processes can be changed in both top-down and bottom-up ways, individuals can serve as agents for structural transformation in their own work. Take, for instance, Anthony Miyagusuku, former manager of sustainability at Cooperativa Pacífico, a major financial institution in Peru, who started addressing groups as "todos y todas" [Spanish masculine and feminine] instead of defaulting to the masculine "todos." What began as a team-level effort quickly spread to the company's formal communications and sparked a re-examination of other cultural symbols, such as the stereotypical imagery of women and men around Mother's Day and Father's Day.

Moving forward, it will be essential to continue to expand the evidence based on which solutions work (and in which contexts) and which do not to advance women in workplaces so that we can collectively direct our limited resources toward more effective actions. While much is already known, many open questions remain. For example, how should organizations frame their diversity efforts? In some cases, explicitly mentioning diversity as a motivation led to greater behavior change (Arslan et al., 2025); in others, practices like mentoring and self-managed teams were associated with greater increases in diversity than practices that were explicitly branded as "diversity efforts" (Dobbin & Kalev, 2016). We also know much too little about the experiences of various intersectional groups (e.g., women of different races and ethnicities, women with disabilities, LQBTQ+ women) as well as people who don't identify their gender as a woman or a man.

All organizations should start by grounding their practices in the best available evidence today—and then test and share how these research-backed practices perform in their context (Hauser & Luca, 2015). Using actual behaviors (such as who was hired, promoted, or selected for a developmental opportunity) as outcome measures is especially important given that too much measurement thus far has focused on inputs rather than outputs (e.g., the number of people trained rather than any measurable changes in women's experiences as a result of training).

Rigorous experimentation before scaling interventions is also important because even the best-intentioned efforts can backfire in unexpected ways. Global telecommunications and engineering firm Ericsson discovered this when it partnered with UK-based behavioral science consultancy, MoreThanNow, on an experiment to close a gender gap in internal mobility, whereby women were less likely than men to have experience in different geographies, functions, and roles in the organization. Ericsson ran a randomized controlled trial of four different messages to encourage internal mobility among 13,000 employees and found that only one of them—a message that told employees they did not have to be "100% qualified" to explore the opportunities—closed the gender gap in interest. Two other messages ended up exacerbating the gender gap because they increased men's interest but not women's (Chang et al., 2023).

Advancing women on par with men and finally leveling the playing field at work are game-changing opportunities for organizations to benefit from 100% of the talent pool; for people of all genders to thrive in their professions; and for all of society to reap the rewards in terms of prosperity. Simply put, it is both the smart and the right thing to do.

CHAPTER SUMMARY

This chapter addresses the critical question of where to go from here in advancing women at work. It distinguishes between evidence-based methods, proven effective through rigorous research, and widely adopted yet unsupported strategies that persist despite limited impact. The chapter first examines individual-level approaches, such as unconscious bias training and women-centric leadership programs, before turning to organizational levers like process redesign, workplace flexibility, mentorship and sponsorship, and employee resource groups. By contrasting what works with what merely appeals, the chapter highlights the importance of data-driven design and systemic change over symbolic initiatives. Ultimately, it provides a clear, research-backed roadmap for accelerating women's progress at work—one that prioritizes structural change, sustainable impact, and fairness for all.

DISCUSSION QUESTIONS

1. What kinds of women's advancement efforts have you encountered in your own work? Would you categorize them as focused on fixing women or fixing systems?
2. Which of the strategies in this chapter strike you as the most promising for your own organization?
3. What is one way that you could become an agent for systemic change in your work? Even if you do not have the authority to change processes or policies for your whole organization, which of your own everyday work practices could you tweak to level the playing field for everyone?
4. What is your one key takeaway from this chapter?

REFERENCES

Abraham, L. (2023). The gender gap in performance reviews. *Journal of Economic Behavior & Organization*, *214*, 459–492. https://doi.org/10.1016/j.jebo.2023.07.039

Allen, G., & Aweh, B. (2021, September 2). Inside DoorDash's leadership accelerator for women of color. *Harvard Business Review*. https://hbr.org/2021/09/inside-doordashs-leadership-accelerator-for-women-of-color

Alwazzan, L., & Al-Angari, S. S. (2020). Women's leadership in academic medicine: A systematic review of extent, condition and interventions. *BMJ Open*, *10*(1). https://doi.org/10.1136/bmjopen-2019-032232

Angelici, M., & Profeta, P. (2024). Smart working: Work flexibility without constraints. *Management Science*, *70*(3), 1680–1705. https://doi.org/10.1287/mnsc.2023.4767

Arslan, C., Chang, E. H., Chilazi, S., Bohnet, I., & Hauser, O. P. (2025). Behaviorally designed training leads to more diverse hiring. *Science*, *387*(6732), 364–366. https://doi.org/10.1126/science.ads5258

Babcock, L., Peyser, B., Vesterlund, L., & Weingart, L. R. (2022). *The no club: Putting a stop to women's dead-end work*. Simon & Schuster.

Barrero, J. M., Bloom, N., & Davis, S. J. (2023). The evolution of work from home. *The Journal of Economic Perspectives*, *37*(4), 23–50. https://doi.org/10.1257/jep.37.4.23

Baskin, K. (2023, September 14). Working moms are mostly thriving again: Can we finally achieve gender parity? *Harvard Business School*. https://www.library.hbs.edu/working-knowledge/working-moms-are-mostly-thriving-again-can-we-finally-achieve-gender-parity

Beaver, G. R. (2018). Individual outcomes of employee resource group membership. Doctoral dissertation, University of Minnesota.

Bezrukova, K., Spell, C. S., Perry, J. L., Jehn, K. A., & Albarracín, D. (2016). A meta-analytical integration of over 40 years of research on diversity training evaluation. *Psychological Bulletin, 142*(11), 1227–1274. https://doi.org/10.1037/bul0000067

Bloom, N., Liang, J., Roberts, J., & Ying, Z. J. (2015). Does working from home work? Evidence from a Chinese experiment. *The Quarterly Journal of Economics*, *130*(1), 165–218. https://doi.org/10.1093/qje/qju032

Bock, L., & Welle, B. (2014, September 25). *You don't know what you don't know: How our unconscious minds undermine the workplace*. Life at Google. https://blog.google/inside-google/life-at-google/you-dont-know-what-you-dont-know-how/

Bohnet, I. (2016). *What works: Gender equality by design*. Harvard University Press.

Bohnet, I., & Chilazi, S. (2025). *Make work fair: Data-driven design for real results*. Harper Business.

Bohnet, I., Hauser, O. P., & Kristal, A. (2025). *Can gender and race dynamics in performance appraisals be disrupted? The case of social influence* (working paper). https://scholar.harvard.edu/files/iris_bohnet/files/performance_appraisals.11.19.21-full.pdf

Bowles, H. R., & Babcock, L. (2013). How can women escape the compensation negotiation dilemma? Relational accounts are one answer. *Psychology of Women Quarterly*, *37*(1), 80–96. https://doi.org/10.1177/0361684312455524

Castilla, E. J. (2008). Gender, race, and meritocracy in organizational careers. *The American Journal of Sociology*, *113*(6), 1479–1526. https://doi.org/10.1086/588738

Catalino, N., Gardner, N., Goldstein, D., & Wong, J. (2022, December 7). Effective employee resource groups are key to inclusion at work: Here's how to get them right. *McKinsey & Company*. https://www.mckinsey.com/capabilities/people-and-organizational-performance/our-insights/effective-employee-resource-groups-are-key-to-inclusion-at-work-heres-how-to-get-them-right

Chang, E., Chilazi, S., Elfer, J., Arslan, C., Kirgios, E., Hauser, O. P., & Bohnet, I. (2023, September 1). Incorporating DEI into decision-making. *Harvard Business Review*. https://hbr.org/2023/09/incorporating-dei-into-decision-making

Chang, E., Kirgios, E., Elfer, J., Wright, K., & Lindemann, G. (2023, April 18). Why you should start A/B testing your DEI initiatives. *Harvard Business Review*. https://hbr.org/2023/04/why-you-should-start-a-b-testing-your-dei-initiatives

Chang, E. H., Milkman, K. L., Gromet, D. M., Rebele, R. W., Massey, C., Duckworth, A. L., & Grant, A. M. (2019). The mixed effects of online diversity training. *Proceedings of the National Academy of Sciences*, *116*(16), 7778–7783. https://doi.org/10.1073/pnas.1816076116

Chater, N., & Loewenstein, G. (2023). The I-frame and the S-frame: How focusing on individual-level solutions has led behavioral public policy astray. *The Behavioral and Brain Sciences*, *46*. https://doi.org/10.1017/S0140525X22002023

Chilazi, S., & Bohnet, I. (2020, December 3). How to best use data to meet your DE&I goals. *Harvard Business Review*. https://hbr.org/2020/12/how-to-best-use-data-to-meet-your-dei-goals

Chilazi, S., Bohnet, I., & Hauser, O. P. (2021, November 30). Achieving gender balance at all levels of your company. *Harvard Business Review*. https://hbr.org/2021/11/achieving-gender-balance-at-all-levels-of-your-company

Chilazi, S., Kolb, D. M., McGinn, K. L., & Porter, J. L. (2022, January 31). Who pays tolls at work, and who cruises on an open highway? *Harvard Business Review*. https://hbr.org/2022/01/who-pays-tolls-at-work-and-who-cruises-on-an-open-highway

Costa, E. (2024). Examining the effectiveness of interventions to reduce discriminatory behavior at work: An attitude dimension consistency perspective. *Journal of Applied Psychology*, *109*(11), 1669–1692. https://doi.org/10.1037/apl0001215

Cross, E. Y. (2000). *Managing diversity—the courage to lead*. Bloomsbury Publishing.

Cundiff, J. L., Danube, C. L., Zawadzki, M. J., & Shields, S. A. (2018). Testing an intervention for recognizing and reporting subtle gender bias in promotion and tenure decisions. *The Journal of Higher Education*, *89*(5), 611–636. https://doi.org/10.1080/00221546.2018.1437665

Debebe, G., Anderson, D., Bilimoria, D., & Vinnicombe, S. M. (2016). Women's leadership development programs: Lessons learned and new frontiers. *Journal of Management Education*, *40*(3), 231–252. https://doi.org/10.1177/1052562916639079

Devine, P. G., Forscher, P. S., Austin, A. J., & Cox, W. T. L. (2012). Long-term reduction in implicit race bias: A prejudice habit-breaking intervention. *Journal of Experimental Social Psychology*, *48*(6), 1267–1278. https://doi.org/10.1016/j.jesp.2012.06.003

Devine, P. G., Forscher, P. S., Cox, W. T. L., Kaatz, A., Sheridan, J., & Carnes, M. (2017). A gender bias habit-breaking intervention led to increased hiring of female faculty in STEMM departments. *Journal of Experimental Social Psychology*, *73*, 211–215. https://doi.org/10.1016/j.jesp.2017.07.002

Dobbin, F., & Kalev, A. (2016, July–August). Why diversity programs fail. *Harvard Business Review*. https://hbr.org/2016/07/why-diversity-programs-fail

Dobbin, F., & Kalev, A. (2022). *Getting to diversity: What works and what doesn't*. Harvard University Press.

Dow, W. H., Goodman, J. M., & Stewart, H. (2017). *San Francisco's paid parental leave ordinance: The first six months*. Berkeley. https://www.populationsciences.berkeley.edu/sites/default/files/SF%20Paid%20Parental%20Leave%20-%20UC%20Berkeley%20issue%20brief%201.pdf

Dropbox. (2020, October 13). *Dropbox goes virtual first*. https://blog.dropbox.com/topics/company/dropbox-goes-virtual-first

Ely, R. J., Ibarra, H., & Kolb, D. M. (2011). Taking gender into account: Theory and design for women's leadership development programs. *Academy of Management Learning & Education*, *10*(3), 474–493. https://doi.org/10.5465/amle.2010.0046

Eyal, T., & Epley, N. (2017). Exaggerating accessible differences: When gender stereotypes overestimate actual group differences. *Personality and Social Psychology Bulletin*, *43*(9), 1323–1336. https://doi.org/10.1177/0146167217713190

Forscher, P. S., Mitamura, C., Dix, E. L., Cox, W. T. L., & Devine, P. G. (2017). Breaking the prejudice habit: Mechanisms, timecourse, and longevity. *Journal of Experimental Social Psychology*, *72*, 133–146. https://doi.org/10.1016/j.jesp.2017.04.009

Gardiner, A., Chur-Hansen, A., Turnbull, D., & Semmler, C. (2023). Qualitative evaluations of women's leadership programs: A global, multi-sector systematic review. *Australian Journal of Psychology*, *75*(1). https://doi.org/10.1080/00049530.2023.2213781

Goldin, C. (2022). Understanding the economic impact of COVID-19 on women. *Brookings Papers on Economic Activity*, *2022*(1), 65–139. https://doi.org/10.1353/eca.2022.0019

Harvey Mudd College. *Fast facts: Harvey Mudd College*. Retrieved from https://www.hmc.edu/about/facts

Hauser, O. P., & Luca, M. (2015, October 29). How to design (and analyze) a business experiment. *Harvard Business Review*. https://hbr.org/2015/10/how-to-design-and-analyze-a-business-experiment

He, J. C., Kang, S. K., & Lacetera, N. (2021). Opt-out choice framing attenuates gender differences in the decision to compete in the laboratory and in the field. *Proceedings of the National Academy of Sciences*, *118*(42), 1–6. https://doi.org/10.1073/pnas.2108337118

Heilman, M. E., Caleo, S., & Manzi, F. (2024). Women at work: Pathways from gender stereotypes to gender bias and discrimination. *Annual Review of Organizational Psychology and Organizational Behavior*, *11*(1), 165–192. https://doi.org/10.1146/annurev-orgpsych-110721-034105

Hospido, L., Laeven, L., & Lamo, A. (2022). The gender promotion gap: Evidence from central banking. *The Review of Economics and Statistics*, *104*(5), 981–996. https://doi.org/10.1162/rest_a_00988

Ibarra, H. (2019, August 19). A lack of sponsorship is keeping women from advancing into leadership. *Harvard Business Review*. https://hbr.org/2019/08/a-lack-of-sponsorship-is-keeping-women-from-advancing-into-leadership

Ibarra, H. (2022, November–December). How to do sponsorship right. *Harvard Business Review*. https://hbr.org/2022/11/how-to-do-sponsorship-right

Johnson, W. B., Smith, D. G., & Christensen, H. (2023, March 8). Where women's leadership development programs fall short. *Harvard Business Review*. https://hbr.org/2023/03/where-womens-leadership-development-programs-fall-short

Kaiser, C. R., Major, B., Jurcevic, I., Dover, T. L., Brady, L. M., Shapiro, J. R., & Simpson, J. (2013). Presumed fair: Ironic effects of organizational diversity structures. *Journal of Personality and Social Psychology*, *104*(3), 504–519. https://doi.org/10.1037/a0030838

Kelly, E. L., Moen, P., Oakes, J. M., Fan, W., Okechukwu, C., Davis, K. D., Hammer, L. B., Kossek, E. E., King, R. B., Hanson, G. C., Mierzwa, F., & Casper, L. M. (2014). Changing work and work-family conflict: Evidence from the work, family, and health network. *American Sociological Review*, *79*(3), 485–516. https://doi.org/10.1177/0003122414531435

Kim, J. Y., Fitzsimons, G. M., & Kay, A. C. (2018). Lean in messages increase attributions of women's responsibility for gender inequality. *Journal of Personality and Social Psychology*, *115*(6), 974–1001. https://doi.org/10.1037/pspa0000129

Klawe, M. (2013). Increasing female participation in computing: The Harvey Mudd College story. *Computer*, *46*(3), 56–58. https://doi.org/10.1109/MC.2013.4

Kristal, A. S., Nicks, L., Gloor, J. L., & Hauser, O. P. (2023). Reducing discrimination against job seekers with and without employment gaps. *Nature Human Behaviour*, *7*(2), 211–218. https://doi.org/10.1038/s41562-022-01485-6

Legault, L., Gutsell, J. N., & Inzlicht, M. (2011). Ironic effects of antiprejudice messages: How motivational interventions can reduce (but also increase) prejudice. *Psychological Science*, *22*(12), 1472–1477. https://doi.org/10.1177/0956797611427918

Mackenzie, L. N., Wehner, J., & Correll, S. (2019, January 1). Why most performance evaluations are biased, and how to fix them. *Harvard Business Review*. https://hbr.org/2019/01/why-most-performance-evaluations-are-biased-and-how-to-fix-them

Markell-Goldstein, H. (2023, February 22). *What we've learned from our first-ever life in virtual first survey*. Dropbox. https://blog.dropbox.com/topics/company/what-weve-learned-from-our-firstever-life-in-virtual-first-survey

Murphy, B. Jr. (2022, October 29). *Chick-fil-A just introduced a 3-day workweek, and people think it's the best idea ever*. Inc. https://www.inc.com/bill-murphy-jr/chick-fil-a-just-introduced-a-3-day-work-week-people-think-its-best-idea-ever.html

National Girls Collaborative Project. (2024, February 26). *State of girls and women in STEM*. https://ngcproject.org/resources/state-girls-and-women-stem

Paluck, E. L., Porat, R., Clark, C. S., & Green, D. P. (2021). Prejudice reduction: Progress and challenges. *Annual Review of Psychology*, *72*(1), 533–560. https://doi.org/10.1146/annurev-psych-071620-030619

Patnaik, A. (2019). Reserving time for daddy: The consequences of fathers' quotas. *Journal of Labor Economics*, *37*(4), 1009–1059. https://doi.org/10.1086/703115

Pepitone, J. (2015, July 28). Check your privilege: Facebook shares its internal anti-bias training. *NBC News*. https://www.nbcnews.com/tech/social-media/check-your-privilege-facebook-shares-its-internal-anti-bias-training-n399776

PerformYard. (2021, May 3). *3 approaches to performance management: Google, Betterment and IBM*. https://www.performyard.com/articles/3-unique-approaches-to-performance-management-google-betterment-and-ibm

Reed Smith. (2023). *Diversity, equity & inclusion annual report 2023*. https://www.reedsmith.com/en/diversity

Roberts, L. M., Grayson, M., & Rosser, B. D. (2023, May 15). An antidote to microaggressions? Microvalidations. *Harvard Business Review*. https://hbr.org/2023/05/an-antidote-to-microaggressions-microvalidations

Ross, L. D. (1977). The intuitive psychologist and his shortcomings: Distortions in the attribution process. *Advances in Experimental Social Psychology*, *10*, 174–221. https://doi.org/10.1016/S0065-2601(08)60357-3

Sandberg, S. (2013). *Lean in: Women, work, and the will to lead*. Alfred A. Knopf.

Sarsons, H., Gërxhani, K., Reuben, E., & Schram, A. (2021). Gender differences in recognition for group work. *The Journal of Political Economy*, *129*(1), 101–147. https://doi.org/10.1086/711401

Seegars, L. (2021). Sanctioned radicals: A comparative study of gender and race employee resource groups in tech. Doctoral dissertation, Harvard University. https://dash.harvard.edu/handle/1/37368349

Slaughter, A.-M. (2012, July/August). Why women still can't have it all. *Atlantic*. https://www.theatlantic.com/magazine/archive/2012/07/why-women-still-cant-have-it-all/309020/

Thomas, R., Fairchild, C., Fielding-Singh, P., Noble-Tolla, M., Cardazone, G., Brown, H., Cooper, M., Krivkovich, A., Yee, L., Field, E., McConnell, M., & Smith, H. (2024). *Women in the workplace 2024*. McKinsey & Company and LeanIn.Org. https://womenintheworkplace.com

U.S. Bureau of Labor Statistics. *Labor force statistics from the current population survey*. Retrieved from https://data.bls.gov/timeseries/LNS11300062

Welbourne, T. M., Rolf, S., & Schlachter, S. (2017). The case for employee resource groups: A review and social identity theory-based research agenda. *Personnel Review*, *46*(8), 1816–1834. https://doi.org/10.1108/PR-01-2016-0004

World Economic Forum. (2023). *Future of jobs report 2023*. https://www3.weforum.org/docs/WEF_Future_of_Jobs_2023.pdf

Zheng, L. (2025, January 23). What comes after DEI. *Harvard Business Review*. https://hbr.org/2025/01/what-comes-after-dei/

CHAPTER 13

Gender and Leadership Case Studies

Nicole Capehart and Lisa A. Marchiondo

In this chapter, five case studies are provided that span numerous topics from the book. Innovative questions follow each case study, prompting reflections on how one would handle each situation and why. In turn, readers consider complex issues and multiple concepts pertaining to gender and leadership. These reflection questions also prompt readers to consider the roles of intersectional identities and unique contexts.

The case studies can be used as individual writing assignments, team discussions, class debates, or capstone projects. Readers and instructors are encouraged to build on the case study questions and connect the scenarios to relevant or key experiences or even news stories, books, and popular media.

The following table (Table 13.1) outlines the chapters most relevant to each case.

Table 13.1 Overview of Case Studies and Key Topics

Case Number and Title	Key Topics
1. Perplexing promotion	Leadership styles Communication Networking Masculinity contest culture
2. A wider window of opportunity: Reentry and flexibility	Leadership styles Negative work behavior Work–life balance

DOI: 10.4324/9781003488590-13

Case Number and Title	Key Topics
3. Representation on the line	Glass cliff Women of color Negotiation Networking
4. When life intervenes	Negative work behavior Communication Negotiation Work–life balance
5. Opportunity at the precipice	Glass cliff Women of color Negotiation Masculinity contest culture

Note: Chapter 12 (Moving Forward: What Works—and What Doesn't—To Advance Women at Work) is applicable to all cases.

CASE STUDY 1: PERPLEXING PROMOTION

Nicole Capehart

Background: Genuine Sales Group

Genuine Sales Group is a fast-paced, high-revenue sales organization. Specializing in cloud services, B2B sales, and high-end consultancy services, Genuine has earned a reputation as a "pressure cooker for closers." The company's culture is often described as aggressive, cutthroat, and numbers driven.

Recruitment materials boast that "only one in three associates survives the first year," emphasizing the company's desire to be elite and rivalrous. For entry-level sales associates, daily life includes aggressive quotas, intense peer competition, and long hours. At higher levels, however, the environment shifts: big accounts require teamwork, cross-departmental collaboration, and relationship nurturing with clients that can span years. Executives are expected to mentor junior associates, model emotional intelligence, and sustain client loyalty beyond the initial sale.

This dual identity of "lone wolf closer" meets "collaborative leader" is never made explicit in training or policy, but it pervades performance reviews and promotion decisions.

The Mid-Year Evaluation Dilemma

It was 8:15pm on a Wednesday, and Angela Grant was still at her desk, poring over two employee evaluation forms.

Angela had spent more than a decade climbing the ranks at Genuine, starting as a fresh-out-of-college associate and rising steadily through the sales pipeline. She knew the company inside and out. While her tenure was long, her role as Regional Sales Manager was still relatively new. For the first time in her career, she was responsible for evaluating employees for a promotion. It wasn't a decision she took lightly. She didn't want to get it wrong, not for the company, not for her team, and certainly not for her own credibility as a leader.

Promotions at Genuine were still largely subjective. Officially, associates were evaluated on sales performance, team fit, and "leadership potential." Unofficially, "leadership potential" often translated to vague signals of likability, confidence, and whether other senior leaders could see you handling a drink at a client dinner without saying something embarrassing.

Now, with end-of-year promotions looming, she had to nominate one candidate from her team for advancement to Junior Sales Associate, and her two contenders couldn't have been more different.

Judith Bell

Judith joined Genuine after several years working in commercial property sales. She was methodical, data-driven, and direct. From the start, she hit her numbers and then some. In just six months, she had closed two major accounts and led the region in quarterly deal volume.

But she was not a team favorite. Feedback from colleagues included the following:

- "She's cold. She never comes out with us."
- "Judith doesn't seem interested in helping anyone else."
- "She's not collaborative. It's like she's always in her own lane."

Her direct supervisor, Carter Liu, was even more blunt:

> "Judith is a machine, but I wouldn't trust her to mentor. She's not a team player. Zero vibe."

Angela, however, had observed Judith closely. Judith wasn't rude; she just wasn't performatively social. She preferred to work quietly, didn't join happy hours, and declined group barbecues on weekends. When Angela asked her about it, Judith said, "I'm here to sell, not to make best friends. I have people outside of work for that."

Thomas Garrett

Thomas was a Genuine golden boy in the making; or at least that's how it looked on paper.

A former college athlete, Thomas was outgoing, charismatic, and extremely confident. Though his sales numbers were average, he was always "on," high-fiving teammates, joking during team huddles, and often organizing the group's social calendar.

Team feedback included the following:

- "He makes the office better."
- "He's going to be a great leader one day."
- "He's just got that Genuine energy."

But Angela had her reservations. In one instance, a client had called her directly to complain about a miscommunication Thomas had made regarding contract terms. When Angela confronted him, Thomas deflected responsibility, saying, "The client misunderstood. I've seen this before. They say one thing in the meeting and change their tune when legal gets involved."

The Decision Matrix

Angela stared at her performance evaluation dashboard:

Criteria	Judith	Thomas
Sales numbers	Exceeds expectations	Meets expectations
Client feedback	Strong	Mixed
Peer feedback	Poor	Excellent
Mentorship potential	Unclear	Promising (per team)
Team fit	Low	High

Based on sales numbers and client feedback, Judith was the stronger performer. But Angela couldn't shake the feeling that Judith was being judged more harshly by colleagues for behavior that might be overlooked, or even rewarded, in a man.

For example:

- Thomas's confidence was read as leadership; Judith's confidence was read as arrogance.
- Judith's autonomy was labeled as "cold," while Thomas's errors were rationalized as part of his learning curve.

Angela felt stuck. If she promoted Judith, she worried about team morale and whether the promotion would even be sustainable. Would Judith be undermined? Would she be left out of crucial client deals? But if she promoted Thomas, would she be reinforcing a system that rewarded style over substance? And more troubling, would she be endorsing someone who wasn't open to feedback?

Company Culture—Unspoken but Powerful

Genuine didn't have formal leadership development. It had "organic promotion," which really meant Angela's judgment was the final word.

The VP of Sales once told her, "We promote winners, but winners people want to follow." Angela thought about that phrase as she revisited the feedback notes.

Decision Point

Angela saved her progress, shut down her laptop, and sat for a moment in silence.

She had until Friday to submit her decision. She could recommend only one person for promotion.

Her options:

- Promote Judith, the stronger individual performer, but risk a cultural mismatch and possible resistance.
- Promote Thomas, the team favorite, but whose performance was uneven and potentially un-coachable.
- Push back against the system and ask leadership to consider promoting both or neither.

But in her gut, she knew: this decision was about more than one promotion.

DISCUSSION QUESTIONS

1. Who would you promote? Why?
2. What implicit norms are operating in this case? How do they intersect with gender?
3. How might this decision shape the team's perceptions of fairness and leadership?
4. If Judith was a man and Thomas was a woman, might the feedback and dynamics differ?
5. How can performance evaluation systems be adjusted to account for both contribution and bias?

CASE STUDY 2: A WIDER WINDOW OF OPPORTUNITY: REENTRY AND FLEXIBILITY

Nicole Capehart

The Managers' Meeting

Melanie shifted uncomfortably in her seat as the conversation at the conference table veered sharply. It was the monthly property managers' meeting at Lasso Land Inc., a chance for Melanie, as District Manager, to coach her three direct reports, review occupancy metrics, talk through employee issues, and support their development as leaders.

Mentorship and internal promotion were a point of pride at Lasso Land Inc. Since joining the company seven years ago, Melanie had seen junior leasing agents rise to management, supported by a structure that emphasized cross-training, open-door policies, and a strong work–life balance initiative, one of the rare pandemic-era policies that had stuck around.

But now, as her three property managers debated whether an employee should be terminated for using too much of her earned paid time off (PTO), Melanie found herself questioning whether the company's policies and practices were truly aligned.

The Company Context

Lasso Land Inc. owned and operated luxury apartment properties across a three-city radius in the Southwestern USA. With approximately 200 employees and $50 million in annual revenue, the company positioned itself as a premium housing provider with boutique-style amenities and a highly curated tenant experience. Internally, Lasso Land emphasized culture, flexibility, internal mobility, and an inclusive workplace.

Melanie managed three of the company's properties, overseeing three property managers, three assistant managers, and around 20 employees across leasing, maintenance, and customer service. Of the three property managers:

> Angela was a 15-year property management veteran and widely respected. Blunt and results-driven, she ran a tight ship and consistently delivered the highest occupancy and renewal rates in the region. Leadership loved her. Staff often found her abrasive.
>
> Janine, similarly experienced, was outspoken and sharp-tongued but known for loyalty to her team. She had a strict sense of "professionalism" and valued hard work above all else.

Beth, the youngest and newest of the three, had recently been promoted from assistant manager. She often tried to emulate Angela and Janine's more authoritative style, though she hadn't quite found her own voice yet.

A New Kind of Hire

The employee in question was Lois, an entry-level leasing agent hired through Lasso Land's new partnership with a nonprofit that supported reentry employment for women with criminal records. In exchange for participation, the company received tax incentives and a potential recruitment pipeline. Internally, it was marketed as a win–win: the company demonstrated its commitment to second chances, and the nonprofit provided pre-vetted candidates.

Lois had joined two months earlier. A single mother of a 5-month-old, she was juggling parenting, parole requirements, and the adjustment to full-time employment. According to Angela, Lois had already used all her PTO.

"Between parole meetings, court check-ins, and her new baby," Angela said, "she's gone as soon as she gets the time. I don't think she's grateful for the opportunity. I can tell when someone's not a fit . . . and Lois isn't a fit."

Janine jumped in. "Exactly. It's not like other companies are lining up to hire someone with a criminal background. She should be bending over backward to show she belongs here. I don't care if she's not at my property. It's just basic work ethic."

Beth frowned. "Isn't PTO meant to be used, though?" she asked hesitantly. "I mean, unless someone's asking for time they haven't earned, I don't see the issue. I thought that was the point of our flexibility policy?"

Angela leaned forward. "It's not just about using time. It's about abusing it. Lois keeps asking for her schedule early and asks if she can come in late on court days. I can't just shift the entire schedule every time she has something personal come up."

Janine nodded. "You have to be firm with people like that. If you make exceptions, you'll have the whole team asking for special treatment. I have ten employees. How am I supposed to accommodate everyone's personal schedule?"

Beth glanced between the two, looking less sure than when she'd spoken. "I guess I don't fully understand what the policy really means," she said. "We talk about work–life balance and flexibility, but what does that look like for on-site staff like ours? We're not office workers. We can't telecommute."

Melanie felt the tension rising in the room—and inside herself. The company's work–life balance policy had always been aspirational. But this situation exposed a deeper problem: no one had defined how it should apply to frontline, reentry, or hourly employees.

Leadership and the Policy–Practice Gap

Melanie tried to slow the conversation down. "Before we go further, Angela, can we pull your property's payroll report?" she asked. "Let's see how Lois's PTO use compares to other team members. Are there others using all their PTO as they earn it?"

Angela shrugged. "Sure, there are a few. And it looks like they have similar performance. But none of them are asking me to rewrite the schedule."

Melanie nodded. "Still, we should be careful not to punish employees for using benefits they've earned. PTO is part of our retention strategy and our work–life balance commitment."

"And what happens if she needs emergency time and doesn't have any left?" Angela added. "She's setting herself up to fail. If she burns all her PTO, what do I do when she needs more time off in a month?"

Melanie didn't have a ready answer. Beth's earlier point still rang in her ears. What does flexibility look like when there are no remote options? When frontline roles can't be covered without staffing impacts?

She also couldn't shake the sense that Lois was being held to a higher standard. Plenty of employees had used their PTO quickly. No one else had been scrutinized like this. Melanie suspected that if Lois didn't have a criminal record this conversation might be different.

Forks in the Road

Melanie had decisions to make—and quickly:

- Should she intervene directly and prevent Angela from disciplining or terminating Lois?
- Should she elevate the issue to senior HR and push for clarity on how work–life balance applies to reentry employees?
- Should she offer to coach the managers privately on bias, or require all three to undergo training on inclusive supervision?
- Should she allow her property managers to continue handling things autonomously, trusting their instincts?

More broadly, Melanie wondered whether Lasso Land was truly ready to support second chance hiring, as well as work–life balance. The policy might say one thing, but the culture was sending another message entirely.

DISCUSSION QUESTIONS

1. If you were Melanie, what would you do? Why?
2. What are the unspoken norms around flexibility, work ethic, and professionalism that show up in this case? How do they intersect with identity and background?
3. How can managers differentiate between performance issues and structural barriers in employment?
4. What does meaningful work–life balance look like for frontline, in-person roles?
5. How can organizations close the gap between policy and practice when implementing inclusion initiatives?

CASE STUDY 3: REPRESENTATION ON THE LINE

Nicole Capehart

Scene: Tension Peaks

Mark, Alicia, Jess, and Paul sat in silence around the conference table. The mood was tense, the air heavy with frustration and fatigue. The group had been at this for hours, and they had nothing. Their proposal to the Board of Directors was due Friday. It was Wednesday afternoon.

"This is a disaster," Alicia whispered to Paul. "I don't even understand why we were chosen for this project. It's not like we have any authority."

Paul sighed. "Of course not. But we all look the part. If we endorse a plan, the Board gets to pat itself on the back for being 'diverse and inclusive.'"

Jess, overhearing, rolled her eyes. "Of course, that's what this is. It's performative politics. They're not going to accept anything that makes real change, so we should figure out what compromises we can live with."

"That's what I'm saying!" Mark said, more animated than usual. "Why should we clean this up for them? We aren't spokespeople for every marginalized group. This is offensive. And embarrassing."

Alicia rubbed her forehead. "Don't you get it though? Who cares what their motive was? We've been handed an opportunity. This could be the start of something real."

The room fell quiet again. Each person sat with their own blend of anger, doubt, and obligation, trapped between what they wanted to do and what they felt they could do.

Four Weeks Earlier: The Assignment

Dixon Marketing was a 7-year-old mid-sized marketing firm with a reputation for delivering bold campaigns and attracting ambitious talent. With roughly 50 employees, it had enjoyed steady growth—until the past year. As momentum slowed, company leadership began turning inward, looking for ways to sharpen strategy, boost morale, and "reignite the culture."

Mark, Alicia, Jess, and Paul, four employees from different departments, were invited to a meeting with Gary Henderson, the Vice President of Human Resources. The subject: developing a new recruitment strategy to "ensure diversity and inclusion in all hiring practices."

At first, the invitation was flattering. Each of the four had joined Dixon in part because of the firm's public commitment to inclusion. The company's recruitment materials spoke of "excellence through diversity" and celebrated resource groups, LGBT-QIA+ leadership, and intersectional values. In interviews, recruiters emphasized a "thriving culture of equity and inclusion."

But once inside the company, reality felt different.

The recruiters, they learned, had been external contractors, not Dixon employees. Internally, while there was a gender balance and women held visible leadership roles, representation flattened quickly beyond that. Employees from underrepresented racial/ethnic backgrounds, LGBTQIA+ identities, neurodivergent communities, or other underrepresented groups were rare.

The Mandate

Gary Henderson was enthusiastic. "You're a talented group with insight we can't get from anywhere else," he told them. "The Board wants real ideas—fresh, grounded in lived experience. Your plan could shape the future of hiring at Dixon."

The group would have 30 days. They'd present directly to the Board of Directors, a rare opportunity for employees at their level.

The team accepted. They met weekly, then daily. They brainstormed campaigns, sourcing tactics, and internship pipelines. But as they dug deeper, they hit a wall.

"There's no point recruiting people into a broken system," Jess said one afternoon. "Retention is terrible. There's no mentoring. No sponsorship. We're just plugging holes."

The more they researched, the clearer it became: the problem wasn't sourcing. It was culture.

They drafted a plan that went far beyond recruitment: internal audits, accountability metrics, inclusive leadership training, mentorship networks, and employee resource group funding. But as the plan grew more ambitious, so did the disagreements.

Four Perspectives, One Deadline

Alicia had been at Dixon for two years. As a Black woman and marketing strategist, she had spent most of that time being the only woman of color in client meetings. She saw the project as a breakthrough.

"We have access to the Board," she argued. "Even if they don't accept the whole plan, we can lay groundwork. We can make a case for deeper change. If we don't show up with something unified, they'll dismiss us entirely."

Jess, a queer White woman from operations, was skeptical but pragmatic. "They want window dressing," she said. "Let's give them what they asked for but slip in a few things that actually matter. Maybe a mentorship initiative. Baby steps."

Paul, a Latino analyst, was offended by the entire premise. "We were selected because of how we look," he said. "Not for our skills. That's the problem. We shouldn't pretend this is inclusion. It's tokenism. I'm not putting my name on that."

Mark, a biracial Asian and White product manager, agreed. Though more senior than the others, he, too, felt used. "They don't want change," he said. "They want cover. If we present this plan, we're giving them exactly what they want: plausible deniability. They can say they 'listened' to us while doing nothing."

Interpersonal Undercurrents

As the deadline loomed, so did the tension, not just about the project, but about power.

Alicia and Jess had started to feel that Mark and Paul held more influence, whether they acknowledged it or not. Mark had more tenure. Paul had closer relationships with key decision-makers. Both, Alicia noted, were men.

"It's easy to walk away from a plan when you've already got a seat at the table," she said one night to Jess. "But some of us are still trying to get in the room."

Mark pushed back, "That's not fair. Just because I've been here longer doesn't mean they listen to me. If anything, they tolerate me."

Paul agreed. "You think we have power? We're being used."

The conversation went in circles. The group's dynamic was strained by intersecting identities, unequal influence, and clashing philosophies.

The Board Awaits a Decision

It was now two days before the presentation. The draft was a mess. The proposal was half-polished, filled with redlines, incomplete sections, and contradictory recommendations.

They had to decide:

- Present a unified but diluted plan, hoping to get a foot in the door for future changes.
- Take a bold, principled stand, even if it meant alienating the Board.
- Disband the group, telling leadership they wouldn't participate in a performative process.

Or something in between.

Back in the conference room, Alicia broke the silence. "I think we have to decide who we're doing this for. Is it for us? For them? Or for the people who come after us?"

No one answered right away.

The Board would be waiting.

DISCUSSION QUESTIONS

1. What would you do? Explain why.
2. How do various identities and power shape each team member's perception of influence and responsibility?
3. Even if procedures related to diversity, equity, and inclusion aren't ideal at the company, are their efforts better than ignoring DEI? Or are they creating unintended negative consequences? Or some combination of the two?
4. Is presenting a partial plan a compromise or a capitulation?
5. How can teams balance individual values with collective action under institutional pressure?

CASE STUDY 4: WHEN LIFE INTERVENES

Lisa A. Marchiondo

The Introduction

Blue Oak Advisory is a mid-size financial services firm that has been notably growing. Both William and Heather are introductory managers with promising records for progressing to higher positions. They report to Darren, a regional director, who has been assessing their managerial performance and providing guidance to them for several years.

Darren knew William as an ambitious manager. He worked hard, focused on results-oriented outcomes, and centered his energy on ensuring employees reporting to him completed their key tasks, all while rallying them to feel excited about the work. In terms of areas for improvement, his subordinates reported that William could sometimes be dismissive and didn't always respond to their emails.

Darren knew Heather as a team-oriented and mentoring manager. She focused on collective outcomes and centered her energy on ensuring employees reporting to her felt motivated to contribute and voice ideas. For areas for improvement, her subordinates reported that Heather could be slow to make decisions at times and that some employees found her sarcasm off-putting.

William and Heather each faced personal issues affecting their time and energy at work. They both planned to contact their supervisor, Darren, about these concerns and to request additional paid time off.

Life Intervenes

William had a 4-year-old who was recently diagnosed with autism spectrum disorder. William was trying to enroll her in a program for Applied Behavior Analysis (ABA) therapy, which required a lot of research, calls, visits, evaluations, and coordination with insurance programs. In addition, he was looking for a reputable orthotist for his daughter's musculoskeletal issues, a speech-language pathologist for her speech delays, and an occupational therapist for her delayed fine motor skills. Beyond the time involved in her care, William had become anxious about her future and well-being. He lay awake at night contemplating and worrying: Will she be able to live independently? Will she be able to establish caring friendships, and/or will she be exposed to bullying? How will her education be affected? He was seeking support groups online.

Meanwhile, Heather had a 7-year-old who was recently diagnosed with an early-stage cancer. The cancer was most likely treatable, but this diagnosis had significantly shaken her family. They spent years investigating her son's symptoms, seeking numerous opinions from specialists, and determining this diagnosis. Watching her son cry as blood was repeatedly drawn brought her to tears. Even with a hopeful outcome, her son would undergo many uncomfortable medical procedures. He wouldn't have "kid time" or attend school for months. Heather would have to work with her local school to obtain lesson plans and personally teach her son—that is, when he was feeling well enough to learn. The situation caused Heather great anguish. She and her family would be spending every day at the hospital in the coming months, including sleeping on couches in the hospital room many nights.

Both parents were facing fear, uncertainty, sadness, heightened protectiveness, and financial concerns. They needed to discuss their situations with their boss, Darren.

William's Email

William knew he needed to contact Darren about his situation. He finally emailed him, saying:

> Darren,
>
> I need your attention right away for a special favor. I know you're typically really busy, but this is more important than the business operations.
>
> There is a critical issue I need to discuss, and I need to talk tomorrow morning.
>
> Because you receive a lot of emails, I'll just plan to be at your office at 7:30am.
>
> William

Darren found the message forthright but assumed William had something critical to discuss. He responded, saying he would be in his office by 7:30 am for the discussion.

William's Meeting

The next morning, Darren invited William into his office to discuss his email. William explained the situation regarding his daughter and all relevant details. He needed an extended leave and was ready to negotiate.

Prior to this meeting, William discussed his situation with many colleagues at the firm. They told him about exceptions that could be made in different circumstances, providing examples like, "Mark did this 5 years ago . . ." and "Sue did this 7 years ago . . ." They mentioned negotiations that could be helpful to make his case more appealing. One coworker, in particular, told him how much money the company was paying for Software Q, mentioning that it was really eating into the annual budget. He suggested that William leverage it as a cost-cutting mechanism to offset his extended leave. William ran this idea by a few other coworkers who agreed it was a good strategy. Overall, colleagues told him to be confident about getting the accommodations he needed to care for his daughter.

Sitting in Darren's office, William referenced his notes. He now had a sense of which issues mattered most to his division and had taken time to brainstorm strategies for a win-win solution.

"Darren, if given an extended leave, I could cut Software Q to compensate for the additional paid time off. No one really uses it, and it costs a fortune. In fact, we'd save money regardless of my additional paid time off, if it was cut. What do you think?"

Heather's Email

After debating when to contact Darren, Heather emailed him, saying:

> Hi Darren,
>
> I'm sorry to contact you on a Sunday. I realize it's the weekend, and I'm sure you're with your family. I apologize if this has interrupted you.
>
> There is something important I would like to discuss whenever it is convenient. Would it be okay to talk tomorrow (or another time this week)?
>
> I look forward to hearing from you when you have time.
>
> Thank you,
>
> Heather

Darren found the message vague but was interested in what Heather needed to discuss. He said he would be available the following day for the discussion.

Heather's Meeting

Heather entered Darren's office the next day to discuss her situation. She explained her son's diagnosis and the future steps she needed to address. She explained that she would need to negotiate an extended leave to accomplish it all.

Prior to this meeting, Heather had confided in one coworker about her son's cancer diagnosis. She didn't want to draw attention to herself by revealing it to too many colleagues, and she didn't want to make employees feel sorry for her. Her closest colleague, Wendy, advised her to be honest with Darren and outline all the details of her situation to him. She offered support, inviting Heather over to her house for coffee. Wendy actively listened, and when Heather asked her to keep the situation private, Wendy agreed.

Sitting in Darren's office, Heather wrung her hands. She knew her situation was serious, but she worried about placing an onus on others by taking an extended leave. Would colleagues have to work overtime to cover for her? Would she cost the company significant money? Would her image be tarnished, and would she appear as self-serving and artificially "special"?

After a lengthy silence during her meeting with Darren, Heather finally offered a pitch:

> "Darren, I realize the extended leave policy is often limited, but I really need at least two months. I know it isn't ideal, but . . . please? Can you help me and my family out? I would be so grateful. I'm sure I can make up for it in some other way."

The Dilemma

Darren approached his supervisor about his employees' requests. His supervisor considered the proposals and returned saying, "Unfortunately, we aren't in a position to provide extended leaves to two employees right now. However, think about it and decide which employee needs the extended leave the most. Then, I'll approve that one exception."

Darren pored over his notes. He praised William as a hard-working manager with great results. His subordinates were energetic working under him, yet Darren was aware he would need to work with William on his email responses and dismissiveness. He noted that William had presented a solid idea for exchanging his time off with winnowing expenses in other areas of the company. Darren was empathetic about William's situation that involved numerous specialists and an uncertain future for his young daughter with autism.

Reviewing Heather's case, Darren was impressed with her ability to intrinsically motivate her employees and boost team-oriented outcomes, even if he would need to talk with her about reducing sarcasm and making faster decisions at times. He noted that she hadn't offered ways to make up for her leave. Darren felt terrible that her son had been diagnosed with cancer. Her tepid request made him wonder how critical the leave was in her case or if she could make do without it.

Darren faced an uncomfortable decision.

DISCUSSION QUESTIONS

1. What would you decide, and why?
2. To what extent do course topics help explain perceptions of William and Heather? How might these dynamics intersect?
3. How might insidious workplace mistreatment, such as ignoring emails from coworkers, be interpreted differently based on gender?
   a. What about being forthright in emails and excluding pleasantries? When are these actions perceived as rude versus business-minded and necessary?
4. Do you think that perceptions about accommodation needs are shaped by mental/cognitive versus physical conditions? Temporary versus permanent (or long-term) conditions?
   a. How might gender intersect with these perceptions about disability accommodations?
5. How might perceptions have differed based on additional information about Heather and William's identities, such as race/ethnicity, sexual orientation, disability, age?

CASE STUDY 5: OPPORTUNITY AT THE PRECIPICE

Nicole Capehart

Lisa A. Marchiondo

Adventure Awaits

Adventure Awaits was a respected wilderness survival company. With a storefront selling outdoor gear, popular wilderness survival and medical courses, and youth and adult backpacking excursions, the company had built a loyal customer base. But its most profitable arm was its long-standing contract work with military and emergency services, providing training simulations and high-stakes survival exercises.

Though it had been acquired by a larger parent company, Adventure Awaits retained its local identity. It was community-rooted and prided itself on loyalty. The company had a reputation for promoting from within.

Being a stereotypically masculine industry, wilderness survival typically involved showing toughness, endurance, and resilience. Internally, the company culture of Adventure Awaits also encouraged confidence, mastering one's job, and being able to answer any customer question. Competition between employees often cropped up. Nonetheless, employees took pride in their accomplishments and expertise.

Elena's Path

Elena spent most of her young adulthood with Adventure Awaits. Her parents had immigrated from Mexico before she was born. They valued hard work and the outdoors, drawing her to the company from an early age.

At 17, she took her first survival course and was immediately hooked. Her curiosity, confidence, and cool-headed problem-solving made her a natural in the field. By 18, she was working as a cashier in the gear shop, where her bilingual skills proved beneficial. By 25, she was one of the company's most requested instructors, especially by the military units they served.

Elena's style was direct, precise, and high-energy. She held trainees accountable and pushed them to perform. Her reputation for no-nonsense leadership and innovative ideas made her a go-to for high-profile trainings. Her long-term goal was to become Vice President of Military and Emergency Services, and she had ideas for expanding into national security training and federal contracts. She had now been with the company for decades and was a key employee.

The Opportunity: Trekking on Thin Ice

Adventure Awaits had been treading steadily since its acquisition. However, some divisions were performing better than others. Merchandise sales were high, especially after a notable magazine highlighted the company and its regional hiking trails. Military and emergency programs—one of the more profitable divisions—were tanking though. Government funding for third-party training had recently declined, so the company's military consultancy was substantially reduced. Employees had been discussing this shift and worrying about the future of this division.

One Tuesday, the company's founder, Leo, called Elena into his office. "I have an exciting opportunity. You've been with the company a long time and have had consistently high performance. After talking with the executive team, I would like to offer you a leadership opportunity at the company."

"Really?!" Elena eagerly replied. "Thank you for considering me, Leo. Which leadership opportunity?"

Leo continued, "You've been involved in our training programs for years, with great success, so I'd like to invite you to serve as the new Vice President of Military and Emergency Services."

Elena was speechless. This had been one of her dreams. She felt confident about progressing to leadership.

Yet, doubt quickly seeped in. This division was performing poorly. This area had had negative profit for several years. The solution might be out of their hands, given that government funding was low. There was no indication that this situation would change in the coming years.

Being the first woman—and Latina—VP at the company would be a meaningful "first"—for both her and the company. But what if she couldn't turn around this division? Would she look bad for leading the lowest-performing division at the company? Would this affect her future career negatively or positively?

The Debacle

That night, Elena lay awake, her mind racing. She had spent years rising through the ranks of a company she loved. She had always dreamed of a leadership position. Yet, she felt unsure about this opportunity. Her brainstorming toggled:

- Should she accept the position? If so, would it affect her long-term career portfolio, if the division didn't improve?
- Should she decline the position? If so, would her career become stagnant at the company? Would it appear that she wasn't ready for leadership?
- Should she start looking for opportunities elsewhere?

She didn't know the answer. But she did know one thing: this wouldn't be an easy decision.

DISCUSSION QUESTIONS

1. If you were Elena, what steps would you consider next, and what decision would you make? Why?
2. Is it unethical for the company to offer this position to Elena, given that she would be the first woman and first Latina leader? Why or why not?
3. What facets of masculinity contest cultures are present? Do those features seem to affect Elena's situation?
4. What concepts from the book are relevant to this issue and the decision-making involved?

Index

Note: Page numbers in *italics* indicate a figure, page numbers in **bold** indicate a table, and page numbers followed by an "n" indicate a number on the corresponding page.

For Product Safety Concerns and Information please contact our
EU representative GPSR@taylorandfrancis.com Taylor & Francis
Verlag GmbH, Kaufingerstraße 24, 80331 München, Germany